THE FLIGHT OF THE YOUNG SPARROW

TRUDI SPATZ

ISIS
LARGE PRINT
Oxford

First published in Great Britain 2008
by
Isis Publishing Ltd.

Published in Large Print 2008 by ISIS Publishing Ltd.,
7 Centremead, Osney Mead, Oxford OX2 0ES
by arrangement with the Author

British Library Cataloguing in Publication Data
Spatz, Trudi
   The flight of the young sparrow. – Large print ed.
   (Isis reminiscence series)
   1. Spatz, Trudi
   2. Refugees – Great Britain – Biography
   3. Germans – Great Britain – Biography
   4. World War, 1939–1945 – Great Britain
   5. Large type books
   I. Title
   941'.084'092

ISBN 978–0–7531–9488–1 (hb)
ISBN 978–0–7531–9489–8 (pb)

Printed and bound in Great Britain by
T. J. International Ltd., Padstow, Cornwall

THE FLIGHT OF THE YOUNG SPARROW

DEDICATION

With love and gratitude to my
parents and brother.

CONTENTS

FOREWORD

In 1935, my family, the Spatz family, fell into disgrace and my father was transported to a labour camp for three years.

This is not a story about concentration camps, but about how a German family survived persecution in Germany, escaped with their lives and came to live in England during the Second World War. When the war broke out between England and Germany, my parents, brother and I just kept praying, wondering and asking, "What will become of us? What does fate hold in store for us now?"

Many books have been written and films made about prisoners of war and how they tried to escape, about Germans interned on the Isle of Man, about Jewish refugees, but so far no one has told the story of Germans living in their own home in Britain, facing war and all its implications.

We had to get used to, and accept with as much good grace as we could muster, words such as "Jerry", or more usually "bloody Jerry", and "the only good Germans are dead Germans".

I was 13 years old and a refugee from Germany, not a Jewess. In Germany, Jews had to wear a star on their clothes, but in England the words "enemy alien" became an invisible star, and perhaps harder to bear as they aroused not the sympathy of the people but scepticism and sometimes open hostility.

ACKNOWLEDGEMENTS

I am grateful to my sons for encouraging me to put my memoirs in chronological order and to write this book.

For many years that I belonged to the Cambridge U3A [University of the Third Age] writers group, who gently criticised my efforts and helped and guided me, thus improving each chapter. The group was ably led by Elizabeth Bray, who was supportive and had the patience to listen to the altered script and always encouraged me to carry on.

Many thanks to Hugh Hillyard-Parker who put the manuscript on a computer in the requested and correct format.

CHAPTER
ONE

Hamburg Easter 1935

A visit from the Gestapo.

It was 1935, the last day of the Easter holiday. My family — the Spatz (which means "sparrow" in German) family — was driving back home after visiting my uncle and aunt in Frankfurt am Main. It was a long drive as we lived in Hamburg in northern Germany. My brother and I were excited to be going back and were looking forward to seeing our friends again. My father ("Papa") stopped the car so that he could stretch his legs. He asked my mother ("Mutti"), my brother, Kurt, and me to join him, to stand and stare and admire the glorious colour display of the sunset. The sky was aflame. Papa put his arms lovingly around our shoulders and said, "Look and take in the beauty of this sunset. Be thankful that as a family we can enjoy it together. Savour this moment. Who knows when and where we shall have the opportunity again." Arriving home, the neighbour's children greeted us happily. Little did we guess that the storm clouds were gathering for us and that we would eventually flee from Germany.

It was the following night. All was quiet and peaceful, and the Spatz family had gone to bed. The grandfather clock chimed midnight. Suddenly, the stillness was shattered by cars stopping noisily and the car doors banging. Then stamping boots hurrying into our building. Tramp, tramp, tramp. We listened, frightened, our hearts pounding. At whose door would these stamping boots stop tonight? They passed the first floor, now coming up to our floor. There were two flats to each floor and two more flats above us. As they noisily mounted the stairs, each family whose door they passed gave a sigh of relief. Then they came to our floor. We listened, terrified. Mutti said, "Oh God, please let them go by." Which of the doors to the two flats would they knock at? We hardly dared to breathe and for a few seconds, an eternity, we were all in a state of suspended animation. Then a loud banging at our door and shouting, "Aufmachen, sofort aufmachen!" — "Open the door, open the door at once." We all froze and could not move. Then Papa went to the door and looked through the peephole. He turned back to us and said to Mutti with a hopeless expression, "The Gestapo. It's the Gestapo. It must be a mistake, keep calm!"

Mutti was the first to react. She took her wallet from her handbag and pushed it under the mattress. The banging on the door and shouting became menacingly loud and continued until Papa opened the door. Pushing him aside, the Gestapo men stamped in. The leader of the group was dressed in the recognisable long black leather coat. He was a small man with hard steely eyes. He clicked his heels and saluted, "Heil Hitler."

Then he bowed his head sharply and introduced himself. "Schmidt. Get dressed." A pause, and then, "You will accompany me." Papa kept repeating, "There must be a mistake — we are not Jewish or Communists. What have I done?"

Schmidt's next words sent shivers down our spines as he replied, "You will find out." Turning to his men, he said, "Search the flat."

By now I was crying helplessly. As Kurt was 13 years old and I was 10, Mutti begged if my brother and I could be together and get into my parents' bed. As she tucked me in, she whispered that she had put some money under the mattress. Then in her normal voice she added, "Don't cry, Trudi. It will not help any of us."

After that she got dressed and sat quietly on the edge of the bed, holding my hand.

Schmidt moved over to the dressing table and rummaged in the drawers. His fingers suddenly picked something up, a piece of jewellery, and put it into his pocket. I shall never forget those hands with their long, spidery fingers, which, when they touched anything, looked to me like a spider pouncing on its prey.

In the meantime, the men had emptied all shelves, cupboards and drawers, and thrown everything on the floor. After they had spent several hours searching the flat, they decided it was a hopeless task. Searching for what? We never found out what they were looking for, but they left devastation behind. Later, we often wondered if they were looking for communist leaflets or newspapers.

The Gestapo stamped out as noisily as they had come in, but this time they took our parents with them.

Kurt and I were left behind in the flat and after they had driven away, there was silence, stunned, deathly silence. We both just sat there, staring at each other. We sat silently on the bed, confused and bewildered, listening and wondering, "What now?" The silence became oppressive and I started to cry quietly. What could two helpless children do in a situation like this?

Kurt, being the elder, made a decision. He suggested that I should stop crying and help him to tidy up the turmoil the Gestapo had left behind, so that when and if our parents returned, they would find an orderly home again. Kurt was still wearing his pyjamas and I my nightie. We sorted everything out and put it back in its place, which took the rest of the night and well into the next morning. All the time we made sure that we moved quietly, silently and carefully. If we heard any noise, we would rush to the door and peer through the letterbox, and Kurt would look through the peephole to see who was coming up those stairs. Was it Papa or Mutti, or perhaps both of them?

It seemed strange as life went on its usual way. The milkman delivered a litre of milk and the baker left eight bread rolls by the door. We opened the door gently and took the provisions in. We were glad of them as in those days people did not possess a refrigerator and Mutti used to buy fresh and perishable food daily.

We drank some milk and ate a roll. Then tiredness overtook us and all we wanted was sleep — to sleep and forget what had happened, and perhaps, when we woke

4

up, we realised that it was not a nightmare, but reality. I started to weep again, out of tiredness, fear and despair. We stayed on our parents' bed and Kurt put his arms around me and held my hand, saying some encouraging words.

"Ever since you were born, Spätzchen (my nickname, meaning "little sparrow"), Mutti taught me to look after you and to take care of you, and I will do this now."

We lay down and fell asleep. We slept for hours. Being on our parents' bed gave us a feeling of comfort as it was the only piece of furniture not tarnished by Gestapo hands. Because of this, it was a like a refuge, reassuring us despite our feelings of loneliness, desolation, being abandoned and forsaken. When we awoke, to pass the time, we reminisced and told each other about the happy hours spent with our parents.

Papa was just under six feet tall. We often teased him that if he put a newspaper into his shoes, he would reach the longed-for height. He was from Hanover, with broad shoulders and a thick neck, and Mutti used to laugh at him as he had a rather plump nose to go with those features. Mutti said it looked like a potato nose, but it was his eyes that held you. The palest blue eyes, like the sky on a lovely summer's day, and his hair was very pale ash blond. To us he stood ten feet tall. He had a good sense of humour and was full of fun.

"Do you remember the walks in the country and how they always became an adventure?" I said.

Using his pocket knife, Papa would cut a twig from a branch and another one from another bush. With his pocket knife he would make three little holes in each one. Then he would hit the little sticks against his knee and chant a magic verse, shaking the little sticks. The pith of these twigs would fall out and they became two flutes with three notes, each one of a different tone. Then he would take his harmonica out of his pocket and the three of us would play a tune. Mutti was not left out because she would sing as we wandered along country lanes.

Mutti, in contrast, was dainty and petite. I loved to brush her pale chestnut-coloured hair. No one ever knew the colour of her eyes. They were grey blue and the iris had a brown ring around it. When she was happy, the blue dominated, but when she was not well or unhappy, the brown and blue seemed to merge and the eyes would become a deep grey, fathomless — as deep as the ocean. Mutti saw beauty everywhere, and life and laughter oozed out of her. Would this night change my parents?

All next day we stayed in the flat listening to every movement on the stairs. Strangely, life seemed to go on in its usual way. The milkman delivered the milk and the baker left fresh bread rolls by the door. The same this morning as always. Kurt and I ate what was left over from the previous day and the eight bread rolls and drank half the milk. Twenty-four hours had passed and not a word from our parents. What should we do? Again, Kurt decided that we should try and sleep, and then in the morning should go to school as if nothing had happened.

6

The milkman and the baker delivered their wares as usual. We took special care in dressing and combing our hair. We left the flat and as soon as we stepped into the street, the other children, our friends, came running towards us. We were happy to see them and hoped that we could all walk to school together. To our dismay, these friends picked up stones and threw them at us. Some children came over to me, kicking me and pulling my hair and shouting, "Verräter, Verräter!" — "Traitors, traitors!"

Kurt and I fought to get free from them. We noticed that the parents of these children stood by their windows, pulling the net curtains aside and watching it all happening. We ran back to the flat and safety.

More waiting, just waiting. Another 24 hours went by. No news. There was no food left, only the daily delivery of the milk and rolls. This would cease on Saturday when we would have to pay for them. Kurt and I had decided that we would not do this, but use the money from under the mattress for the rail fare to Uncle and Auntie in Frankfurt, or as far as it would take us towards Frankfurt am Main.

Another 24 hours passed. What could 10- and 13-year-old children do all day without making a sound, so that no one would hear us, especially the people living in the flat below. We felt so alone in the world and despair replaced the feeling of desolation. We tried to hide our feelings of fear from each other, terrified at what the next hours would bring and what the future might hold. I did not cry any more. There were no tears left to shed. How we wished and prayed that our parents would come through the front door.

Hitler's theories and speeches were full of propaganda about the youths that would help him to build his Third Reich, especially the blond-haired, blue-eyed Arians. Both Kurt and I were blond — Kurt's hair was golden blond, while mine was white blonde like Papa's, but where was help coming from for us, after Hitler's henchmen had destroyed our family?

Was it only a week ago that my family had had that carefree holiday? Life can change overnight into a nightmare. How often, in happier times, did I wish "for time to stand still". Now, time dragged on slowly. I tried to keep control of my emotions as they changed from fear to panic to hopelessness. Even those feelings died, leaving me with a drained, empty void of blankness.

Three days became four days — an eternity. Kurt and I had decided to pack a small case and a rucksack with some of our clothes and write a note for our parents, in case they returned home after we left, saying that we were on our way to Uncle and Auntie in Frankfurt. This should prevent them from worrying about us. We decided to sneak out in the middle of the night, afraid that the children would attack us if they saw us. We did not know how far that money under the mattress would get us towards our goal.

We waited for midnight to arrive. I was amazed to see how my brother had changed from a happy, carefree schoolboy into a person with a too-old head on

8

his young shoulders as he tried to keep control of the situation as best he could.

Late in the afternoon we heard a noise at our door. We froze, too frightened to see who it was scratching at the door. What were they trying to do? We crept silently to it and looked out through the letterbox. Kurt pushed me roughly aside and opened the door quickly. Mutti stood there. Our mother had come home. Our lovely mother was with us again. We could not believe our eyes. Somehow she looked so different. We asked the obvious questions.

"Mutti, is it really you? Where is Papa? Why did they take you away?"

She could not speak, but put her arms around us. Kurt noticed that she swayed, so he helped her to the lounge and to sit down. Then we could tell each other what had happened.

Mutti looked so tired and exhausted, years and years older. Her big eyes looked like huge pools, too big to fit in their sockets. Eyes that had the life squeezed out of them, they told of suffering and crying. Kurt thought she might want a drink and fetched a cupful of milk for her, which she drank very slowly, just a sip at a time. Then she finally shook her head and spoke, but she would not talk about those days. She called them "the four lost days". She thought that we had had enough trauma of our own for our age. All she said was, "Papa is not coming home. They sent him to a labour camp". The authorities had confiscated all our money from the bank as well as any outstanding money from the firms Papa dealt with.

We had nothing to live on and so had to make plans how to get through this troubled time and survive.

Mutti had begged Schmidt to let her go home and look after us. As they had not found any incriminating evidence in the flat and as nothing had come to light during the four days of interrogation that they could pin on Mutti, the Gestapo let her go, with the threat that if she did not bring us up as good German citizens of the New Order, she too would be sent to a labour camp, while Kurt and I would be sent to a Nazi school in Berlin.

Up to this moment, we had had a happy life. All Kurt and I had to worry about was going to school and getting good marks and a good report so that our parents could be proud of us.

After Mutti had rested, we had the first of many conferences during which we decided what our next move had to be. Mutti thought that these consultations were important. She believed that Kurt and I, even though still children, had a right to express our opinions and should know exactly what we were going to do.

The first action was to send a telegram to my father's business friends in Holland. The message read, "Halt all business and freeze money until we contact you again."

The next biggest decision was quickly made — to leave the flat — as we could no longer afford the rent and the neighbours were no longer friendly towards us. The next practical step was to sell most of the furniture and paintings. This would make us some money to live on for the time being.

Our maternal grandparents were dead, so Mutti wrote to Papa's parents in the hope that they might offer us a home or help us by supporting us with some money.

A reply came quickly by return post. "Sorry, we do not want to get involved in any way as it might have repercussions. For the moment we enclose £10.00 hoping this may help you a little."

In Germany, there were many different support groups which operated via the Nazi regime and nobody had to go hungry, but people like us, with a member of the family in the labour camps, were ostracised. We lived under the constant fear of the consequences of our situation — that my grandparents might lose their freedom too if they helped us. They had made their views known and disowned us, telling us that they did not want to hear from us again.

What was our crime? We were not Communists, nor Jewish — both heinous crimes in Nazi Germany of the 1930s. We just surmised that we were the victims of the envy of one man, a "good party member", who had the power to destroy a whole family.

Mutti started to search for accommodation, but where could we find somewhere cheap to live as we had so little money? A change of school was essential for me. Kurt's school was in the centre of the city and therefore the other schoolboys did not realise what had happened to us. If possible, Mutti wanted to find accommodation in that area as this would save on fares, but where would we start to look?

Mutti would get up early in the morning to search for a new flat. She walked up and down the streets, looking in shop windows for advertisements, hoping that somewhere rooms were being offered cheaply.

After a few days, Mutti came home very excited. Quite by chance, she had seen an advertisement to share a large flat. It was near the big lake, the Aussen Alster. This accommodation consisted of a large lounge, two bedrooms, the use of the kitchen and bathroom. Mutti told the owner, Herr Schulz, that she was a widow. Herr Schulz was an elderly gentleman and was pleased to have a family to share his flat. He agreed that if Mutti looked after his rooms, we could live rent-free. We began to hope that life would be a little easier. We were safe for now. But for how long?

The move to our new home went smoothly. We kept only the essential furniture, but so far we had been able to hang on to Mutti's piano. It had belonged to her since childhood. Mutti sometimes said, "If that piano could talk, it would tell many stories." She would sit hour after hour and play, sometimes singing or humming a melody. At other times she would just sit and rest her hands on the keyboard with her thoughts far away. Then, ever so softly, she would start to play again. Was she dreaming of the past or the future? Playing on the piano would help her to calm her emotions, and she would regain her composure and inner strength.

I had to face going to a new school and meeting the girls of my form. They often teased me for being so quiet, but at home Mutti would drum into us, "Don't talk about the past and what happened. Maybe all will go well. Always do as you're told, behave and be polite. Remember, our lives may depend on your actions. Always remember the conditions under which I was allowed home after those terrifying four days at the Gestapo Headquarters. I promised to bring you up as good citizens in the true new German spirit." We had to think about every word before we spoke and watch every action we took. Just one wrong or thoughtless word spoken could mean our death.

Hamburg is a Hanseatic City, a free city. This allowed it to have its own police force and laws, and educational system. My new school was an education-ally experimental one, under Hamburg's new law, but it had the same Nazi discipline as all the other schools.

Every Monday morning, weather permitting, assembly took place in the playground, otherwise in the gym. We sang several Nazi songs, one girl would recite a political poem, and assembly would conclude with the National Anthem and the Horst Wessel song, the Nazi Anthem. We stood to attention, our right hands raised in the Hitler salute as the Swastika flag was raised.

On Saturdays, the same type of assembly took place, only this time the flag was lowered. The girl who was given the honour of reciting a poem and raising or lowering the flag would be the one who had excelled during that week, or had the best class marks for her work or good behaviour, or was a member of the BDM

13

(the Bund Deutscher Mädel — the Hitler youth movement for girls). Age did not matter; it could be the youngest or the oldest girl in school.

The other days of the week we had to pass the caretaker, a little tin-pot general, who would take the salute. "Heil Hitler!" The right arm outstretched, the hand raised to eye level. He was the watchdog. If he thought that a girl saluted in a slovenly way, he would report her to the teacher or headmistress. If a girl was caught out too often and reported for this misdemeanour, the parents' political outlook to the party could be checked and this could have serious consequences. I became a model saluter.

Once a month on a Saturday, the teachers organised a walk in the country or by Lake Alster. Although Hamburg is a harbour city, a large lake enriches the city. The Alster is divided by a bridge and so its two parts are known as Binnen Alster ("Inner Alster") and Aussen Alster ("Outer Alster"). The larger part is the Aussen Alster and along the lake edges are many trees, footpaths, grass verges and parks. Swans, ducks and grey geese glide along on the water. The swans are conscious of their privilege as the symbols of Hamburg's independence. Alster boats, sailing boats, cruise on the water. The Alster is connected to the river Elbe by many canals and locks. Because of all these waterways, Hamburg is known as the "Venice of the North". In fact, Hamburg has about 2000 bridges, compared to Amsterdam's 650 and Venice's mere 450.

During these class outings, we would walk somewhere along the Alster at a leisurely pace with time to stand and stare at nature. As Hitler's time in power grew longer, more and more girls joined the BDM and would be seen wearing the uniform. Black skirt, white blouse, black scarf rolled up to make a tie and held in place by a leather knot (similar to the scout's scarf and woggle). Finally, a khaki jacket, on its sleeve the Nazi emblem. Our happy and carefree strolls became more and more regimented, turning into long marches with rucksacks on our backs containing sandwiches and a drink. As we marched along, we would burst out in song — traditional folk songs as well as party songs — always marching in step, never admitting to being tired. The rhythm of the songs would keep our flagging spirits going. The greatest humiliation was if one of us developed a blister.

The school had a unique arrangement with a local piggery, which would buy potato peelings and stale bread that we collected from our own homes and brought to school. In the basement of the school were two large rooms. We had to throw the bread into one room and the potato peelings into the other, without the paper bags. These were thrown into a dustbin. The items were kept apart as more money was paid for the bread. First thing in the morning, when the register was called, we replied, "Yes, here", "Here, potatoes" or "Here, bread". We were given extra marks for bringing these items. We needed no encouragement to remember to seek out every last scrap.

The money earned from this went into a school fund called "holiday home". Each class enjoyed three weeks' stay in this holiday home, an old 18th-century Frisian farmhouse on the Isle of Sylt. Parents had to pay only for food and the fare. Any other overheads, such as the Matron, staff and upkeep of the house, were paid for out of the piggery fund. If for some reason parents could not afford this basic price, then the money from the holiday fund would be used to subsidise the cost.

Life had taken on a calmer aspect, but we had to be careful and on our guard all the time. One day I was not feeling well. Mutti took me to our family doctor for a check-up. We noticed two men standing on the other side of the pavement watching the doctor's house. When we wanted to go into the surgery, Dr Preis refused us entry. He pointed to the two men on the other side of the street and told us that they were from the anti-Jewish paper, Stürmer. Anyone, especially blonde German children, being examined by a Jewish doctor would be contravening the Nuremberg Race Pollution Act. The patients would be photographed and the photos would be published in Stürmer. The doctor would be sent to a concentration camp. He pointed out that in our circumstances it would be doubly dangerous for all concerned as he had been warned to keep his hands off Aryan children.

We all felt more secure in our new flat. Mutti was trying hard to get employment. She walked from shop to shop but always received the same reply, "You have no references." She also applied for jobs minding and looking after children as she was a trained nanny, but when prospective employers saw her last testimonials, they would invariably say that while she was obviously a very capable person, the references were too old and out of date, and so were of no value any more.

Mutti became very secretive. She stopped eating with us when she served the meals. She always made an excuse, "I had my meal while preparing it" or "Don't tempt me, remember I'm on a diet."

Then one day, Mutti was not at home to welcome us back from school. Had she been successful and found a job? How we wished this had happened. The doorbell rang. When we opened the door, a naval officer stood there, supporting our Mutti. He suggested that we should make a cup of coffee for her. Then he told us that Mutti had collapsed at his feet.

When he looked in her handbag to find her name and address to give to a taxi driver, he noticed that Mutti's purse was empty — not even a single pfennig in it. From Mutti's appearance he could see that she looked as if she came from a respectable family and was not a vagrant. This made him feel responsible and he didn't want just to put her in a taxi, but decided to accompany her and pay the fare. After Mutti had had a drink of coffee, he suggested that he should come back the next day to see how things were with us. While we made the coffee, he noticed that the cupboards were bare and there was no food for anyone. He was very thoughtful and gave some money to Kurt to buy some food.

Mutti had prayed and prayed for some help and guidance on how to get some money for food for the family. In her darkest and most dismal hours, she always believed and said that God would send a sunbeam to guide us.

The next morning, true to his word, the naval officer visited us and asked if he could advise us. When Mutti told him our story, he suggested that we contact our solicitor and ask him to help us to retrieve some of our confiscated money, instead of becoming a burden on the state. Mutti mentioned that at this time in our lives she feared going to the solicitor. To our surprise, the officer offered to accompany Mutti to give her moral support and to show the solicitor that Mutti was not on her own. Both Kurt and I thought that he was a hero as he did not seem to be afraid of anyone.

How happy we three were when, a few days later, a letter arrived notifying us that once a week we were to collect some money from the solicitor. We were grateful, but when Mutti saw the amount allowed us from our own confiscated money, she sighed and said, "Too little to live on, too much to die on." Months later, when Mutti investigated what had happened to all our money, she noticed that the money allowed us by the Gestapo was more than she received from the solicitor. Mutti challenged him on this matter. He was not embarrassed and admitted freely that he kept this money. He subtracted a certain sum from our small allowance to pay for his services in getting the allowance.

This discrepancy with the money made Mutti pensive and for days she was preoccupied with her thoughts. Then one evening she told us that she was going to find out what had happened to our money and how much had been actually handed over to the State. She checked Papa's books carefully and rechecked the figures over and over again. She took note of the accounts outstanding on that dreadful night when they took Papa away and compared them with the statement from the Gestapo and the amount paid to the state. Her thorough investigation showed that money was missing. This was much more difficult to trace and Mutti surmised that some of our money had found its way into the Gestapos' personal accounts. Everybody seemed to be lining their own pockets, while we had to go without.

One account had been paid to the state. Neither had a small account in a savings bank been mentioned. Mutti asked Kurt and me to sit down and listen to her ideas. She wanted us to help her analyse them and find fault with them. It was important to make the right decision. Kurt was 14 years old and I was 11.

As we made plans and altered them, scrapped them and started again, a letter arrived from the Gestapo man Schmidt, telling her to divorce Papa as she was very attractive and still young. She would then be free to marry another man who could provide for the family, especially as Papa was going to be transferred from the labour camp to one of the dreaded concentration camps.

This stung Mutti into action. Without hesitation she replied that she would not divorce Papa as he would need his family and home, if and when he was released to come home. Then she sat down, wrote letters and rewrote them, sitting for a long time and staring at what she had written. When we asked what she was up to, she gave us a short, sharp answer, telling us to keep out of this and thatthe less we knew about it, the better it would be for my brother and me. It hurt us terribly to see our petite, fragile Mutti, who was always kind and gentle, loving and helpful, turning into a hard, scheming person, but then she was fighting the only way she knewhow , to give her small family the best chance of surviving.

Mutti arranged for me to spend a weekend with one of the few friends she had left. Mutti would only avail herself of friendship in an emergency. Kurt and I could not understand Mutti's change of principles as we could not see the crisis at that moment. All she would say was, "You will enjoy the change when you go with Mrs Pfennig to their allotment and chalet in Olsendorf."

It was a lovely weekend and for short moments I forgot our trouble and spent a few carefree hours filled with laughter. I got drunk on laughter — it was infectious — and I was allowed to eat to my heart's content. Food. Glorious food. Scrumptious food.

When I arrived home on Sunday evening, my brother opened the door of the flat and looked as if he had been crying for hours. I don't think that I had ever seen him crying before. When he played a boy's prank and Papa spanked him for it, or if he hurt his knee, the reaction was always the same — biting his lips together. So, seeing tears on his white, drawn face, I knew immediately that something tremendous must have happened. My heart stood still and I dared not ask what was wrong.

Kurt made me sit down on the sofa. "Mutti is in hospital," he remarked, and then he explained from the beginning.

Mutti made sure that I was out of the way and in safe hands with the Pfennigs. She then asked Kurt to take a letter to a schoolfriend's mother. He thought this a strange request as neither mother had ever contacted other before. Being a dutiful son he went on his way and kept thinking about the way Mutti had said goodbye to him. Finally he came to the conclusion that something was wrong and he turned round and ran home as fast he could. When he opened the door of the flat, he could smell gas and rushed to the kitchen to check the gas cooker. Horror struck him when he saw Mutti lying in front of the cooker with her head in the oven. With his youth and inexperience, he did not know what to do first. He turned the gas off and opened the window. Then he dragged Mutti into the bedroom and tried to revive her. Blinded by tears, he ran to the nearest telephone booth and rang for an ambulance. As we lived near the hospital, the ambulance arrived at the flat at the same time as Kurt did. After that it became a muddle. While Kurt was waiting at the hospital, Herr Schmidt of the Gestapo unexpectedly arrived. He was very agitated and shouted at the doctors, "If you do not revive that woman and keep her alive, you will lose your jobs."

The doctors told Kurt to go home as everything was being taken care of.

In the flat Kurt found a letter from Mutti explaining her action. She had written to Schmidt pointing out the discrepancies in the accounts and saying she would use this information if Schmidt did not prevent Papa from being sent from the labour camp to a concentration camp. Also, that she had written to a prominent SS officer from her home town. The letter was sealed with sealing wax and embossed with our seal with a message, "To be opened on my death or disappearance", written on the outside. This is what had agitated Schmidt.

Is there any love greater than the love of a wife who is prepared to forfeit and sacrifice her own life to save the life of her husband? Even at the point of facing death, her only thoughts were to try and save her husband. I think at that moment, though, she had not thought about us. Kurt had spent 24 hours on his own, waiting for me to come home and share this fate with him. Once again, we were alone! The first time it was the Gestapo that had caused this, but now it was our Mutti's action that had broken faith and trust with us. Had she not given a moment's thought as to what would happen to us? How could she desert us like this, to save Papa's life. What about ours? We were sitting in the living room as her action confounded us. We had no thoughts or feelings, only loneliness and numbness. We felt all alone in the world. One cannot find the right words to describe how we felt. How could Mutti do this to us if she loved us? We felt abandoned, unloved — apparently, we were not worth being considered. We were deserted, we felt desperate and desolate. We were so hurt that we could not even cry. There was not even a farewell note. Emotionally, we could not sink any lower.

I remember looking around the room, gazing at the familiar furniture and bits and pieces, but they gave no comfort, no answers. I went over to the piano. I had had a few lessons from Mutti and could play a few finger exercises and scales. I asked Kurt whether playing these might help us and give us an intuition of what to do as often happened when Mutti played. All we could do was pray and go to the hospital and wait there for days, but we were not allowed to see Mutti. Waiting and hanging around near her door might annoy Schmidt of the Gestapo. At home, all we could think about was, "Oh God, please let Mutti come home again."

Finally, the doctor assured us that Mutti had pulled through, but he could not understand why the Gestapo had threatened him with deportation.

I think that we were on our own, during that time when a strong bond was forged between us. We had to rely on each other and later in life, if one of us needed help or advice, we always turned to the other.

After a long, long time — an eternity for Kurt and me — Mutti came home again. Before she was discharged from the hospital, Schmidt informed her that for the time being Papa would remain in the labour camp and should Mutti pull another stunt like this, it would be fatal for all of us.

We shared with Mutti her relief at the outcome of this drama, but it took its toll emotionally on Kurt as he became very quiet and withdrawn.

To cheer us up, our landlord, Herr Schulz, tried to give us all a break and invited the three of us to accompany him to the Munich Hofbrau Haus. As soon as we entered, we saw a Bavarian band playing folk songs. People had linked arms and were swaying in rhythm to the music. We soon found a table and Kurt and I drank apple juice. Everybody was happy. The band leader honoured regular customers by taking the band to their table and offering them the baton, thus showing everyone else that conducting was not that easy. The conductor pointed out that the band would only play as the guest conductor indicated. The music started, but only one instrument played. The guest conductor had not indicated that the whole orchestra should play. Well-known melodies became distorted as he conducted a waltz at the speed of a funeral march! As soon as the guest conductor had worked out the speed and how to conduct all the instruments, the baton was passed on to the next guest. We all laughed and laughed until the tears ran down our cheeks. Everybody was enjoying themselves immensely.

We sat at an oblong refectory table and shared it with several other people. All of a sudden, people were whispering to each other and finally the news reached us that Captain Langsdorff (later captain of the battleship *Graf Spee*) had arrived. Everyone knew about his great achievements — the latest was a cruise round the world with very little modern equipment on board the ship, not only to find out how old-time seafarers coped, but also to discover new sea lanes.

The people at our table suggested that I should go and ask him for an autograph. At first, we resisted, but to keep everyone calm Mutti suggested that I buy a picture postcard from the Hofbrau Haus and take that over. I vividly remember the postcard, with its picture of the Hofbrau Haus symbols — a beer tankard, a radish and a pretzel.

Shyly, I approached the Captain's table, curtseyed and asked for his autograph. He looked at me quizzically for a while; then a gentle smile of recognition crossed his face and he nodded his head ever so slightly. Yes, he remembered me. Taking the picture postcard, he asked me for my name. Then in Plattdeutsch, a dialect used in Hamburg and by sailors, he wrote: "Dear Trudi, don't look into a mousehole, but, head up high, look at the sun."

While he wrote this, I realised that this was the officer that had helped us months before. He looked at me thoughtfully when, with a gentle smile, he handed the card back to me. Again, I curtseyed as I thanked him for his kindness. It was a German custom for well-brought-up little girls to curtsey when greeting a person. This custom died out soon afterwards as the "Heil Hitler" greeting replaced it. Excited, I returned to our table, but Mutti shook her head and so I waited till we got home to tell her about the Captain.

Amongst all this joviality, a man got up and stood on top of his table. He was slightly tipsy. He picked up two ashtrays, made of the rounded ends of 1914–18 cannon balls. Putting the flat sides together, he opened and closed the two halves asking, "Who is this talking?" Everybody was laughing as he answered his own question, "Dr Goebbels." Suddenly, a hush fell over the hall as four men came to the table and pulled the man roughly down and dragged him away. One can only guess what happened to him. The saying went, "Three years in concentration camp for a bad joke — five years for a good one." Even amongst a happy crowd, the sinister overtones were always present. As soon as it was possible, without drawing attention to ourselves, we left for home.

CHAPTER
TWO

Trips to Frankfurt and Sylt

Christmas 1935 — Hard times continue

A letter arrived from Auntie, inviting me to stay with them for four weeks. I did not want to go to Frankfurt. It was so far away, and I didn't want to leave Mutti and Kurt alone. What if trouble flared up again, who could help them if I was away? Mutti was firm. I cried, begged and even stamped my foot, something normally not in my nature. Mutti explained that while I stayed with Auntie, she could save the money I would cost to feed and spend it on Kurt. He was still suffering from the shock of finding Mutti nearly dead.

So came the dreaded day and I was seen off at the station. I had to travel on my own, but Mutti asked the guard on the train to keep an eye on me and put me off at the right station. Auntie was waiting there and welcomed me. She hugged me and cried a little, and kept saying, "You poor little soul, poor little sparrow. You must forget about it all while you are staying with us."

From that moment life rushed past me. My three cousins kept me busy all the time and I learned to laugh again. There was so much to see in Frankfurt: the well-known Palm Gardens, for example, and the old houses in the centre of the city (Römer). As my cousins knew how little money we had, they took me round the different ice cream parlours, something we did not have in Hamburg, and I remarked that the ice cream tasted different from ours up north, so I was spoiled and was given ice cream several times a day, eating ice cream till I could not face another cone or spoonful!

A few days later, we packed our luggage and Uncle drove us all to their country house in the Taunus mountains. Auntie hoped that this would build me up, with the fresh mountain air and the scent of the many pines and other trees.

It was a small village and we soon adapted to the ways of the country folk, searching for mushrooms for breakfast and picking wild berries. My cousins were Victoria, four years older than me, Elsie, two years younger, and Bernhard, three and a half years younger. Instead of resting after lunch in our bedrooms, we preferred to put up tents and rest in them. When Uncle could take time off from work, he would drive from Frankfurt and join us. He would take us out in the car. It must have been quite large as we all seemed to fit in easily, Auntie sitting in the front and the four of us on the back seat. Passing through towns and villages, again these looked so different from houses in the north. They were timber-framed and had many window boxes planted with geraniums and begonias. I remember seeing many flags and placards proclaiming, "Vote for Hitler, if you want to be free."

I had never seen so much fanaticism and political propaganda. I mentioned this to my relatives and their reply was simple. "You northerners, especially Hamburgers with all your shipyards, you are brushed a little red" — a reference to communism.

Uncle's hobby was stalking deer. He would get up at 4 a.m. and drive out to the country to a spot where grass fields and if possible a brook bordered the forest. The deer would leave the forest to graze and drink from the stream. Uncle would not literally shoot them, but he had a good camera and would "shoot" with that. One fine morning, he insisted that we come with him, leaving at 4 a.m. as usual. When we arrived at his favourite spot, we all got out, leaving the car behind, and walked for the next hour through the forest. We were not allowed to talk and had to watch where we trod as the breaking of a twig would warn the deer of our presence. We finally arrived at the meadow, but something alarmed the deer, because all we saw were their backsides as they ran away. By now it had started to rain and we had to walk all the way back to the car, looking and feeling like drowned rats.

Victoria's school had an outing, a cruise down the Rhine, and Auntie thought that I would enjoy this. Just as we were leaving, Victoria rushed back and picked up the large bottle of Eau de Cologne 4711, which was a gift from me. To start with, I was rather melancholic as I remembered my family's car journey in that happy time before Papa was taken from us. The countryside looked quite different from the boat. It was the middle of the summer and very hot. The girls from Victoria's form thought that I was quaint, so pale and fair, and with the way I spoke so different from the dialect of the Rhineland. As we cruised along, they sang lots of songs about the Rhine.

When we arrived at St Goar, we disembarked and had to climb the narrow path up the mountain. It was the quick way up to the top of the massive Lorelei rock. As the sides of this passage were made of slate that reflected the absorbed heat of the day, it became very hot and I could hardly keep up with them. Then my cousin produced the bottle of Eau de Cologne, sprinkled some on a handkerchief and wiped my face with it. This revived me a little. Finally we reached the top and the bottle was empty. All the others cheered that the girl from the north coast had managed to keep up with these suntanned girls. Looking down onto the Rhine, we could see the Lorelei rock thrusting dangerously into the river, causing a sharp bend and creating lots of whirlpools. It was easy to see how the legend had sprung up of a golden blonde mermaid, sitting on the rock and combing her hair. Sailors would look up at the rock, entranced, instead of watching the dangerous currents, and so the boat would sink.

Time passed very quickly and the carefree holiday came to an end. Auntie packed an extra suitcase filled with dresses from her and my eldest cousin. Auntie was much taller than Mutti and quite plump. She said, "Your mother is wonderful with needle and thread, and can soon alter the dresses to fit her and you." She also packed a suit from Uncle. Mutti could alter this for Kurt as he had outgrown his clothes.

Then at the station came the goodbyes. I remember we all shed a tear, hugging each other. Just as the train was leaving, Auntie called out, "Remember where we live, if you need help. You fitted in so well — just like one of the family."

This time the train journey was more enjoyable as I was going home. Both Mutti and Kurt were waiting at the station and they looked fine. What a relief. Mutti hugged and kissed me over and over again. Finally she said, "Let's look at you. What a lot of sunshine you must have had — you are so suntanned. My little brown mermaid!"

During the first three weeks of school, my class was supposed to visit the school's holiday home on the island of Sylt. Mutti pointed out to the headmaster that the cost of food and travel was too much for her to pay and she would prefer it if I could go to school as usual. The headmaster explained to her that in cases of hardship, the school fund would sponsor everything. So Mutti sat up a couple of nights and altered some of the dresses Auntie had sent. I felt as nicely dressed as all the other girls. We had no school uniform.

We all met at the Hauptbahnhof (main railway station). Two teachers were in charge of us. We were all so excited and busy waving goodbye to our families. This time I left in a happier frame of mind than when I had travelled to Frankfurt as the weeks there had shown me that Mutti and Kurt could cope on their own.

Time passed quickly as we sang and munched our sandwiches. At last we arrived at the Hindenburg Dam, which connects the island with the mainland. It is a single rail track and as the tide was in, the water reached right up to the top of the dam and we seemed to be floating on the water. What excitement. As soon as we reached land again, the train slowed up. We had arrived at our destination, the village of Keitum. The teachers had their hands full trying to calm us girls down and getting us to walk in an orderly formation to the home, "Friesenhof". It was a big 18th-century Frisian farmhouse. The walls were painted white and were surmounted by a thatched roof. To complete the picture, a large cartwheel had been placed on the top of the roof to encourage storks to build their nest. In front of the house, along the white wall, grew pink and red hollyhocks. To us it looked just like a fairyland house.

Our beds were in a large dormitory and as soon as we had unpacked, the bell rang to let us know that tea was served. The teachers took this opportunity to lay down some strict house rules, which they expected us to obey instantly — as we were near so much water, it could be dangerous if we didn't. If every girl behaved as was expected of her, every one could relax and enjoy the holiday. It was not all playtime, however. Every morning we had school lessons adapted to our surroundings. German literature, geography and history of the island, then biology to learn about the natural life of the island and the sea around us. We had to find sea stars and different shells, spot different types of birds and, finally, try out map reading. These lessons took place every morning and in the afternoon we were allowed on the beach. On Sunday mornings we went to the church service wearing our best dresses and a wreath of flowers in our hair. On the beach, we took great pride in building a castle, and as the tide never covered the beach except during storms, we claimed that bit of the beach as our own. We held competitions for who could decorate the walls of the castle with shells most artistically. We left our clothes in our castle and we squealed with delight as we entered the cold water.

Then came the first outing, to the other side of the island facing the North Sea. Westerland is the rich people's resort, with elegant promenades and beach basket chairs. This part of the beach was not for us as you had to pay an entrance fee, so we walked further along the dunes to the free beach. Again, we had a lesson on nature study and then we were allowed in the water. It was a child's paradise. The water was so clear and clean that if you were knee-deep in the water, you could still see your toes perfectly. We splashed in the water as it was too shallow to swim in.

One stormy day the teachers took us to Westerland again. We stood on the dunes watching the waves rushing up towards us. The beach was covered by the sea water. The waves fought restlessly with each other, each one trying to outdo the other, getting higher and higher — as high as a house. They came rushing, roaring, crashing towards us, all covered with white foam. If we half closed our eyes, the foam looked like wild white stallions with flowing manes. When the sea is like this, it is so powerful and frightening. The sky was not to be left out of this battle, with the gale force winds and dramatic clouds. The whole firmament was a spectacular, powerful scene and we felt so small and helpless watching it.

Then came a day when we were told to go to bed in the afternoon and sleep. This was to prepare us for a test, to see if we could read the map and find our way around part of the island at night. We carried our rucksacks with sandwiches and a drink, along with soap and a towel, while in our jacket pockets we carried a compass and map.

The sea and beach looked quite different from during the day, dark and mysterious. No sea gulls shrieking. We walked for hours along the beach and inland. We were getting very tired so the teachers told us to dig a hollow in the sand and lie in it to get some sleep. The hollow would protect us from the wind. We looked at the stars shining brightly in the night sky and soon fell asleep. As we woke up in the morning, we went to the sea to wash ourselves. We blinked our eyes as we couldn't believe what we saw. There were lots of men and women either sleeping or walking, but all of them stark naked. We looked and looked again, and started to giggle — our giggles became bashful, girlish squeals. This woke the teachers up, and when they realised what was causing this giggling session, they told us to pack our things and march on without looking sideways. When we were alone again, we rested and had our packed breakfast. Then we checked our maps. Soon we found out that we had left the path too early and so strayed into a nudist colony!

By now we had been a week in Keitum and having all behaved as was expected of us, we were given

34

unsupervised free time in the evenings. Most girls would walk as far as the village and go window-shopping. Several of my friends wanted to see what was beyond the village. We reached open country and we noticed a campsite for the Arbeitsdienst soldiers ("soldiers with a spade", whose task was building roads and houses). Two soldiers stood on guard at the gate. As we passed them, we saluted "Heil Hitler!" To our surprise they jumped to attention and saluted back. We were impressed. On our way home we once again saluted and again they stood to attention. We were thrilled that we had so much influence, remembering that we were just 11 to 12 years of age. To us young girls this was great fun. We told several other girls about it and formed some groups. It became a game for us. As each group passed these solders, saluting took place. The other group watched from a distance. Soon after tea, full of mischief we would rush out to play this game. We thought that perhaps on the third day they would tell us to stop and get lost, but no, perfect saluting continued!

On the fourth day, we noticed that a man in civilian clothes was following us. Later we realised that it was to find out where we lived. Then the next day, at lunchtime, we had to face an officer from the camp who demanded, in very strong words, that we stop our behaviour or else he would take drastic measures. He put the fear of God into us. The teachers made sure that we obeyed this order as our free time privilege was taken away and we were given extra duties as punishment.

We also visited different churches and the teachers explained why they were so strongly built. They had to serve a double purpose. They were places of worship, but they also had to act as fortresses to protect the people from the Vikings and Danes when they invaded the island.

After three weeks we were all brown as chestnuts and looking much healthier. Returning to school, we were all very enthusiastic about collecting the potato peelings and stale bread as this is what had helped us have this wonderful open-air adventure holiday.

Herr Schulz, the owner of the house and with whom we shared the flat, had a crippled foot as the result of a car accident. All the bones in the foot had been broken and they had healed badly and deformed the foot. The point is that it was not an inherited disease and no genes would pass this deformity on. Under the Nazi law, however, a cripple was not allowed to produce children. People with any deformities were either sterilised or castrated, depending on the severity. Herr Schulz received a letter from the authorities, ordering him to report to the hospital for an operation. When he returned from this ordeal, he turned into a recluse and asked Mutti to find other accommodation now as he no longer desired to look after himself. He left as soon as possible for a residential home.

The reasonable calmness of our existence was once again shattered and another restless period started for us.

Mutti began searching for other accommodation that we could afford and finally found somewhere in a suburb. It was a very modern flat providing hot and cold running water and central heating from a boiler room looked after by a caretaker. Also in the basement was a laundry room with washing machines, spin dryers, warm air dryers and a large hot mangle — and to give the laundry the finishing touch, we could use the iron. All you had to do was to book the time and day, saying which equipment you wanted to use, and supply your own soap powder. It was one of the new blocks of flats built by the Arbeitsdienst. This being so, a very patriotic warden was put in charge to look after the tenants.

It was one of those many days when we were expected to put the Swastika flag out of the window. We did not own one as Herr Schulz had taken care of this in the previous apartment, and we definitely could not afford to buy one. Early in the morning the block warden came to see Mutti and pointed out the absence of the cherished flag. Mutti explained that she could not afford to buy one. The block warden offered one to us and hoped that in future we would hang the flag out of the window with pride.

The flat was small, consisting of a lounge, one large and one small bedroom, bathroom and kitchen. Mutti and I shared the large bedroom and Kurt slept in the small one. Once again, we had money trouble as we had to pay rent and so food was once more scarce.

Mutti became thoughtful, her mind working overtime. Christmas was drawing nearer and the three of us would go window-shopping, looking at all the goodies. Christmas specialities included marzipan breads, Christmas biscuits, bananas, shiny red apples and oranges. We also had a look at the toy department. Looking didn't cost any money. Finally, Mutti asked us what we would like for Christmas, but it must not be too expensive. I closed my eyes and wished for one big shiny apple. Just one. Sadly Mutti shook her head. "We cannot afford it." I think at that moment her heart must have broken as she saw my disappointed face. Home again, we railed at Mutti. "Must you send that monthly parcel to Papa? With all that delicatessen we can hardly afford." The parcel contained a whole salami sausage, a liver sausage and a few of the cigars that Papa used to smoke. But in the last of his letters (which were few and far between), he had made a point of requesting Turkish cigarettes. Papa never mentioned the parcels and Mutti surmised that these cigarettes were for whoever checked the parcels, perhaps also the sausages. Mutti pointed out that if a few cigarettes and sausages made Papa's life a little easier, we should be grateful and do our bit. He was confined in a labour camp with all its evil and hardship, while we had our freedom and so far had survived. I don't remember us getting anything.

A few days before Christmas Eve, however, a huge parcel arrived for us from Mutti's sister in Frankfurt. Dresses from Auntie for Mutti. She could easily alter them to fit herself. Dresses from my cousin for me and a suit from Uncle that would make nice plus-fours and a jacket for Kurt. Mutti could work wonders with a needle. We took our time to unpack the parcel. Everything was touched and admired. Then we came to small packets wrapped in Christmas paper. We turned them over and over, and tried to guess what they

38

contained. We decided to leave these small parcels till Christmas Eve. That is when Father Christmas arrives. The parcel proved Mutti's theory once again. When things look really black, God sends a ray of sunshine.

We celebrated Christmas Eve in the usual ritual way: Mutti playing carols on the piano and us singing them. Then my brother and I had to recite a Christmas poem and Mutti would tell or read a Christmas fable. Only then were we allowed to unwrap our presents. We were so excited, showing each other what wonderful gifts we had received. Apples, more than the single one I had wished for, and yes, many other Christmas specialities as well, stollen, gingerbreads, marzipan sweets covered with chocolate and shaped like a miniature loaf, honey and some continental sausages. The table was laden with all these good foods fit for a king.

After Christmas, Mutti once again became very thoughtful. She checked Papa's books and kept saying to herself over and over again, "All that money. The savings bank account hasn't been confiscated and one firm has not yet paid our money to the state. Dare I try and draw some money out of the bank account?"

She knew the consequences if she were caught. Which one was best to tackle first, the bank or the firm? Many evenings we sat round the table trying to work out a scheme. The three of us agreed that the bank did not involve anyone else, and also that this time I should help Mutti as so far Kurt had taken the brunt of the trouble and he was still suffering emotionally from the previous episode. I was still only 11 and a half years old.

We had some dummy runs to the bank and found out the best way in which to get away from there. Lots of trams passed by and we decided to use these, taking the first one that came along to wherever it was going.

One fine spring morning Mutti said to me, "Today is B-day. Bank day."

The plan was that she would go into the bank on her own. We had previously decided that I should wait outside for ten minutes and then follow her into the bank. This was a precaution in case this account was a trap for us and the bank notified the Gestapo. If there was any trouble at the counter or if some men came for her, then I should walk straight out again. If all went well, I should go to her. It would look more harmless with mother and daughter walking out together. Those ten minutes passed very slowly for me until, with apprehensive feelings, I entered the bank. All looked calm, but as I approached the counter where Mutti stood I noticed that she kept shaking her head, so I looked round for somewhere I could wait unobserved. I could feel my heart pounding in my ears. I saw a table and chair, and I pretended that I wanted to write something while watching Mutti. Then she turned round and waved to me with a happy smile. I wanted to run up to her, so that we could get away as quickly as possible, but Mutti's last instructions were, "Don't run or rush. Don't draw attention to yourself. Cashing money from the bank is routine for us. Remember, nothing extraordinary." So, to keep myself under control, I kept saying to myself, "Walk, walk, just walk," counting the rhythm "1, 2, 3, 4, walk." When I reached

Mutti she introduced me to the cashier smiling, "Ah, my big daughter has come to take me shopping." With that, she said farewell and we walked slowly to the door and out of the bank, pretending to talk about the forthcoming shopping spree. Outside we looked for the first tram that stopped and we jumped on, going away from the danger spot. Once home we hugged each other, delighted at the outcome of our intrigue.

Next day we went to a savings bank and Mutti opened two accounts to safeguard the money. One was in Kurt's name and one was in mine. We hoped that the Gestapo would not think of checking accounts in our names and should Mutti get into trouble with the Gestapo, Kurt and I would have a little money to help us along.

Mutti had drawn out only some of the money from the bank and several weeks later she thought that we should have another go and try to get more money out, while still leaving a reasonable amount in that account. This time we reversed the arrangements. I should go in and she would wait for me outside the bank. Last minute instructions: "Go to the same cashier. Smile in a friendly way. Don't talk unless you are spoken to. Let him put the money into the brown leather bag and lock it. Don't run, whatever you do."

I went in and followed Mutti's instructions. So far, so good. The cashier made a remark about not spending all the money at once. "Oh no, it's going to be our holiday money," I said. Then came the unexpected reply, "Where are you going for your holidays?" Without hesitation I responded quickly, thinking about the school holiday in Keitum on Sylt. He seemed satisfied, nodding his head, "Yes, Sylt is rather expensive. Enjoy yourselves."

Now leave the bank, slowly does it. All had gone well again. Mutti said that we would not touch the rest of the money, but it would give us a small kitty for when Papa came home again. When would that be? When the powers that be thought that he was educated in the true Nazi spirit.

One day Mutti confronted us with her next plan. She wanted to contact the one firm that had not paid its debts either to the state or to us. Dared she tackle the managing director of the firm, the owner? But needs must. Again she had the idea of contacting her childhood friend, now in the SS. Would he come to Hamburg and help her? All he had to do was sit at a table in the Second Class restaurant in the main station and give her moral support. She arranged to meet the proprietor of the firm at the same time. I was to accompany her. As it happened, he was Jewish. Mutti asked him nicely why he had not paid us or handed the money over to the state. He made several different excuses, but finally told the truth. He pointed out that he knew Papa was in a labour camp and rather than getting involved, he preferred to remain silent. Mutti told him how hard up we were and asked him please to give us half of our money. The rest he could keep for himself. He refused, saying that if the Gestapo were to find out that he had had business dealings with us, he would need the money to hand over to them. Mutti begged and begged him for part of our money, but to

42

no avail. Mutti's thoughts were fixed on her family and its future and survival, and especially on that time when Papa would come home again. That was when we would need money.

It was painful for me to see my gentle mother, who never hurt a soul, becoming so hard. She pointed out to the businessman that not far from our table sat an SS man in his black uniform who was a friend of ours. To prove this last point, Mutti looked over to him and he waved to us. The businessman then became very agitated and wanted to leave, but Mutti was determined to get some of our money from him. It was money that belonged to us. She stopped him from leaving and said that it would be in his own interest to pay her. She again asked for half the money, saying he could keep the rest. If he didn't agree to these terms, he would have to pay it all to the state as she would call her friend over and tell him the situation. The businessman became very angry, but finally paid her the requested half of what he owed us. They then parted as amicable acquaintances. It seems strange to me that, regardless of creed or race, when people have possession of other people's money, they are loath to part with it, but prefer to line their own pockets.

Before leaving the restaurant, we went over to the friend and Mutti thanked him for just being there. He smiled and said, "What are friends for, if they cannot sometimes give a helping hand?"

Again this money went into the special accounts. "This will be very helpful for when Papa comes home again," Mutti said. "We shall use just a little of it to keep body and soul together. At least it will prevent us going to bed hungry."

Our way of life was now established. As long as we did not make any ripples but disappeared into the crowd, we stood a chance of surviving, but the fear of being found out haunted us continually. Constant fear is a draining emotion.

CHAPTER
THREE

Easter 1938

Papa released — Escape from Germany

A few weeks before Easter 1938, before the school term ended, the headmaster warned us that Baldur von Schirach, the leader of the Hitler Youth, would be visiting the senior schools in Hamburg and that he had "sent us a message", as he put it. He had notified us in good time so that we would do something about it. He would visit the schools after Easter and all those girls who were not in the BDM (the Bund Deutscher Mädel — the Union of German Girls, part of the Hitler Youth) — would be questioned by him personally about the reason why they were not in the movement. If, in his opinion, there was no valid reason, then the girl would be asked to leave the school. This was not the end of the tale. Anyone drummed out for not being a member of the party would also not be able to get a job. No employer would voluntarily ask for trouble and stir up a hornets' nest. The message was doubly important for us. So, the next week, I asked if I might join the BDM group where several girls from my class were members.

Much propaganda was being made about the Anschluss (annexation) of Austria to Germany. At school we had to draw maps of Germany and Austria — "Greater Germany" as it now was. The Anschluss map. The best map would win the prize of a visit to Austria. Patriotic Germans in both countries reached fever pitch about it all. The news about the Anschluss began to dominate everything. History lessons, geography, literature — all were based on Austria and how the Austrians had begged to become part of Germany and wanted to embrace Hitlerism. On 14th March 1938 there were great celebrations and jubilation, with film shows of Hitler marching into Austria and Vienna. Crowds cheered wildly and young girls threw flowers at the marching troops. Older people wept with joy and the crowds called fanatically for Hitler.

While all this excitement was taking place, we too had ours. A letter arrived from the Gestapo informing us that Papa would be coming home at the beginning of April. We too joined in celebrating the Anschluss — but in a different sense. For us it was the Anschluss of Papa to the family. We too were excited and we planned our welcome. I was especially excited because it was well known in the family that my brother was Mutti's favourite. She had been brought up by her mother, a young widow, to long for a boy. Granny had had three daughters, so when my brother was born, the baby boy so longed for by Mutti and Granny was treated like a gift from heaven. I did not take much notice of this favouritism as Papa always gave me that extra bit of attention and love. When he was taken from us, it hit me especially hard, but now he was coming home.

Mutti made a suggestion. "When Papa comes, both of you children go into the bedroom. It may be too emotional and overpowering if the three of us greet him and he sees how much the two of you have grown in those years lost to him."

The doorbell rang.

"Hush, hush, children. Into the bedroom and don't come out till I call you."

By now we had learned how to wait quietly. Eventually Mutti's voice called us. I ran out of the bedroom first. I ran to meet Papa. The moment I saw him, I stopped dead in my tracks. That was not my Papa. He looked so different. As he stood up, he needed to support himself and he had difficulty in moving one leg and arm which seemed stiff. Mutti saw my face and explained that Papa had had a stroke. I wanted to embrace him, hug him, but this was a different father from the one that had left us. Even his eyes were different. They were still blue, but not the clear azure blue of before, but paler, a watery blue, and they seemed smaller. His hair was so short and his skin looked dirty-greyish. He held out his hand and it shook and trembled. I could not touch it and shake it. Then I remembered that he would be sent home when he had been re-educated into the new German spirit, so I quickly stood to attention and saluted him — "Heil Hitler" — and ran from the room. Somehow that bond between us never grew again. In later years I grew bitter towards him because of all the hardship we had been through and still had to face. Bitter because he had never given a thought to making the family secure, should fate deal us a bad hand. It would have been easy to put some money into a special account as Mutti had, in my brother's and my name.

From the moment Papa came home again, things happened fast. Family conference after family conference. Papa would not talk about his experiences, his time away from us, in order not to burden our minds unnecessarily, so that we could start looking forward to the future. All the time Papa kept telling us not to breathe a word to anyone about our family conferences, decisions and plans. I don't think he realised the good training we had had in staying silent, keeping secrets and waiting for hours and even days on end.

As far as Papa could see, there would be no chance of a job for him. We had to consider emigration. But where to? Papa's choice was Africa. Mutti opposed this suggestion, and Kurt and I agreed with her, saying that those wild open spaces were not for us. America? This seemed feasible, but how would we get there?

No one must know about our plans. A good German does not leave his country. Ships sailing from Hamburg were mostly German. Apart from that, we dared not go through the customs in Hamburg. Papa did not have a passport. The Gestapo had taken it, and mine, a child's passport, had expired as they were issued for one year only. Mutti and Kurt still had theirs. Thanks to a little luck, the Gestapo had overlooked these. Finally, the plans were made that Papa should ask the Gestapo to organise a passport for him and me. In return Papa offered to try and see if the Dutch business contacts would do business with the rival Nazi firm, something they had wanted to start three years before. As Papa applied for just the two of us, the authorities thought all would be well as Mutti and Kurt would be staying behind. After we got our passports, Papa decided to do everything by the book as he did not want any trouble when crossing the border. All men in the age group for military service had to have military permission to leave the country, so he applied for this. Now we had to think carefully. Were there any other obstacles to overcome?

Next came the planning and packing of our clothes. One case per person. Some summer clothes and some for the winter.

The woman living in the flat below us was married to a Dutchman living in Holland and when she met my father she took a fancy to him. My parents took the risk of asking her whether she would help us. Could she send some of our things in her name by boat to Holland and store them in the port? Further instructions would follow. For this help she could choose anything from our home that she wanted.

The timing of sending these goods was very important. They must not cross the customs in Hamburg before we crossed the Dutch border. The customs officers might check out the address of the sender and so find out about our escape plan. If we were lucky enough to get these goods to Holland, it would help us and give us a fresh start in a new country.

The items were carefully chosen. Some household linen, bed linen, towels and tablecloths, a dinner and tea service, some saucepans. Some of Mutti's favourite books. Some photos. Two leather armchairs, a long case clock and a Singer sewing machine. The household linen, photos and books were packed in a large oblong wicker basket and the breakable goods into a large oak box. It was Mutti's, in which she had collected years ago for her dowry.

The rule in Germany was that when a person left their flat overnight, it had to be reported to the block warden. My parents even did this, telling the warden that we were going to visit Mutti's sister and family in south Germany.

Papa used some of the saved-up money to buy himself a new suit, coat, shirt and shoes as well as the rail tickets. Then he even visited some of the farmers he used to do business with and bought some horseradish. This was one of the foods he used to export to Scotland. When this was sold abroad, it would give us some money to start with as taking money out of Germany was restricted.

As the hours passed and minutes were ticking away, Mutti and Papa made a last check that we had packed all the necessary papers — passport, military permission for Papa, birth certificates and my parents' marriage licence. I was hugging and hanging onto my baby doll.

Late in the evening we made our way to the main station to catch the train for Holland. The first suggestion was that we should split up and travel at

50

different times and then meet again in Holland. Mutti was against this. "We should go as a family and help each other over difficult moments." All the furniture and carpets, and Mutti's piano, were left in the flat. Papa locked the door and put the key through the letterbox.

This was the moment of no return. No one spoke a word and tears were streaming down Mutti's face. As we descended the stairs, Papa said to her, "Don't look back!" He realised that if Mutti did so, she would not be able to step out into the unknown, especially as she did not speak a word of English. Papa spoke some, and Kurt had passed his Higher School Certificate in English, while I had been learning it for one year. With heavy hearts and fearful of the future, we travelled by taxi to the station. Mutti sat very still and had her eyes closed.

Kurt's school friend, Otto, who knew our history, was asked if he would give us a helping hand in carrying our luggage. We had packed one case per person and a small one for our documents. I was not strong enough to carry a big case and Papa could not carry two cases with his paralysed arm. Otto was also told that we were going south to stay at my Auntie's, to try and see whether we could make a new start there. My parents thought that it would look better if someone saw us off, but even he must not know our real destination.

We took a last look at the station. The guard blew the whistle and the express train's wheels started. As the train passed Otto, he spotted the board on the compartment — Amsterdam. He ran to catch up with us and shouted, "God bless, safe journey to Amsterdam." A last farewell wave from my brother and me.

We sat down. No one spoke a word as we all had our own thoughts about the unknown future. Kurt and I looked out of the window, a last glimpse of Hamburg, and we wondered whether we would ever see it again. (Kurt died in 1961. He never returned to Germany for a visit.) Even the rhythm of the wheels seemed to forecast the future, with their repetitive chant, "Never come again, never come again." Once again it was in the dark of the night that our lives changed.

My parents suggested that Kurt and I should try to sleep because none of us had been able to for the past few nights. I clutched my baby doll tightly as I would not leave her behind. She was all soft and cuddly. Digging my nose into her shoulder, I pretended to sleep. Fortunately, there were only two other occupants in the compartment. Mutti pretended to help us to sit comfortably. She put her finger across her mouth and said, "Not a word."

The other occupants of the compartment wanted to talk, but my parents made some excuse that the children were too full of excitement and it had worn them out, so they needed a rest themselves before we children had replenished our stocks of energy.

It was a long journey. A noise woke us from our slumber. The shutting and opening of compartment doors. The customs men. There were two of them, greeting everybody with the usual "Heil Hitler! Passports please!"

One of the customs men was angry with the other man in the compartment. He shouted that no German so far had had a military permit to leave the country. They were going to stop the train at the next station, a small station, and would make sure that all German men who were without permits left the train and returned to Germany. They would hold up the train till they had checked that every man had got off. His angry voice boomed into the compartment. I clutched my doll tighter and tighter, and started to cry. I could not cope with this situation as I knew the consequences if we were sent back to Germany. The customs man wanted to know why I was crying. Mutti replied quickly, "My daughter is just over-tired through the excitement of going on a foreign holiday."

Papa had shrunk emotionally into his shell. The shouting had brought back bad memories from the labour camp. Mutti laughed and said, "Ah, Heinrich. We're the lucky ones. We can go on because you have the military permission for leave of absence from Germany. Please show it to the officer."

Mutti's voice seemed to shake him out of his emotional freeze. After the customs men had checked our passports and the military permit, he pointed out to the other man in the compartment what a good and law-abiding citizen Papa was and he wished there were more like him.

The train halted at the small station while the customs men completed the checking of the rest of the passengers. He then returned and told the other man in our compartment to get off. Naturally, his wife left with him. The train stopped a long, long time. Our hearts were pounding. No one spoke a word during the waiting time as our thoughts ran riot. Had the furniture gone through the Hamburg customs and been loaded onto a ship? Did anyone suspect anything yet? As the minutes ticked away, they seemed like hours. At last the guard blew the whistle. Mutti asked us to look out of the window and wave to the customs officers.

After a short while, the compartment door opened again. The Dutch customs officers came in and greeted us with, "Guten Morgen. You are in Holland."

We all cried with relief. Mutti gave the customs officer a big hug. Again she took the lead and simply said, "You are the most welcome sight." I think they guessed why we were so emotional and replied, "Welcome to Holland. Hope you will be happy here."

The train took us to Amsterdam. We booked into a hotel and Papa contacted his business associate to talk about business and the money he held for us, money he was to have paid for goods received from us three years before. All the family was invited and then plans were made about how we could get to America. Mr Jan pointed out that the money was invested and he could not get at it easily. He had to give notice to release it and this would take some time. Papa suggested that he should give us some of his own money and use our invested money to repay himself. There was no risk involved that he would be out of pocket because he already held our money.

Our visit was very different from the one three years earlier, when my parents had been fêted, wined and dined, and Kurt and I given so much chocolate. This time the atmosphere was cold and indifferent, not at all friendly. My brother and I were not invited to play with their sons as before. All the time Mr Jan tried to hurry our departure to England, and even suggested that Kurt and Papa should go on their own and secure a place on an English ship bound for America. Mutti and I could travel later and join them in England. It sounded sensible, but Mutti dug her heels in, pointing out that we had agreed before leaving Hamburg that we wouldn't split up when crossing the Dutch-German border and that we should always travel together. The timing was crucial as many Austrian refugees were arriving in England and the British government was introducing restrictions, with entry by visa only. They did not give an exact date when they would enforce this new law. All we were waiting for was our money — or at least some of it — from Mr Jan. It always surprises me how decent people, when they get hold of some extra money that does not belong to them, are loath to part with it. They tell all sorts of lies to wriggle out of an obligation. Finally, Mr Jan offered us some money to get rid of us and promised to send the rest on when we had a settled address. He knew very well that once we had left Holland, we could not return and collect it. We never received that promised money. He refused to send it. Mutti decided that the moment we had some money, we should leave.

While waiting for the money, my parents thought it would be a pleasant change if we joined the musical evening in the hotel and had a drink. A girl band was playing all the familiar melodies. One girl in the band played an accordion. This was an instrument that I longed to play. I hoped that when I was old enough to hold the instrument and my fingers were long enough and strong enough to manage the keys that perhaps my parents would be able to afford to buy one for me. I was hypnotised, listening and watching her perform. She noticed this and came to our table and played just for me. I still remember the song, "Hear my song, Violetta!". I was on cloud nine!

Just before we had gone downstairs to the musical evening, Papa had insisted that he should look after my passport. I felt very hurt and indignant. I pointed out that I was a big girl — 13 years and 9 months old. Still Papa insisted and reluctantly, I took my passport out of my handbag and handed it over to him. When we joined the musical party, I put my handbag behind me on the chair. When it was time to go to bed, we all went to our rooms. I was busy dreaming girlish dreams and forgot to pick up my bag. Arriving in our rooms, I had a sneezing attack and needed a handkerchief, when I realised that I had left my bag downstairs on the chair. I ran as fast as I could to the restaurant, but the people who had occupied the table and chairs after us had already left, taking my handbag with them. I went to the waiter and asked if those people had handed my bag to him. They had not. Oh dear, I had lost it. I was very upset and my grown-up dignity suffered badly. As a result of this episode I still have a phobia of losing my handbag and wherever I go, my handbag goes with me, even from room to room inside my own house. I thanked Papa for his foresight and wisdom. If I had lost my passport, God only knows what we would have done then.

Mutti, however, with her acute sixth sense, had a feeling of foreboding and she was determined to act on it. "We must leave tonight or it will be too late," she said. Although it seemed irrational, it turned out that her instincts were accurate. Our final escape from the turmoil of mainland Europe was about to take place. Mutti had made up her mind that we should leave, but it was very difficult to act on such a random decision as this as we dared not sail by the ferry. Some kind of secret, private crossing was needed, so Papa went to the docks to see if he could arrange something. By good fortune he found a fisherman with a trawler who was prepared to take us across the North Sea to Harwich.

Again it was in the dark of the night that our lives changed direction. How I hated those dark nights — and still do. Any noise frightens me and sends shivers down my back. We made our way to the harbour and boarded the trawler with our four cases and my baby doll. The fisherman laughed, "You have chosen a blustery night — I hope you are good sailors." As we left the harbour, the boat was tossed up and down on the waves. It felt as if it was a small nutshell bobbing on the water. The cabin was too small to give all four of us shelter. To shut out the dark stormy clouds and keep us dry from the spray from the waves, we crept under the tarpaulin. Everything smelt of fish. It made me feel quite sick. Oh how we prayed to see land soon again. I have no detailed memories of that night — only darkness, stormy black sea, tarpaulin and the reek of fish. While hiding under the tarpaulin, my thoughts went round and round. What was to become of us? Where would we find a home, or would we be like "nomads", wandering from place to place?

Early in the morning the sea became calmer and the trawler skipper called out to us, "You can see the coast of England. A lovely sight in the morning light."

We watched the sun rising as we finally arrived in Harwich.

CHAPTER
FOUR

Granted permission to enter England

The future: USA or England?

When we had found our land legs again, we made our way to the Immigration and Customs Office. Here our joy and happiness were short-lived. That morning, just two hours before we arrived, the visa restrictions had come into force. We spent hours in the Immigration Office begging, pleading for permission to enter the country, so that we could book a cabin on a ship bound for America. Nothing my parents said seemed to help. Papa pointed out that he had had business dealings in Scotland before and that he had sent horseradish to Hull where it was waiting to be forwarded on to a purchaser, and then we would be on our way to America. But it was hopeless. We needed a visa from Germany. Papa tried to explain that we would never get a visa and that he had been discharged from a labour camp only a few weeks before. If we returned to Germany, it would be the labour camp or a concentration camp for all the family. The immigration officer might as well sign our death certificates.

When Papa realised that the immigration officer was refusing us entry, he became silent and made a hopeless gesture, shrugging his shoulders and turning his hands up helplessly. Mutti kept pleading with the officer to let us stay for just a few days to book a boat bound for America. Even she finally realised that this was the end of the road. She went on her bended knees to the man.

Papa kept apologising to us that he had brought us to this bitter end.

The ferry berthed and many tourists came happily rushing towards the Customs Office. It would be the ferry that would take us back to Holland.

Suddenly, the immigration officer picked up the rubber stamp and brought it down on our passports. Neither Mutti nor Paper held out their hands to collect them. We just stood there, numbed mentally and physically. Our minds were blank. No thoughts of what to do next. Everything hinged on this visa.

The immigration officer laughed and said, "After hours of confrontation, it looks as if you have changed your minds and don't want to enter any more!" Now it dawned on us that he had stamped and signed our passports to enter England, to freedom and safety. As Mutti grasped the passports, she held the man's hand for a minute to her cheek. We were granted six weeks' stay in England to clear up the business and book passages for the next part of our journey. So on 20th April 1938, we set foot in England. We crossed the invisible line from danger to safety, and we were truly in

England. Oh, England! We embraced and kissed each other. At last we were out of danger.

As the other travellers rushed past us, Papa decided to find out the time of a train that would take us to Hull and from which platform. We all moved forward slowly because of that fourth case. There was nobody to help us, so I pushed it along. Finally, a porter spotted our predicament and helped us to the train. Our first train journey in England. What luxury — the seats in the compartment were all upholstered, not just wooden seats like in the German trains. Then we snuggled down to get warm and relax. After a little while we became curious and had a good look at the English people in their own country. Somehow they looked different from the people we saw in Hamburg. We noticed that the passengers were scrutinising us as well. We must have looked a sight to them as if we had come from another planet. Tired, unkempt and untidy, we had not had a chance to have a wash or comb our hair. Perhaps we even smelt of fish and tarpaulin.

The first thing I noticed about our fellow travellers was that some had slightly protruding or false teeth. This was a rarity in Germany, because as soon as you lost a tooth or perhaps two, a gold crown would be fitted to fill the gap. Papa explained that the slightly protruding teeth were caused by speaking English, with its "th" sound, the tongue pushing the teeth forward.

I was fascinated by the ladies in the compartment who wore so much make-up. Only ladies of questionable character would use it so obviously in Germany. Some passengers held shopping baskets on their laps. You never saw these in German towns or cities. Papa tried to make conversation with some people in the compartment, but they just stared at him. No one smiled and they hardly spoke to each other. We decided on first impressions that the English were a strange breed.

As the journey progressed, we sat back and in our thoughts we tried to sort it all out. What did the word "freedom" mean? And what would it mean for us to be really "free"? No more fear and watching every word and action. No more having to use the Hitler salute. Freedom — a magical word, yet in my child's eyes was now a different fear, one I dared not voice to my parents: we didn't belong to any country. Where would fate take us? Would we be like the autumn leaves, blown about by the wind? Would we be restless, nomads wandering from place to place?

Our interest was diverted as the train rushed through the countryside and we looked out of the windows. We were amazed by the many houses: small ones, terraced ones, large ones and villas. In German towns and cities, people lived in blocks of flats, but here there were all different types of houses, each one with its own garden, from some the size of a pocket handkerchief to large ones, some even the size of parks. The houses had several chimneys and if you shut your eyes slightly, the passing houses gave the illusion of castles, the chimneys being the turrets.

When we arrived at a station, our fellow travellers would open the windows and lean out, giving a shy sort of wave, before opening the door and getting out.

Finally, we were the only passengers in the compartment. When we arrived at our destination, we wanted to open the door, but we could not find a door handle or latch. We waved to people on the platform, hoping that they would help us by opening the door, but no, they thought it great fun and waved back. The more frantically we waved, the more they smiled at us and even laughed at our childish behaviour. The guard blew the whistle and the train moved on with us still in the compartment. What now? At the next station, fortunately, people were getting on and as they opened the door, we took our four trunks and my baby doll and hurried out. The guard had not yet blown the whistle, so Papa had time to ask how to open the compartment door. Now it was our turn to smile as the strange actions of the earlier passengers were explained. When they opened the window and leant out of it, it was to open the door from the outside. This movement was the strange little wave as their hands reached for the door handle.

By lunchtime we had arrived in Hull and we decided to get something to eat in a restaurant. As Papa spoke English, he decided that he would go to the harbour and check whether the horseradish had arrived. He left Kurt in charge as he also spoke good English, having passed his Higher School Certificate, and we would wait for Papa in the restaurant. While Papa was studying the menu, he noticed some money left on the table next to a dirty plate. He picked it up and put it into his pocket, expressing his opinion, "The English seem to be careless with money." After the waitress had cleared the table, Papa ordered the meal for us. It was our first taste of fish and chips. It was food cooked very differently from German food and we had never tasted chips before, but we enjoyed them.

We went back to the station as our next destination was Nottingham. Mr Jan, the Dutch businessman, had a business associate there and he would welcome us. We arrived at about 11p.m. By now we were seasoned travellers. The station looked deserted and only the left luggage department was open. When the attendant heard that we came from Germany, he got very excited, because that day Germany had played England in a football international. He told us all about the football team, the match and the goals, while all we wanted to do was find a hotel, fall into bed and sleep to make up for the previous sleepless night of our stormy crossing. After a while, he looked at his watch and said, "Ah, it's midnight. Now I can lock up and then the station will be locked up too." We asked about the station restaurant. Hamburg's station restaurant was open 24 hours a day.

"Sorry, the cafeteria closes at 10p.m." What about the station hotel? "That closes at 10.30p.m. — 11p.m. at the latest — and they don't open the doors for anyone at midnight."

Where were we to go if the hotels all closed at midnight? What a sleepy city! So we went outside the station and the gates were bolted after us. Papa and Kurt decided to look round the city to find some hotel or somewhere for us to go. Mutti and I and our four trunks and my baby doll stayed outside the station. In no time, a car drove up from the main road into the station lay-by and slowed up where we were standing. The driver looked at us and then drove off. A couple of minutes later, the same car appeared again and did the same manoeuvre. Mutti pointed out the black and white check pattern round the middle of the car and mentioned that the previous car had had the same pattern. The car came a third and then a fourth time. Mutti started to get worked up, thinking it must be a German car, a fifth columnist in the car spying on us — otherwise why would they keep coming up to us, slow down, look at us and drive on? Mutti was all for escaping and running away. I stopped her, pointing out that this was impossible. We could not carry all four cases. She insisted.

"Leave them. Let's save ourselves."

"How can we? Papa and Kurt won't know where to find us."

This seemed to make sense to Mutti, and we moved as far as possible from the pavement and huddled in a corner. Then we saw Papa and Kurt return, accompanied by a policeman. Our first reaction was "trouble", but they seemed to be talking to each other in a friendly enough way. The policeman looked like the photo in our school textbook, showing us how kind British policemen were, even stopping the traffic to let a duck and her ducklings cross the road.

Papa explained that they had seen the police officer and asked for help. He knew the owner of a small hotel and would wake up the night porter. At that moment, the same car with the check pattern drew up again.

Mutti grabbed hold of Papa, telling him that the driver was spying on us. Papa translated what she had said and the police officer just laughed good-naturedly. "Nay, nay. You're as safe as houses. Those are the taxis. The checked border round the car is so that people can recognise them easily." Of course, they would drive up, seeing a woman and child outside the station with luggage, and were hoping for a fare.

So all was calm again. Once in the hotel and in our room, we had no trouble falling asleep even in strange beds.

Next morning we had our first English breakfast. Many a time Papa had told us about the good and tasty English breakfast. We were ready for it as we had not eaten since lunch the day before.

We looked at the breakfast menu. The continental way was a buffet table filled with a variety of breads and rolls, continental sausages and different cheeses, a variety of jams and honey, and fruits. Papa kept saying, "You wait for the English breakfast."

The menu. Grapefruit, porridge.

We did not know any fruit by that name. Kurt had an idea — grapes. Perhaps different varieties, black and green grapes, making it up into fruits. "Yes, please, four times grapefruits."

When they were served, we looked at them in amazement — so different from what we had been expecting. We tasted them. The bitter flavour was a shock to our taste buds so we asked if we could try the porridge.

"Sorry, no. You can only choose between one or the other."

The next items were fried haddock, bacon and eggs or kippers. We asked what these kippers were. "Smoked herrings," came the reply.

We should enjoy these as in Hamburg smoked herrings were a speciality, known as Bückling. When the kippers were served, we didn't recognise them. To us they did not look like smoked herrings. How we were supposed to eat these kippers? "Please may we try the bacon and eggs?"

"Sorry, only one choice for each course."

So once more no food. Then the toast, butter and marmalade were served. The marmalade had a bitter taste and we asked if we could have strawberry or raspberry marmalade. The waiter shook his head and said that he had not heard of strawberry marmalade. So our great wonderful tasty English breakfast consisted of a slice of toast and butter. In our mind's eye we could see the Dutch breakfasts we had once enjoyed, the table laden with all that delicatessen, where you could have as much food as you wanted. We left the table as very hungry, disappointed visitors.

Papa rang the business associate whose name Mr Jan, the Dutchman, had given us — a Mr Meyers. He would be pleased to meet us at the hotel and would assist us in booking a passage to America. In the meantime he thought it advisable for us to find a guesthouse and move to there. It would be more economical, more comfortable and we would find the meals more to our liking. Also, we would be able to catch up on our sleep. Mr Meyers spoke fluent German as he had been with the British Occupation Forces stationed in Cologne after the First World War. Suddenly he remarked that he was of the Jewish faith and hoped that we would have no objection to that. Papa replied that we had many Jewish friends and also that he had been in a labour camp. From that moment we were friends. Mr Meyers helped us to transfer to a guesthouse. He then invited us for tea, cakes and scones, and also invited us to his home to meet his family.

In the restaurant Papa again found some money by the plate on the table. He showed this to Mr Meyers, saying how careless people were in England. Mr Meyers laughed at Papa's quaint idea about the careless habits of the British, explaining that it was a tip for the waitress. Another curiosity! On the continent, the tip is automatically added to the bill.

We returned to our new guesthouse and went to bed. For the first time in many days, we fell asleep and had a sound and peaceful rest.

CHAPTER
FIVE

Permission to stay in Britain

A farm. Learning new ways of living

After a good night's sleep in comfortable beds, we greeted the dawn with new hope and courage. The sun was shining and we said to each other, "This will be a wonderful day, a new beginning." Going downstairs for breakfast, we could smell tasty food and we wondered what it could be. Papa thought it smelt like eggs and bacon. When the breakfast was served, it was that talked-about special English breakfast, the full works: egg and bacon, fried bread, sausages, mushrooms and tomatoes. We all agreed that this was truly a hearty breakfast. This treat was followed by toast, butter and honey.

This was a good start to the day. Well-rested and nourished, we felt that we could face any trouble coming our way. Mr Meyers was as good as his word and arrived to meet us in the morning. From the moment we met him, we felt at ease with him and trusted him. So we discussed our plan of going to

America to start a new life there. We soon discovered that Mr Meyers had a great talent for persuasion. He thought England would be a much better place and safer haven for us. "There are too many fifth columnists in America," he said. "Stay here and make England your new home." We could not see how we could achieve this as all we had was visitors' permits that would expire after six weeks. Still Mr Meyers persisted and eventually he convinced us that England was the future for us.

He helped us to draw up our application to the Home Office. Then the correspondence started. Because of the influx of the many Austrian refugees and with the unemployment situation in spring 1938, foreigners could not get a work permit. They were not allowed to take any job that might deprive English people of a livelihood. Refugees had to prove that they had enough money to live off for several years, unless a charity, such as the Quakers or a similar organisation, would adopt them and help out. As we had come over on our own and were not Jewish, no such help was available to us.

We fulfilled the necessary requirements and at last came the great day when a permit to stay indefinitely was granted to my family. A great burden dropped from my parents' shoulders as by now we had started to understand and absorb some of the British way of living. My parents said, "When in Rome, do as the Romans do," so right from the start we tried to get to know the customs and culture of this, our new country.

Now came the big question: what were we going to do? We couldn't just still sit still and use up all our money. What would happen to us then? So we had to use the money to help us earn more. But what could we do? Should we open a shop? Fine, we could employ someone, but none of us in the family knew enough English. Papa spoke it reasonably well — with a Scottish accent as he had done business with a Scottish firm and had been to Scotland several times. My brother had just passed his Higher Certificate in English. I had one year of school English, but Mutti did not speak one word of the language. Nor did we know enough about English tastes in the different foods to become successful shopkeepers.

Perhaps Papa could start an import-export business again, but he had no contacts here in England and we certainly could not deal with Germany. One of the Nazis' tricks was to import goods and not pay for them as Hitler had put a ban on money leaving the country.

Papa was a farmer's son, so farming seemed a feasible possibility and thus the search began. Mr Meyers, Papa and Kurt viewed several farms. Those available were either too big or too expensive, and those we could afford were of a poor quality and miles and miles from a town.

While the search continued, we learnt how English people lived. They were very kind to us and well-meaning, and would speak to us very slowly and in a loud voice. Mutti would cover her ears with her hands saying that she was not deaf or mentally retarded. She realised that some words were similar to the

Hamburger plattdeutsch, a dialect of Northern Germany. For example, "Pipe" is spelt the same in English and plattdeutsch, but in Hamburg they would pronounce the "e" at the end of the word. "Eaten and drinken" in plattdeutsch is "eat and drink" in English. So Mutti jumped to the conclusion that if she pronounced plattdeutsch badly, it could pass for English!

One day, while we were having lunch, Mr and Mrs Moore, the landlord and landlady, told a funny story. We all laughed heartily. Mutti had not understood a word. She picked up the carving knife, holding it in her hand with the blade upright. She went up to Mr Moore and with a serious expression asked him, "Shall I kill you with this knife?" Shocked and perplexed, he looked at Mutti and ran frightened from the room. Now it was Mutti's turn to look puzzled. In German, "kitzeln" means "to tickle"; badly pronounced in Platt-Deutsch, it becomes "killen". To tickle a person with a knife means to make them aware, tease them or pull their leg! Papa had his hands full trying to explain this to Mr and Mrs Moore and getting them to calm down. They insisted that she must have had a nervous breakdown or gone mad.

When the Moores addressed Mutti, they would call her "Mrs Spatz". Often she wouldn't react and so our family decided to call Mutti "Mrs" and as time went by, it became our pet name for her. For example, we would say "Mrs, let's have some tea"!

We used to look forward to lunches at the Moores. Many of the main courses were similar to ours, but the sweet course was something new. We were used to blancmange or jellies and fruit, but Mrs Moore would serve up sponge flans with stewed rhubarb and custard. As time passed, it might be strawberries or raspberries. Every day we waited for our surprises. Syrup pudding, lemon meringue pie. Too many tasty desserts to mention. Mutti even went into the kitchen to watch Mrs Moore preparing and cooking the sweets.

While Papa and Kurt carried on the search for a farm, "Mrs" and I would go window-shopping. One day we spotted strawberry jam in the window of a shop, but when we went in and asked for "strawberry marmalade", we were told that they did not stock that item. We asked the assistant to come with us and pointed to the jar. "Ah well, that is strawberry jam." Returning to the guesthouse we showed off that jar of strawberry jam as if it was a prize given to conquering heroes.

Time dragged as we searched for a farm. So we explored Nottingham and learnt about the legend of Robin Hood, and visited the castle and museum. One day Mr and Mrs Meyers took us to Sherwood Park. It was a lovely sunny day and we sat down to watch the game "cricket". They tried to explain what was happening, but to us it seemed a very slow-moving game. Still, we enjoyed sitting in the sunshine and feeling wonderfully relaxed. After a while we walked through the park and came to another lawn. Again, the players were wearing all white, the same as the cricketers, but this game was played with big wooden balls. The players rolled these into the distance, while they watched the ball rolling along as if hypnotised, often with one hand on their back and slowly walking forward. This game was very, very slow.

Nottingham is a beautiful city and people told us that the girls were the prettiest in England. They wore pretty dresses, even though they worked in factories making lace or cigarettes. Neither type of work required protective clothing and the work did not soil the clothes.

Our greatest adventures were when we went shopping, mostly window-shopping. This way we found a treasure of a shop selling delicatessen and continental foods. We missed these, especially at tea time — liver sausage, salami and, perhaps hard to understand, rye bread. The white bread was delicious but was served up too fresh and too soft. Having eaten it for several weeks, we noticed that our digestion suffered.

When we paid for our purchases and were given the change, we would query it. As the shop assistants had seen us before, they would smile and remind us, "Twelve pence to one shilling, twenty shillings to one pound."

One day a farm was advertised in Doncaster, a mixed farm including some cows. It looked promising so we all travelled together to see it. "Mrs" and I went along to see a little of England. Mr Meyers, Papa and Kurt went to visit the farm, while Mutti and I went to look around the town. Walking along the high street, we came up to a crossroads where the corners of the pavement were protected by railings. Some men were sitting in a squat position by the railings watching the traffic go by. What strange people, we thought. How could they be comfortable in such an uncomfortable position? Yet it did not seem to bother them. Later, when we lived in Doncaster, it was explained to us that these men were coal-miners. When they were underground they would sit in this crouched position while working on a coal seam.

Anxiously we waited and waited for six weeks to hear whether the Home Office would grant us permission to stay permanently in Britain and allow us to live on the farm. If permission came, Papa would be able to sign the final contracts, and we would be able to move and live on the farm.

During this wait, the tensions were so strong and we were so excited that Papa decided to give us a treat. He took us to a restaurant to have tea and cakes. Yes, cakes. During the previous three years, when Papa was in the camp, we would only have cakes as a special treat when we had saved up enough to afford one small cake. We would divide one piece of cake into three pieces, one piece for each of us, Mutti, Kurt and me. Now we were going to get one whole cake each! What luxury! The waitress brought a selection of mouth-watering cakes. We were astonished and our eyes nearly popped out of their sockets. Papa said, "Tuck in. Don't waste good money and leave any." Kurt and I looked at each other, hardly believing that this was true — that we were allowed to eat three, even four cakes each. I remember Papa having two, but Mutti only had one. When we asked for the bill, it was the waitress's turn to be surprised as she looked at the empty plate. She asked us how many cakes we had eaten. The look on Papa's face spoke volumes as he realised his mistake. You only paid for the cakes eaten and not for those left on the plate! Different countries, different customs. In Germany, the waitress would serve only those cakes you had chosen and when they were brought to your table you had to pay for them.

The waiting came to an end when at last the official letter from the Home Office arrived. With trembling fingers, Papa opened the letter. What news would it bring? Good or bad? Had we been wasting our time and should we have been making enquiries about passage to America? Papa was so emotional, he could not speak. He looked at the letter and read it over and over again. Finally, he handed the precious paper to Kurt to translate it for Mutti. When we realised the importance of it, we jumped for joy and hugged each other. This letter was official notice informing us that we could stay in England and live on the farm. England! Oh, what a long sigh. England would be our country and we could build our home here. We would learn to live free from fear. Only those who have faced this constant threat can understand what it means to have freedom and what a priceless gift it is.

Having planned every move carefully, we were now exerting ourselves physically and mentally, rushing around trying to get as much done as we could and working out what to do next. Papa wrote a letter to the Dutch Harbour Authority to inform them of our new address and asking them to forward our bits and pieces to England. At last came the day when we could move and take possession of the farm. It was the Friday before Whit Monday 1938.

Early in the morning we said our farewell to Mr and Mrs Moore, while they wished us every happiness in our new home. We left with our four cases and my baby doll, and travelled to Doncaster. Before going to the farm, we left our luggage at the station and went shopping in the town. We bought some food and then went to a furniture shop to buy two double beds to start with. Papa and Kurt would have one, and Mutti and I would sleep in the second bed (it wasn't appropriate for Kurt and me to share a bed). Then we bought blankets, pillows, bed linen, pots and pans, and cutlery. We made sure that the shops would deliver on the same day in the afternoon. Unfortunately, the gas company refused to deliver before Whitsun, so we bought a single gas ring. With this we could at least boil some water and make some hot drinks, or even heat some tinned soup. The previous farmer had promised to leave four plates, cups and saucers, and a small table and four chairs.

So now we were ready to go to our new home.

Mutti and I had not seen it, but all four of us were very excited and happy to have a home to go to after all the weeks of uncertainty.

The taxi took us and our luggage to the farm. It was in the middle of the suburbs, opposite the village pump and next to a park, which gave the farm its name, Park House Farm. As we stood in front of the house, our emotions were very powerful. We were thankful to God that he had given us a chance to live happily in this new home and new country.

We stood and surveyed the house. A big, stone 18th-century building. The entrance door was in the centre of the house with a gable over it. The house was surrounded by a three-foot high wall, topped by six-foot high iron railings, with a large iron gate in the centre. My first reaction was that the house was fenced in like a prison. Were the local people (mostly miners) not friendly towards farmers? We did not enter the house by the front door. In all our time there we never used it, but entered by the wooden gate at the side. Next to this gate was a small building, the dairy. The path led past the side of the house and a small garden. We came to the side door of the building. Papa fished a four-inch long key out of his pocket, held it up and ceremoniously put it into the keyhole, saying cheerfully, "Open, Sesame." We all had different thoughts as we entered the large farmhouse kitchen. Under the window was a large brown sink and above it two taps for hot and cold water — an unexpected luxury. Another wall was taken up by a huge black fireplace which consisted of a firebox, two black doors for ovens and a black container for heating extra water. I think it was known as a "Yorkshire Range" with a back boiler. Mutti shook her head and wondered how she was ever going to cook in such a fireplace. The kitchen floor was laid with red quarry tiles and the walls were whitewashed.

We explored the house. From the kitchen a passage led to a large room, the breakfast room. It too had a red quarry-tiled floor and white-washed walls, which were covered with patches of grey and green. The floor was filthy and was covered with an even dirtier carpet. The windows were high and had a box seat. This showed the thickness of the walls. On the window side, the wall was covered by wooden shutters. The room was dominated by a huge brick fireplace. Mutti started to worry how much coal it would need to make a decent fire in it. Later we found out that we could buy coal cheaply from the miners as they were allowed to buy an allocation cheaply, some of which they would sell on, thus making a profit and helping them out financially.

There were two doors from the breakfast room. The first one led to the entrance, central hall and main staircase. A thick iron bar had been fixed across the front door. Someone must have been very nervous living here to protect themselves with high metal fences and metal bars. We carried on viewing the house. Two more rooms, the dining room and lounge. Back to the breakfast room. The second door opened up to a spiral staircase leading to five bedrooms, bathroom and toilet. The whole house was damp and the walls were covered with large patches of mildew.

Then there came a loud knock on the front door. Our first visitor! The furniture van had arrived and at the same time, the groceries were delivered. We were getting more and more excited as it was no longer a dream or vision, but reality. This was to be our home for the future.

Looking at the house, we realised that it needed a lot of hard work to make it into a comfortable, clean home.

There was another knock, this time on the kitchen door. A young man in working clothes and a cloth cap stood there. This was Arthur, our first employee, who greeted us with the words, "Cows are here. Who's going to help with the milking?" We stared at each other. We were city people and wearing clothes suitable for wearing in town, where milk was delivered in bottles to the door. Never for a moment had we thought that we would be thrown in at the deep end so quickly. Papa was a farmer's son, so he offered to have a go and help, but he was wearing his best and only suit. When Arthur spoke, we had to listen carefully as he pronounced the words so differently. "Aye, it's Yorkshire," he explained. Papa went into the shed and found an old overall and a pair of wellington boots. So Papa changed into these working clothes. Arthur showed Papa how to use the milking machine and finish the process of milking by hand. Then help was needed in the dairy, to filter and cool the milk and put it into churns. Mutti decided that this was going to be her job and she might as well start right now. At the end all the milking equipment would need to be washed — hopefully in hot water.

Hot water! Kurt put the kettle on the gas ring and then we both tried to light the fire in the Yorkshire Range. However hard we both tried, the fire kept going out while smoke bellowed out of the different parts and joints of the range. We asked Arthur for help. "Aye, once you've got the knack, you'll be all right," he said.

80

He went out to the shed and brought a flue brush back and a long-handled scraper. He showed us how to use them. Kurt thought that I should do this job as my dress was washable. Indeed, I made a thorough job of it. I found that all the different flues were choc-a-bloc with soot and so once they were clear, we tried to light the fire. Success! I jumped for joy. I had managed to cope with this job. Soon we realised why it was called a back boiler as the water in the taps was getting warm. I ran out to the dairy to tell Mutti that soon there would be enough hot water for her to wash all the milking equipment. She just looked at me and burst out laughing. She laughed and laughed. The tears were streaming down her face. I had not seen or heard her laugh like this during the previous three years. Mind you, I could not see what was so funny, until she said, "Look at you! You look like you have been up the chimney!"

I was covered in soot from head to toe, hands and dress as well — but I had managed to light the fire! Then I dared to laugh at Mutti. She stood barefoot, no stockings on and just wearing her thin petticoat which clung to her drenched body. She explained that her thin high-heeled shoes could never stand up to all that water splashing about and she had taken off her best dress in order to take care of it. We were often in stitches laughing at our predicaments and amateurish attempts to conquer our new work.

Quickly we learned to adapt to our new lifestyle. After my first effort at cleaning the range, it became routine that I would clean out the flues every week. I became an expert at it and could wear my ordinary dress without getting a single spot of soot on it.

After milking, the cows were let out of the cowshed into the orchard. Here they could graze until they could be taken to the meadows. Arthur and Papa cleaned the cowshed first and then Kurt joined them. With the help of the two dogs, they guided the cows past the park to the meadow. Arthur pointed out that each gate must be securely closed after the cows had walked through.

Arthur suggested that both Papa and Kurt should make friends with the two dogs, hoping that they would accept their commands. The next piece of advice was, "Don't lock the dogs up. They are working dogs and not pets for playing with."

My next job was to prepare a meal for tea. I had never cooked before, so anything could happen. I heated a tin of soup on the gas ring, put the sausages (not Frankfurters!) onto a baking tin into the Yorkshire Range, laid the table and then finally called the family for their meal. It tasted as good as a feast. The work had made us all really hungry. It was our first meal in our new home.

So the work was allocated. Papa and Kurt helped with the milking and farm work. Mutti looked after the dairy, making sure that the filtered and cooled milk was in the churns and outside the gate for the milk lorry to collect. The lorry driver would not wait if the churns were not at the collection point. The milk would be wasted and we would lose the money we could have earned. Whenever possible, Mutti would give me a helping hand with the housework as I had to learn what to do and how to do it. I was just 14 years old. I found it very hard to change over from being a schoolgirl to doing a full day's work as a mature woman would do.

Kurt was not expected to work as hard as the three of us. He worked as much as his strength would let him. We tried to protect him without his realising this. He had not fully recovered from an illness he had had in spring 1935. The doctors hadn't been able to do anything and had diagnosed that a 'flu germ had attacked his heart. Medicine had failed to help him. On the Friday when the doctor made his visit, he warned my parents that on his next visit on Monday morning he would have to write out a death certificate. Mutti thought and thought about where she could find help. Finally, in desperation, she visited a homoeopath, who prescribed "Raw, fresh carrot juice". It had to be freshly grated and the juice squeezed out through muslin. It had to be drunk before it had the chance to oxidise, when it would change to a brownish colour. Mutti and I could not grate carrots quickly enough. Kurt was so weak that he could not drink from a cup, so Mutti coaxed him into taking just a teaspoonful of juice at a time. After a short while, he had half a cupful of this carrot juice medicine. An hour later we grated some more carrots, for another half cupful.

Come Monday morning, Kurt was sitting up in bed and eating a little breakfast. When the doctor arrived and saw this, he asked Mutti if we had called in another doctor. Mutti said no. The medical profession does not recognise homoeopathy. The doctor just stood and kept looking at Kurt and finally said, "A miracle has happened here." However, the illness had left him with a weak heart. Many years later in England, his illness was diagnosed as rheumatic fever.

As yet I had not been in the cowshed, so I plucked up my courage and ventured in. The cows were bigger than I had imagined. I wanted to touch them, but each time I got near a cow, she would swish her tail and it would hit me. The cows reacted so differently to me than to the men. Again Arthur gave me an explanation. "You shouldn't approach the cows too close from behind. Instead, be firm when you pat her, otherwise it feels to her as if you're tickling her, like flies bothering her. That's why she swishes her tail in self-defence." He also advised me to talk to the cows as I approached them, saying softly several times "gushla, gushla" — translated it means "good lass". Yes, his advice worked wonders. Now I really felt like a seasoned farmer.

My brother enjoyed milking the cows and I heard him humming. I asked why he did this. "I feel relaxed," he answered, "and the cows find it soothing and relaxing. I noticed that they're easier to milk and they yield more."

Although I started work at 6.30–7.00a.m, just doing the housework, I asked if I could help with the farm work too. Papa was very pleased with my offer. He simply said, "Yes, that's wonderful. Your job will be to collect the eggs, feed the chickens and let them out of the stable. After that, let the calves out and take them round the back to the orchard. In the evening, see to it that they all go back into the cowshed."

84

Papa was proud that we were all helping as best we could. Because of my offer he would be able to save some more money. We had to be very careful about spending our funds as they had to last till the autumn, when, hopefully, we would have a good wheat harvest. The Milk Marketing Board paid only monthly for the milk and eggs.

When the time came to put the chickens and calves back into the stable, Arthur helped and taught me how to call them. The previous farmer had not liked work and had not cleaned the chickens' nests, so the chickens had found other nests in the yard in hollows under bushes or by the haystack. I had to search for them and take the eggs to the kitchen, carefully wiping them clean and then storing them on egg trays.

Then came the job of fetching the four calves from the orchard and the difficult task of letting them climb into their cowshed. The straw was so high that it was practically impossible for them to climb up. Shouting at them and pushing them from behind helped, but then I screamed as several big fat rats came out of the straw. Papa came running over wondering if I had had an accident. When he saw those huge rats sauntering away as if they owned the yard, Papa decided that no one must go into the yard unless they were wearing wellington boots.

Before going to bed, Papa wanted to check the yard to see that all was well and to look at the stars from his own front door. To his horror, he did not see the stars, but was greeted by the sight of lots of rats having playtime in the yard. He shut the door quickly and announced that we must declare war on the rats. The first task would be to remove the manure heap behind the cowshed and also clean out the empty sheds and the ones the chickens and calves were in, transporting the manure all on a lorry into the fields.

We were emotionally and physically exhausted, so we decided to have an early night as in the morning it would be early to rise. I slept soundly and when the alarm clock rang at 5.30a.m, for a moment I did not know where I was. Then memory flooded back and it dawned on me that a lot of work was waiting for me.

My first job was to make sandwiches and a pot of tea for Papa and Kurt before they started their outside work. Then came the frightening job of lighting the fire in the Yorkshire Range. Mutti insisted that even though we were on a farm, the house inside had to be spick and span. So, every morning, with a deck brush and floor cloth, I had to scrub the red quarry tiles in the kitchen and breakfast room. Kurt and Papa had rolled up the filthy carpet.

Papa had gone into the yard to call the two dogs, Bessy and Flossy, her puppy. He came back into the kitchen looking very angry. "Those two damned dogs have run away! And we paid a high price for them. Well-trained be damned!" So Papa and Kurt hurried away, half running and then walking for a bit to catch their breath. They were worried that it would take some time to herd the cows and walk them back to the farm. You cannot hurry cows or they will lose some of their milk. Herding them without the dogs would mean they would lose some time for milking. Surprise, surprise!

Papa and Kurt returned very quickly and Papa had a broad smile on his face. Those two "damned dogs" were already in the field. They had herded the cows together and were waiting patiently at the gate. Papa said, "Mutti, please feed the rascals well. They are good dogs and have earned a good breakfast." Many a summer evening when we walked across the meadows, we could see the dogs with the cows, guarding and protecting them.

During our second breakfast in our new home, at about 10 a.m., we were discussing the order of the day, and Mutti said only one word, "shopping". That meant another trip into Doncaster to buy working clothes and wellington boots. As we returned home, all looked quiet in the yard, but then Papa saw several rats walking in a leisurely fashion across it. One rat had jumped onto the back of a chicken. Papa hurried to get a spade to kill the rat, and the chicken as well, as the rat had eaten a lot of flesh between its shoulder blades and neck.

I was sent to a neighbouring farm to see if they had any cats they could spare and let us have. I was lucky, they gave me two mature cats and two kittens. Again, it was pointed out that these animals were working cats and we should not confuse them with pets. The four felines were put into a large basket and I took them home. My parents thought that even though they were not pets, they should know where their home was. Mutti soaked some bread in milk and then Papa took the first cat out of the basket. He laughed, "My word, you're a big, black devil!" He had just a little white bib under his chin. Then Papa pointed out the cat's claws.

They were huge. On each of his toes he had two claws. Papa went on to say, "We'll call you Tommy. The rats will flee when they see your size." The other cat was grey with black stripes like a tiger. We named her Muschi. The kittens were playful — the sign of good ratters. The farmer had advised me that when Muschi had kittens, we should keep them all, because catching and fighting rats shortens their life span as the rats fight back and bite the cats, sometimes causing their death.

Mutti offered the cats the bread soaked in milk, which they devoured greedily. We all took a turn to stroke them. They seemed to like being with us as they purred loudly. Mutti gave them their orders: "In the evening you go out to work — catch your meat and guard the yard. In the morning you come home for bread and milk, and have a good sleep in your basket." Next morning Mutti called them, "Muschi, Muschi". She used a teaspoon, knocking it against a saucer. The cats must have been bilingual as they seemed to understand what was said to them!

We also opened a second front against the rats. As soon as the offices were open again after the Whit Bank Holiday, we asked the pest control department of the local council to help us and they put out rat poison. In a very short time we were rid of the vermin and the danger that the rats would bring disease to the farm.

Following our Whit Saturday shopping expedition, we changed into our new working clothes. There was a loud knock at the main front door. We wondered who that could be as the local people would use the side gate and kitchen door. Kurt ran round to the front and a lorry driver said, "Goods from Holland". Now we were excited, wondering which of our things managed to get through the German customs in Hamburg. We stood and watched as they brought the items into the house. Two leather chairs, one long case clock, one Singer sewing machine, one large wooden box and a big wicker basket. We felt as if Christmas had arrived. Mutti cried and cried, and kept touching each item. The clock was put across one corner of the room. Then we decided it would look better in the other corner, while the two armchairs were put on each side of the fireplace. This made the room look really homely. We only opened the wooden box and wicker basked to begin with, to see if the contents were undamaged. The pleasure of unpacking these had to wait till the evening. It is amazing how these few items from our past home made us feel that this was the beginning of our new home.

We all learnt to work hard and adapt to our new way of life. Kurt and I had grown up emotionally very quickly, but now we had to grow up overnight from being schoolchildren as a full day's work was expected from us. We both had just had birthdays: Kurt was 17 years old and I was 14. There was no gentle transition from childhood to teenagers to adulthood. But we always remembered that our parents did not expect any more from us than they themselves were prepared to do. Perhaps it was hardest on Papa as he was slightly paralysed down one side from the stroke he had had in the labour camp. He also had to be especially careful as his weeping eczema had to be bandaged every morning and every night. It was on both arms and legs as well as on his forehead. Again, it was caused by being in the labour camp. If the bandages got dirty, he had to change them immediately to protect himself from the dust and dirt. To keep the bandages as clean as possible, he always wore a long-sleeved shirt over them. Taking the cows to the meadows and back again was like a therapy for him and after a while he could move more freely again. Even with these handicaps, he felt that he still had to take the lead.

Whit Sunday arrived with a bang. We were still busy with our chores when the first visitors, Mr and Mrs Meyers from Nottingham, arrived. We decided to have a walk through the orchard and then have a cup of tea and sandwiches. We apologised that we could not stop our work as you cannot give money to the animals and tell them, "Go and get yourselves something to eat." Also, we had only four cups, saucers and plates, so tea was served in a first and a second sitting.

During mid-morning and in the afternoon, people gathered by the yard gate and watched us carefully. Finally, Papa asked Arthur what these people wanted. Arthur explained that while drinking a pint of beer in the pub, he had told the story about his new employers: that they were crazy foreigners — city people, but hard-working. He had described how we tackled obstacles during our first days. In 1938, especially in this suburb of Doncaster full of miners, foreigners were a novelty and so they had come for a stare. If they could hear us talking, it would be an extra bonus. The miners had treated Arthur to an extra pint while he was telling the story. In short, we were the latest local news and interest.

Slowly we started to make the farm ours. To encourage the big brown hens to lay more eggs, Papa brought a brown cockerel from another farmer. Now we did not need an alarm clock as at sunrise the cockerel crowed so loudly to herald the day that he woke us and all the other animals up.

Lunch and evening meals became our discussion time.

Before Arthur left the farm on Whit Monday evening, Papa asked him if he would be able to find three or four men — just casual labour — to help clean the small stables and put the manure onto the lorry. The previous farmer had had no horses as he preferred machinery. They would also need to remove the manure heap by the cowshed and transfer it to the fields. On Tuesday morning, four men turned up for work. They were out-of-work miners, very keen to have this chance to earn some money. In 1938 there was high unemployment and dole money was very little. Papa pointed out that he could afford to pay only minimum wages as money was very limited. The miners sang as they worked. To them it was a treat to work above ground and in the open air. While they cleared the manure, Papa and Kurt stood by with spades. As the rats came out of their hiding places, they would kill them. They also destroyed several rats' nests. After this the walls were washed and then whitewashed. This also acted as a disinfectant.

A neighbouring farmer paid us a visit to welcome us to the neighbourhood and he brought us a house-warming present, four goose eggs. He advised Papa to put these under a broody hen and make sure that we had another one ready when the first hen was over her broodiness as goose eggs take longer to hatch. The farmer told us that we had just enough time to get them ready for Christmas. Also, chickens and young cockerels sold well during the Christmas season. Papa acted on this advice and the next broody hen had eight eggs to sit on. All being well, we would have eight golden fluffy little chicks.

When Arthur saw this, he showed Papa an incubator that could hold fifty eggs at a time. He also showed Papa an artificial hen. It looked like a large saucer with warming bulbs fixed under the canopy. Now the question was where we should keep these two valuable pieces of equipment, not to mention the chicks after they had hatched. Mutti suggested the room above the kitchen. A separate staircase led to it. Apparently it used to be the maid's room. It was ideal for our purpose because it was lovely and warm as the hot water tank was in it. Mutti and I cleaned the equipment and aired it. We put all the eggs into it, but we needed another two dozen to fill it, so we took a walk round to our neighbour to buy some fertilised eggs. There was no need to worry about whether or not they were fertile as several cockerels were running around in the yard.

I was so excited about holding the first golden fluffy chicks in my hand. Every morning I would dash up those stairs to see if the hen had hatched her eggs. Then came the red letter day. Our own first little fluffy chicks were chirping under the mother hen. She was quite safe in that room, free from rats. After that I kept a strict eye on the incubator. The next time I looked, I saw several more chirpy little fluffy balls in the incubator. My parents suggested that I should put another fifty eggs in it. Nature is wonderful! From the moment they hatch, the chicks can run and hop and seem to know exactly what they can eat.

We had exchanged the first broody hen, but even the second one was getting tired of sitting on the goose eggs. Mutti said the goslings inside the eggs needed some help in cracking the shells. She took a hot water bottle and a damp towel to her bed and then put the goose eggs on the damp towel. Once the shell was really cracked, Mutti gently helped to peel away the pieces of shell. While doing this she would softly talk, little realising that her voice was being imprinted on the goslings. Later on, when their hen "mother" would call them, they would follow her across the yard, but the moment Mutti was outside and spoke, they would abandon the mother hen and rush over to her, their real "mother"! Many a time she would flee into the kitchen to escape the noisy greeting. As they grew older, these three geese and one gander became better than any watchdog as they would charge towards the gate or the house door, squeaking and hissing, wings outspread. We had to put a notice on the gate and side door, "Beware. Geese on duty!"

Not everything went so well, however. Papa had arranged for the horseradish he had bought to be delivered to the farm. We hoped that Papa could sell it to the firm he used to deal with, but to our horror a catastrophe had happened. The horseradish were ten-inch-long sticks, ten to a bundle. They had been packed into a wooden barrel and, so that the horseradish could breathe, a strong hessian cloth had been nailed over the top in place of the wooden lid. With it being spring, and with the barrels having been stored all those weeks in storerooms, first in Holland and then in Hull, the horseradish had sprouted and green leaves were growing through the hessian. When Papa broke the barrels open, he found a solid mass. All the bundles were entwined with sprouting leaves, and of course it was unusable. Papa did not know how to plant these sticks to make them grow and develop into new plants. We all just stood and stared, each lost in our own thoughts. I started to cry, remembering how Mutti and I had taken such risks to get some of our money. Now it was all wasted. Tears were streaming down Mutti's face. Even Papa wiped away the odd tear. My thoughts ran on how we had scrimped and saved and gone without food in order to save money for Papa to start a business again. Mutti finally said, "If only we had used some of that money to buy new clothes and an extra suit and another pair of shoes for Papa."

This blow meant that somehow we had to save extra money now on labour costs. Mutti offered to go into the field with the labourers. My petite, delicate Mutti struggling with heavy, rough work. When she came in in the evening, she would go upstairs to the bathroom, just wash her hands and then fall onto the bed. I would take some food up to her and remove her shoes. Next morning she would get up and go out again. The hardest part was that she had to keep up the speed at which the others worked, or else she would slow everybody down. This was our first setback, although over the years more were to follow.

Although we had adapted well to our new life, so far we had had no time to clean the extra rooms in the house or decorate the ones we were living in.

One day the geese and two dogs went rushing towards the gate from the kitchen yard, making so much noise that Mutti suggested that I should check what the reason was for this wild behaviour.

A stranger stood by the kitchen gate, obviously wanting to come into the yard. He was very smartly dressed and you could see that it was not another farmer paying us a visit. I asked if I could help him and what his business was. He looked at me in a kindly way. I could read his thoughts: "She's just a child."

"Can I see your parents?" he asked.

"Well, yes and no," I replied. "My father is busy taking the cows back to the meadow and my mother is in the house, but you cannot talk to her. If you tell me your business, I will convey your message."

A sterner look came into his eyes and he said, "I am your landlord."

My reply was, "How is that possible, because the local colliery owns our farm?"

"Correct. I am the Managing Director of the colliery."

This is when my youth and inexperience let me down as I did not know what to say. I was frightened that a visit from him meant that something had gone wrong. I invited him into the house and asked him to sit in the armchair while I ran to the dairy to fetch Mutti.

When we both returned, we saw that he had been walking around the room and studying everything he saw. Mutti, with her few words of English, greeted him and asked if he would like a cup of tea. I think he realised now why I acted like a grown-up person because he asked me if I would be kind enough to translate for him. He had heard some strange stories about us and he wondered if he could help us, but first he would like to see the house and outbuildings. Perhaps the house first as then Papa might be back by the time we got outside.

He noticed the damp patches on the walls and that we had washed them. With all the work we had not had time to decorate any of the rooms, but they were clean from the fungus. He took notes as we walked from room to room. We were just returning to the kitchen when Papa came home. What a relief! The two men seemed to get on well. The outcome of this visit was that the Managing Director suggested that he send some workmen round to hack two and a half feet of the plaster away right round the house, to put a damp-proof layer in. Then painters and decorators would paint the walls. This was a wonderful offer. It would save us a lot of money and time. Then Papa showed him the clean sheds. When the colliery director finally left, he laughed and said, "Goodbye. Pleased to have met you crazy foreign city-people. I hope to see you again."

As the goslings grew up, Papa put a large tub filled with water in the orchard. They were very lively, squawking noisily and jumping into the water. They loved to swim. The poor mother hen stood at the edge trying to call them away from danger, but to no avail. Papa decided that it was too cruel and put her in a rabbit hutch so that she would get over her broodiness.

Life on the farm was hard work, but funny moments like these helped us over the difficult times.

Papa and Kurt worked in the fields. As Papa had driven a car in Germany, he now drove the tractor to mow the grass for hay. This would be food for the cows in winter. The previous farmer had been lazy and neglected the farm. He had tried to cover up his reluctance to work by buying the latest machinery and equipment. Papa taught Kurt how to drive the tractor and they would take it in turns. When Papa had his packed lunch, Kurt would take over and drive. Later on he learnt to drive the lorry. In order to harvest the hay, it had to be turned and when dry, it would be brought to the farm yard. Papa would again employ casual labour.

When the corn was ripe and ready to be harvested, the miners or their wives would stook them. When the stooks were dry, they too were brought to the farmyard and stacked. Then the threshing machine was hired for two or three days. A team of workers came with the machine. The corn was sold, the straw stacked and the chaff was put into big sacks. This could be used in the hen house.

Another first event happened. We were all very excited. One of the cows was going to calve. I was not allowed to watch it as it was not suitable for young girls, but as soon as it was born, Papa called me to the stable. It was a miracle of nature. As soon as the calf was born, the cow licked it.

Then it tried to stand up. The legs seemed to be made of rubber and it fell forwards and sideways until all of a sudden it found its legs were firm enough. It found its way to the cow's udder and started to suckle. Then, while the calf rested lying on the ground, the cow licked it clean. This bonded mother and calf. The calf was allowed to suckle for a few days and then they were separated. The calf was fed reconstituted milk. To make the calf drink out of a bucket, you put one hand in the bucket of milk and let the calf suckle on some fingers and so suck up the milk. The little tongue was ever so rough and the first time I had to do it, I had the strangest sensation.

As Papa got to know the cows and their yield of milk, he sold the poor milkers and brought some Friesian cows, with their familiar black and white markings. As no neighbouring farmer had a Friesian bull, he bought one too, which we called Caesar. Papa's idea was to build up a pedigree herd. Also, the Friesian cows were guaranteed TB-tested.

Eventually, the first Friesian calf was born, prematurely after seven months instead of the usual nine. We named her Dolly. The vet thought that a young calf like that would not survive. She was so fragile. Her legs stayed rubbery and her spine was not strong enough to support her. We got a large enough cardboard box and lined it with a blanket and towels, and brought her into the kitchen so that we could keep an eye on her. To keep her warm we put the cardboard box near the Yorkshire Range. We had to feed her, every two hours at first, then extended to every three hours. As with a human baby, we used a bottle, a large one, and a special strong teat provided by the vet. We had to make sure that the teat stayed on the bottle. We could see her getting stronger day by day, and then one morning she tried to stand up. After several attempts she managed it. Dolly was petted and cosseted, and she used to follow us like a faithful puppy dog. Then came the day that we could take her for a walk into the orchard. The vet was amazed at Dolly's progress. Even when she was six months old, she still came to the kitchen to have a handful of cattle cake. Several visitors got a fright when the calf entered the kitchen. Papa decided it was time that he fixed a gate at the end of the house by the farmyard, to keep all our pets from frightening people. Mind you, we missed our occasional visits from the calf, the geese and even the young chickens. The dogs and cats would jump over the gate. After the gander had watched the dogs doing this and still getting into the kitchen, he decided that he too would do this and he flew over the gate, followed by the three geese.

Many of our twelve cows were given names, but if they had no special feature, then they were given a number. The second calf from a Friesian cow was a little late. In contrast to Dolly, he was a tough little bull and we named him "Hansy". We tried to make all our newborn animals our friends and other farmers used to tease us that soon we would be able to start a circus with all our tame animals.

Our farm was next to a park and we had to take the cows round the edge of the park as our orchard fence was also the fence for the park. When we collected the cows for milking, the bull Caesar would accompany his herd but would stay in the orchard with the calves. A corner of the orchard was dug up and turned into a vegetable garden. This particular day I crossed the orchard into the vegetable garden when suddenly Caesar charged towards me, steam coming from his nostrils. There was no tree nearby that I could use as a shelter. Then, from a different part of the orchard, Hansy also came charging towards me. I froze, petrified. Why was this happening? Caesar was only a few yards away when Hansy, our first Friesian bull calf, ran between me and Caesar. The bull's horns tore the side of Hansy's stomach wide open and he fell over. The bull, realising that he had hurt one of his herd, gave a loud unearthly bellow, ran towards the gate and jumped over it. He was not as heavily built and fat and clumsy as some other breeds. As far as I could see, he was running towards the fields. I called for help. Papa and Arthur came running and, seeing the damage that Caesar had done, took me home and phoned for the vet. I was crying and trembling. The vet checked the wound carefully and saw that none of Hansy's vital organs were damaged. He sewed the calf up and also gave him a tranquilliser injection. The vet suggested that Father take some cows that had been milked into the field as this might calm the bull a little. As a precaution, the vet collected a rifle from his car, warning Papa that when a bull has drawn blood, he might become dangerous. When they arrived in the meadow, they found Caesar grazing. He must have jumped several gates to get there. They approached him carefully, speaking to him in a very calm voice. The vet wanted to examine him to find out the reason for this unusual behaviour. As the vet ran his hand over the animal, he noticed several paper clips embedded in his skin. We assumed that some boys had thought it great fun to use a catapult and aim it at the bull. It looked as if I had arrived at the wrong moment — or perhaps the right one as Caesar could easily have jumped the fence into the park.

The drawback of being next to a park was that mischievous children could hurt and frighten the animals. Another of their sports was to send their pet dogs to chase the animals. On the plus side, at weekends different colliery brass bands would play in the pavilion and the wind would carry the sound over to me, so I could listen to it while weeding in the vegetable garden.

When we thought that all was running smoothly, surprises were always round the corner and we had to learn a few tricks. All the new cows Papa had bought were guaranteed good milkers. The yield was weighed after each milking. One particular cow was short of the guaranteed quantity, yet the cow looked very healthy with a shiny coat. Mutti was for returning this cow. Papa wondered whether gypsies in the neighbourhood were helping themselves, but he could not believe this with two dogs guarding the cows, not to mention the bull. Papa decided to spend a night in the field. No gypsies visited and yet the yield was still low. Old wives' tales tell of hedgehogs suckling, so the next night Papa decided to take up guard duty in the cowshed. No hedgehogs came into the shed but still there was a very low yield. Papa stayed up the next night too. As dawn was breaking, he heard some strange noises and immediately went to check. He could not believe what he saw. The cow had turned her head round completely and was suckling herself! This of course explained the healthy, sparkling, fit animal! The vet suggested that she wore a triangular wooden collar. This had the hoped-for effect as the milk yield increased. It was amazing how cunning animals could be and what tricks they could play on us.

Several weeks after the Managing Director from the colliery had paid us a visit, six workmen arrived one morning to start work on the walls. They began with the ground floor walls, knocking away the plaster to build in the damp-proof layer. For weeks we lived only in the kitchen. We did not complain as all this work was done for us and the colliery Accounts Department paid for it all. Once the walls were completed they decorated the rooms. As soon as the ground floor rooms were finished, the workmen started upstairs. This was finished much more quickly as they only needed to decorate the rooms. Before the men left, the foreman wanted the worksheets signed by Papa, who was unwilling to do this. He was frightened that if he signed it, the building firm would send him the bill. Ten weeks' work for six men! Papa suggested that they contact the Managing Director of the colliery. He came to see whether the work had been satisfactorily done and whether we were happy with the result. After the workmen left, the house became quiet again. No whistling, no shouting from room to room. Blissful silence.

As we were settling down and the house was in a good condition, Mutti made the suggestion that finally we ought to buy furniture and rugs. Mentioning rugs, Mutti wondered if that filthy carpet was still in the barn. She wondered what it would look like if it was scrubbed and hosed down. Looking at it carefully, Mutti realised that it was a Persian carpet. In its native country, sheep and goats would have walked on it and even soiled it with the results of their natural function of digesting food. Once a day it would be sprayed with water.

Papa and Kurt put it on the cleanest part of the concrete yard and Mutti and I scrubbed it with soap and water, pouring bucketfuls of the stuff over it. The result? A beautiful carpet. Little did we guess that we would still have it thirty years later. Mutti finally sold it when she fancied a more modern look.

For days Mutti wrote down what furniture we needed and in which room each piece would go. Mutti could hardly contain her happiness. She was bubbling over with excitement, trying to explain what she thought we needed. This shopping expedition was one of her rare outings as I did the daily shopping. To go back to Nottingham was an extra bonus. While Mutti and Papa were shopping, Kurt and I saw to the animals, with Kurt dealing with all the milking, filtering and cooling of the milk. We worked extra hard to show our parents how responsible we were.

When she returned, Mutti tried to describe the furniture they had bought:

A dining room suite. The main sideboard and table were made of smoked oak. The sideboard had very straight lines, except for the two doors at the front. On each door was a large curve, the shape of an inverted horseshoe. Above the curve was a walnut veneer; underneath it was smoked oak.

Two more armchairs. This was a luxury as all four of us could now relax in the evening, each one in an armchair.

A bedroom suite, again made of walnut, with two extra wardrobes, one for my brother and one for me.

Curtain material, but only for the rooms we were going to live in.

A radio — real luxury. We gathered round it intently to listen to our first programme.

When the furniture arrived and was put into the different rooms, we felt that at last we had a home again.

As life became more settled, we learned how to become real farmers. Papa would drum into us that, with animals, we should never be complacent. Their health and well-being were our responsibility. At one point, our black devil of a cat, Tommy, became very thin and listless. He would not eat any food but would only drink. He would place his chin and throat onto the warm tiles by the Yorkshire Range. Finally, Mutti asked Papa to have a closer look to try and find out what was ailing him. Papa ran his hands gently round the cat's body and felt a swelling under his chin. Papa decided to shave the area to have a better look. Kurt held the cat, but he did not struggle. I think he guessed that we were trying to help him. Poor Tommy had an enormous boil under his chin and it seemed to be almost choking him. Papa saw some marks and said that a rat must have fought him and bitten him. To release the swelling, Papa used a razor blade to cut the skin under his chin asking Kurt to hold the cat securely so that he could not move. Otherwise Papa might accidentally cut his throat. Tommy just lay still and Papa cut the skin. Blood and pus ran out. Papa washed the cut with disinfectant and put a bandage round his neck. Mutti made him a bed in a cardboard box away from the other cats. Tommy was very weak. Mutti warmed some milk and added a teaspoonful of brandy. She held the saucer close to his mouth and he drank a little. Like an invalid, he was being spoiled and pampered. With an added raw yolk of egg and the brandy in the milk, he soon built up his strength and before too long he became our little black devil again.

CHAPTER
SIX

Making friends

A shock meeting Germans in Doncaster

It was not all endless work. During the eighteen months before the outbreak of war, we made several good friends who stuck to us through thick and thin. They remained true friends, even through the difficult war years and afterwards. Some stayed friends for life.

One of these friendships had a strange beginning. In the morning when we worked, I still wore my hair in curlers. My mother's hair was naturally curly, but mine was straight — very blonde and straight. How I longed to have it curly like hers, so I wore these curlers all night and in the morning till after lunch. It would then be curly for the rest of the day. If I mentioned the word "perm" to her, she would reply that I was too young and it would be a waste of money. The curlers were made of folded paper or strips of material. One wound the hair round it and then knotted it. This would keep it in position. I looked like a strange species of hedgehog.

On Saturday mornings I would help Mutti in the dairy, wearing wellington boots to protect my legs from all the splashing water. It was just one of these Saturday mornings about 10a.m. as we were having breakfast, when someone knocked at the kitchen door. As I had the youngest legs and spoke reasonable English, I always had to answer the door.

A handsome young man stood there, smartly dressed in grey flannel trousers, white shirt and blazer. His eyes were sparkling. I remember that I was wearing a pale blue dress with dark blue spots on it. In my best English I politely asked him, "Can I help you?"

His reply made no sense to me at all, "I liked you from the first moment I saw you."

I looked down at my boots and, coyly touching the curlers in my hair, I said to him, "I beg your pardon, please, I do not understand you." He repeated his sentence a second time and a third time. I did not know how to handle this situation, so I simply said, "Excuse me, please, but I better tell my parents," and closed the kitchen door, returning to the breakfast room.

My parents wanted to know who had knocked at the door. I told them that this young man had repeated the same sentence three times. My mother wondered where this young man was.

"Outside the kitchen door," I replied.

"Well, you had better invite him in and we shall find out what he really wants."

He entered shyly and we offered him a cup of tea. Then my parents asked him what he had said to me and why. He repeated his sentence a fourth time, adding that he would like to take me out. My parents questioned him. "How do you know that you will like her?"

Then he explained that for weeks and months he had watched us, but especially me when I was in the yard. On his way to work he had to pass the farm gate and again on the way home. My parents pointed out that I was not yet 15 years old and in their opinion I was far too young to go out with a young man. However, not wanting to offend him, my parents agreed that the following Saturday he could take me to the pictures.

I was so excited, for several reasons. Going out with Frank made me feel very special, because it was me he had invited out, not my brother's kid sister, but me. Also, it would be the first time I had been to a film show. The night before I could hardly sleep, I was so full of anticipation about this great adventure.

As arranged, Frank called for me. The film we went to see was *Rose Marie* with Nelson Eddy and Jeanette McDonald. The story and music really stirred my emotions and I felt overwhelmed. I thought my heart would burst. During the interval, Frank wanted to talk to me, but as I had never seen advertisements like these I thought they were part of the show and finally I said very politely, "Please excuse me, but if you wanted to talk, we should not have gone to the pictures. I have to concentrate, otherwise I do not understand all the information." Poor young man! We sat in silence for the rest of the show.

This silent treatment did not put him off, however. Going home by trolleybus, he told me that he would like us to go out together again. My parents allowed us to meet once a week and many Saturdays we stayed at home. Frank had learned to play the violin and sometimes he would bring his violin and would play just for me. Just for me! Sometimes my parents joined us and they too enjoyed his performances. I lived from one Saturday to the next.

Opposite the farm was a small grocery shop. I spent many hours there because sometimes I wanted to buy a particular item of food but did not know the correct word for it. I used to stand aside while they served other customers. Mr and Mrs Lawrence, the shopkeepers, had no children and so they enjoyed teaching me colloquial English. One day, my mother wanted some Gries. The dictionary translated this as "grit" or "gravel". So, armed with this information, I went across the road to buy some grit or **gravel**. I took the dictionary with me to show Mr and Mrs Lawrence. They smiled and suggested that I should go next door to the stone-mason. No, no, no, Mutti wanted to make some soup with it. They suggested all kinds of things, barley, rice, salt, even sugar. No, no, I wanted grit or gravel. We argued about it for about half an hour, but I left empty-handed. Weeks later, when shopping in town and passing Lipton's grocery shop, I saw it displayed in the window. It had a strange name, "semolina". Modern dictionaries give this translation too, the grit of wheat!

Going shopping in Donny (the local name for Doncaster) could be fraught with danger for us. One particular large shop sold continental delicatessen. My parents were discussing which of the continental sausages they wanted to buy. They spoke in German to each other. A man had been listening to them and came over to greet them, "Heil Hitler! I have not been notified that another German couple had arrived in Donny. We have a very active Nazi group here."

My parents were speechless and went pale, but my father pulled himself together and answered, "Good day. We came to England to get away from politics."

From that day on, we were very wary and alert, always watching people's actions. We kept wondering how strong and active the fifth columnists were in England and whether they would find out where we lived. Once again, fear became our companion. We mentioned this encounter to the police and they explained that in Doncaster was a German factory, Bamberg, making silk stockings and celanese underwear. The managers and supervisors were German, while the workers were English. The Germans, who had a good position here in England, had to be good party members.

The Farmers Union Secretary suggested that my brother and I should join the Young Farmers Club, so that we could meet other young people. We were invited to join them when some Young Farmers were visiting the Great Yorkshire Show. As we walked round, I talked to my brother in German, when I noticed that a young man was following us. The Secretary of the Young Farmers Club was looking after us and Kurt pointed out this man's strange behaviour to him. He recognised the young man as they had attended the same school. Once again, this young man's father was a manager at the Bamberg factory. The man pointed out that he had heard us talking in German and wanted to know why

110

we had not reported our arrival to the Party. Our friend from the Young Farmers was very good and replied, "These young people are my guests. There was no need for them to contact anybody as they are my visitors."

Of all the places in England, we had to choose our farm and pick a town with a German Bamberg factory in it! This incident only increased our fear and we felt even more insecure. As the political tension between England and Germany grew, so our anxiety grew as well and became more and more noticeable. We did not dare to face the facts — should war break out, what would happen to us?

As Mutti spoke very little English, she was now nervous and too frightened to accompany me when I went shopping in Doncaster. She would venture out only if really necessary.

We had many discussions on the subject of my education. Seeing it had stopped so abruptly, my parents thought that I should go to school again, keeping in mind that I had to help on the farm. The Principal from the Grammar School could not help as my knowledge of English restricted me in some subjects, so I tried the Technical College. The principal there was only too pleased to help me. With careful planning he offered me the chance to join different classes according to my ability and to study only essential subjects so that I need attend only for a few hours in the morning. My timetable consisted of English, Literature, German, Chemistry, Physics, Maths and Cookery. Later in the year I joined a class for engineering drawing. I wanted to learn tracing and how to make blueprints.

For several hours a day I was a schoolgirl again. The English teachers made allowances for me during dictation or note-taking. When I could not remember the sentence, I just looked up and the teacher would repeat it and I could write on.

I found the physics lessons very difficult. I was frightened of the physics master. He spoke through his teeth and never seemed to move his lips. I remember well the first lesson that I understood anything about, after weeks of struggling. We were learning about the law of expansion by heating a metal ball and putting it through an unheated metal ring. It would not pass through the ring after being heated. The teacher called my name and wanted to know the answer, but I just stared at him. He changed the subject.

"So you have come from Germany?"

"Yes, sir."

"You have seen Herman Göring speak?"

"Yes, sir."

"His uniform fits him well and he looks smart?"

"Yes, sir."

"His shirt collar fits him well, but after he has spoken for a while he gets hot. He then puts his fingers into the collar and tries to stretch it?"

I did not know whether he did or not, but I said, "Yes, sir."

"Well, that is the law of expansion. His neck gets hot and swells up, while his collar stays the same size."

112

This was the first physics lesson I understood and afterwards I was no longer afraid of that teacher. Often after a lesson I would ask him to explain certain parts that I had not understood.

At break the teachers would recount to each other the mistakes I had made in English and they were highly amused.

I found the cookery lesson very interesting. We had to bring with us a dish to cook in, for example when making shepherd's pie, we brought a pie dish. I always collected the necessary dish from a friend. One particular day my mother was not well and so I had to miss the cookery class. I rang this friend, Joan, telling her that I did not require any bowels for that day and would she store my bowels until the following week. Joan thought it a good opportunity to tease me and asked, "What do you do with these bowels?"

"You know, I cook in them once a week."

She went on quizzing me about my bowels, until she could no longer control her laughter. She explained that the way I pronounced "bowels" meant "intestines". "It's that little letter 'e' that makes all the difference. What you use in cookery class is a 'bowl'!"

I made many howlers and the teachers loved to share them with each other during their breaks. Certain letters were my stumbling blocks and the teachers often did not correct them as it made my English sound quaint. The letters V and W were the most problematic.

I would pronounce the V with the English rounded pronunciation of W as this was a new sound for me. Thus, "violets" became "wiolets", while "vinegar" became "winegar". Similarly, "I vash in vater" because I visualised the written word "water" and pronounced it with the German "w", which sounds like the English "v". Likewise, "I vear a west". The points of the compass were north, south, east and vest!

There was also the infamous "th", which Papa claimed caused the English people's protruding teeth as their tongue pushed against their teeth. When I concentrated, I would remember to do this, but I spoke at normal speed, then the "th" became a "z". It took many hours of elocution lessons before I finally came to terms with these difficulties.

I learned to understand the language through going to the pictures. Apart from meeting Frank on Saturdays, I was allowed to go to an afternoon performance costing 6d once a week. Two films were always shown, the main feature and the B film. Often I would sit through one film twice. The second time round I would shut my eyes to hear whether I could understand it all. If not, I would open my eyes quickly to see the actions and thus work out what the meaning was. This way I learned the language. I could understand what was said in German or English, but could not translate, not knowing the exact words needed to translate. People realised that I could understand them if they spoke slowly. Little did they realise that I could also understand them when they spoke to each other quickly. I think they would have been embarrassed if they had known.

My brother wanted some relaxation from farm work, and so he decided to join a night class at the Technical

College. Perhaps it seems strange that he chose to join an advanced German class, but he hoped that by doing translations, it would help him to learn colloquial English.

After a few sessions he befriended two students and, when the teacher realised this, she wondered whether she could help this acquaintanceship to progress and invited the three for supper. Kurt was very excited as they found out that they had similar interests, so Kurt invited them to meet the family. This was the beginning of a long friendship. Tim and David became regular visitors as both lived in digs, and spending some time on a Saturday or Sunday with my family helped them to relax.

Mutti welcomed them with open arms as for the first time since coming to England she could join in a conversation in German. These two young men were nine years older than me. To them I was just Kurt's kid sister, but they fell for my mother's charms, which hurt me a little.

David was a real charmer, tall and handsome with blue eyes and blond hair. He was very talkative and spoke fluent German. When he was telling a tale, his eyes would sparkle mischievously. In contrast, Tim was the silent, serious type, with dark brown eyes and brown hair. He looked at life much more seriously and solemnly as his job was a public prosecutor. He said that he saw life in all its sordidness and seediness.

Every so often David would come later in the evening and would bring a gift of flowers or chocolates for Mutti. When he gave her these tokens, how I wished and longed that just once I would be recognised and the gift given to me. He realised that we were pleased to see him at any time as long as he was ready to take us as he found us. When late autumn arrived with its cold foggy evenings, David would visit us at eleven o'clock or even midnight. His explanation was that he felt lonely and miserable, and wanted to stay the night. The family would usually be in bed as we generally had to rise early in the morning. When the door bell rang, Mutti suggested that I should get up and let him in, and make a pot of tea and sandwiches for him. Mutti promised that I could stay a little longer in bed the next morning. On one of the nights he confessed that he had a nickname for me. My heart raced and I held my breath, hoping and wishing that it would be a nice one. I thought to myself that he had waited until we were on our own to tell me this, so that no one would tease him. All I wanted was to be recognised as a young woman, and not just that kid sister. I waited breathlessly, anxiously — and then he told me, "Polly".

Why Polly? Because I reminded him of a song. Oh how lovely and romantic. Then came the explanation. The song was "Polly put the kettle on". "You do this the moment I come into the kitchen."

It was like a slap in the face. Did he not realise that I had been in bed for several hours and wanted to get back to sleep as the new day would bring with it hours of hard work? I kept my head held high and laughed about it, but as soon as I was in my bedroom, I cried and cried and cried myself to sleep. The next time he came late to see us, I did not put the kettle on. He kept

116

looking at his wristwatch. Finally he asked if I would be good enough to make him a cup of tea. "Don't bother this late about sandwiches," he added. I think he realised that he had made a big mistake.

In the cold and wintry evenings, the cows stayed in the shed and at about 9.30p.m. Papa and Kurt would go out to check on them, putting hay into the crib and giving them water to drink. After a long day's work, they were too tired to stay up when David arrived late.

One day David suggested that I ought to meet a young lady called Joan. She was trying to learn German but could not keep up with the tuition in the evening class. I could earn a little pocket money by helping her. As soon as I met her, I pictured her as Snow White. She had raven-black wavy hair and a white complexion with dark brown eyes. To complete the picture, her lips were a lovely red. I was bewitched by her. Joan was eight years older than I was and a friendship was to grow between us that lasted many years until she finally died in 1970 in Africa, where she had been living. As I was emotionally very mature, I got on better with her than with the silly giggly girls at the Technical College. My parents insisted that my brother's friends should also be mine, and that my friends should be my brother's too. I think Kurt fared better by this arrangement as his friends were always too old to take any interest in me. We all enjoyed music and spent many evenings dancing in the breakfast room, pushing the table and chairs against the wall. David and Tim would ask Mutti for a dance, and in the soft low light and the glow of the fire, she would look younger again, her beauty undiminished by all that hard work. When Kurt had to work outside in the stable in order to keep an eye on any cow about to calve, he would wear his wellington boots. If all was well, he would come back into the house for a short while, wearing his freshly washed wellingtons. He would come straight through to the breakfast room and have a couple of dances with Joan. Mutti would moan and groan about her lovely carpet, but Kurt would laugh at her with his head held high, saying "Mutti, these oriental carpets have put up with more than a pair of clean wellingtons walking over them. What about the sheep and goats?" Mutti always gave in because Kurt was so hard-working, and if a few moments' dancing would brighten his life, so be it. Papa would leave us at about 10p.m. and he would get up when Kurt went to bed. They never left a cow on her own to calve, just in case of complications. Looking after the stock was important because it meant looking after our money. The calf was the profit as the Milk Board paid little for a gallon of milk.

We felt as if we were becoming seasoned farmers, but as the seasons went on, we had to learn about harvesting the wheat. As we had no horses, Papa drove the tractor and behind it the reaper/binder, which cut the wheat and bound it into sheaves. Once again the miners would help with the harvest. They would put six to eight sheaves into shocks or stooks to dry, making rows of these but leaving enough space for the tractor and cart to pass between them. The men would then pitchfork the sheaves onto the transport. They would then be driven to the farmyard and stacked ready for the threshing machine. A team of men came with the threshing machine and they would feed the sheaves into it, cutting the twine so that the wheat would fall into the machine. This made a lot of noise and dust as the grain was extracted and poured into bags. The binder would then bind the straw into manageable bales. These were then stacked. Meanwhile some of the chaff would be burnt. So that the harvest would run smoothly, when the men had their short breaks I had to carry out to the men a basket full of sandwiches and an enamelled jug full of tea ready mixed with milk, but not sweetened. They worked until it was dark when the weather was fine as everything depended on the corn being dry. I could do this journey several times during the day as I had summer holidays from school.

The work carried on for Papa and Kurt; as soon as the wheat was harvested, they started to plough the fields and re-sow them. Papa had bought good seed, hoping to reap a good harvest the following year.

Every season brought its problems and we had to learn to cope with them. Nearing Christmas came the big task of killing all the chickens and the four geese. Papa could not face this task, so most of them were sent to the livestock market and auctioned. Still, he was left to kill the geese. He caught one and took the goose into the stable, but quickly came out again, hugging the goose. Papa pointed out that the goose sensed what her fate was going to be as she was crying. So the four geese were taken to the local butcher who killed them and sold three of them. The fourth was for our Christmas dinner. We had to pluck her feathers and then hang her by her feet till we wanted to cook her. Both Mutti and Papa decided that we would never raise geese again. On occasions such as these people could see that we were not toughened farmers!

As Christmas came nearer, we told our friends how we celebrated the festive season. To us it was a religious time and we would spend the Christmas days in a quiet and solemn mood. Then Joan told us about her Christmas, describing how her family celebrated the holiday with a big party for her and her brother John. To me it sounded more like a New Year's occasion. Joan then invited Kurt and me, so that we could experience it. It took place the weekend before Christmas. Joan's mother was a domestic science teacher and she prepared so many tempting dishes, foods that we had never seen before. The table was laden with this delicious food. Before we could taste it, we had to pull crackers and wear the paper hats. Other friends were also invited and we were twelve in all. We helped with clearing the table and then we played party games. We were taught the tradition of mistletoe. As the evening progressed, we were getting tired. Joan's brother John made up the fire and we all sat round it on armchairs and the settee, and on cushions on the floor, and we learned how to roast chestnuts. Eventually a quieter mood came over us and the family sang Christmas carols. We did not know any of them apart from "Silent Night". After a while the singing became quieter as we fell asleep, one by one. The fire had died down, yet no one wanted to go to bed. John went upstairs and returned with some blankets to keep us warm. In the morning we all felt a little stiff and to soothe our aching joints, some of us had hot baths. There was plenty of hot water as the house had a back boiler. After breakfast Joan's parents suggested that we all have a good brisk walk. The cold air woke us up. If I remember correctly, only Joan and John, my brother and I returned home and Mr and Mrs Green had cooked lunch. By now Kurt and I were feeling guilty about staying away from the farm for so long and completely forgetting about our farm work. But what a party it had been! We were invited again for the following year. While sitting around the blazing fire, my thoughts went back to the last few years in Germany, when we could not afford even an apple as a Christmas gift.

Then it was our turn to invite Joan and John, David and Tim for New Year's Eve. We danced the hours away till Big Ben rang in the New Year, 1938. Mutti had prepared some "Grog". This is a mixture of rum, water and spices, and is drunk hot. We toasted in the New Year — "Prosit Neujahr". Then we went outside and lit some sparklers and fireworks. Returning back inside the house, we had some more Grog to warm us up. It gave us a warm glowing feeling inside.

Then Mutti insisted that we should try and see what the future had in store for us. We melted a little lead in an old spoon and then tipped the molten lead into a bowl of water. The result was carefully checked as the shape held the mysteries of the future. As with reading tea leaves, with a little imagination it was possible to see symbols of the future. If its surface was smooth, that was a good omen; protruding spikes meant we would have to be aware of danger. Most of the shapes had a lot of spikes, warning us of trouble and danger ahead.

CHAPTER
SEVEN

1939 — Declaration of war and its effect on us

In 1939 our lives on the farm and the farm work were more or less a repetition of how we had lived from the time we arrived, but with less stress, and we were facing the new year with confidence. We had only one worry, but would never admit to it or even voice it. The political tension between Germany and Britain was growing. We didn't dare think about it, but carried on with our work as usual.

Since bumping into and meeting the different Germans from the Bamberg factory which manufactured underwear and stockings, we lived under a mental strain in case one of them should find out where we lived. We felt very insecure and once again we lived on our nerves. As the prospect of a war between Germany and Britain increased, we dared not face the fact of what would happen to us, and as fears of war intensified, local people would come to see Papa and ask him for his opinion on Hitler and war. All he answered was that everybody should be concerned as Hitlerism was an evil regime and must be destroyed.

Life seemed to go on in its leisurely English way. There seemed to be no movement to mobilise the armed forces. The Prime Minister, Mr Chamberlain, visited Germany to meet Hitler. Returning to Britain, he held his umbrella high and announced "Peace in our time". Papa shook his head and said that Chamberlain was too much of a gentleman and his word was his bond, but agreements signed by Hitler were not worth the paper they were written on. Hitler had bought some time to execute his plans and also he wanted to find out the strength and commitment Britain had to Poland. Didn't Britain realise the military power Hitler had built up to create a mechanical killing machine? We lived from day to day, frightened for our future, but not letting our fear show to the local people.

We worked harder than ever, cutting down on casual labour as our savings were getting less and less. I worked especially hard as Mutti had spells of violent stomach pains. She exacerbated it by working too hard outside. I made her rest and did all the housework on my own. I also helped in the dairy, filtering and cooling the milk and washing the milking equipment. Even I could not keep this up. I was still not yet 15 years old. Every time the news was on the wireless, one of us would sit by it and listen carefully for the latest developments.

Business friends living in Nottingham who had no children of their own invited me to stay with them for a week to give me a break. My parents were very pleased for me.

124

I was in need of a pair of shoes, so my parents suggested that we should buy a pair before going to Nottingham. Mutti and I went to the Saxone shoe shop. The assistants knew us as we had bought the wellington boots there and leather boots for Papa and Kurt to wear during the summer as well as regulation school shoes for me. When the shop assistants saw us, they thought that we must be in a great hurry. They were surprised to see us at all and that we were still in Doncaster. We laughed and said that we lived here. We could not understand their reaction until they asked us why we had not returned to Germany. "Haven't you had a letter from the German Embassy? All the people employed by Bamberg and their families left last week." We explained that we had nothing to do with Bamberg. "We are here on our own. We are farmers." We wanted to do some other shopping, but Mutti had become fearful and wanted to get back home for security.

Next morning I set off for Nottingham. The bus trip was pleasant and Mr and Mrs Curtis met me at the bus station. A few days of sheer luxury followed. They really spoiled me. To be able to stay in bed a little longer and not to have to scrub those red quarry tiles in the kitchen and breakfast room before 7 a.m. was wonderful.I stretched my arms and relaxed. Then the door opened and Mrs Curtis came in carrying a tray with breakfast for me. What a wonderful feeling of being pampered.

We never mentioned the situation between Germany and Britain. I wanted to help and Mr Curtis showed me his lawnmower. Now that I had learned the secret of his beautiful green lawns, I had to have a go with it. Mr and Mrs Curtis kept me busy going shopping and sightseeing, with visits to the castle, so I had no time to brood over the political situation. But however hard they tried to distract me, there was no avoiding the inevitable tension as we sat and listened to the latest news.

Then it happened. The announcer stated that Hitler's troops had marched into Poland. Mr Chamberlain gave his ultimate warning. If Germany did not withdraw its troops, we would be at war. I begged Mr and Mrs Curtis to let me hurry home immediately as I wanted to be with my parents and brother when the dreaded hour arrived. Mrs Curtis gave me a beautiful amethyst ring, saying that should my parents and brother be interned, they would apply for me to live with them or even adopt me as I was under 16 years of age. "Please remember this. You could live with us as our foster child."

The journey home was a nightmarish trip. Whereas I had enjoyed the outward journey, this time I stared out of the window but saw nothing, all my thoughts running feverishly around in circles. What would happen to us now? Why did trouble keep following us? Tears streamed down my face and the lady sitting next to me noticed this. She said, "Never mind, dear. It can't be that bad. It may never happen!" If only this could be true, but "it" had already happened. Even though I was still young, I knew that Hitler would never recall his troops.

My parents were glad to see that I had managed to get home safely and that I had cut the holiday short. Whatever was going to happen, we would all face it together and support each other. We decided to carry on working the same way as always. After all, the animals knew nothing about war.

One of us kept listening to the wireless to make sure that we heard what action Hitler was taking. We worked mechanically, like zombies, lifeless and apathetic. Finally, on Sunday morning, 3rd September 1939 at 11.15 a.m., the Prime Minister, Mr Chamberlain, spoke:

"I am speaking to you from the Cabinet Room at 10 Downing Street. This morning the British Ambassador in Berlin handed the German Government an official note stating that unless we heard from them by eleven o'clock, that they were prepared at once to withdraw their troops from Poland, a state of war would exist between us. I have to tell you now that no such undertaking has been received, and consequently this country is at war with Germany."

The four of us sat next to the wireless and no one uttered a word. I think that we all had the same thoughts. What was to become of us? What now? The same thoughts as we had had twice before: when the Gestapo took my parents away and when we escaped from Germany. We sat motionless, numbed by the news from the wireless. Up to now, England had been the country that had given us shelter and protected us, but now we were people from the enemy country. The silence between us became oppressive. I think none of us knew the right words to break it.

A loud knocking at the kitchen door broke the spell. Papa went to see who it was, who would be coming to see us at this crucial moment. To his amazement, two tall policemen were standing at the threshold. The police station was about five minutes' walk from our farm. They must have left the station while Mr Chamberlain was still making his announcement. Up to this point we had met only a few policemen. Once was on the first night in England when a policeman found a hotel for us to stay in. They had always been friendly and helpful, but now they were here to perform their duty. Papa invited them in. They apologised — yes, apologised — for disturbing us and explained that they had a notice from the Home Office to warn us that we might have to be interned. It was not the wish of the British Government, but might be necessary to protect us from the local people as many of them were miners and might not be able to distinguish between "good Germans" and "bad Germans", and might therefore turn against us. One policeman explained further that, if we were interned, a government seal would be put on the house and the animal stocks would be sold and the money saved for us until after the war. We were to pack four cases, one per person, and be ready to leave at any time. Papa asked if there were several different internment camps, but the reply was a simple "No". We had realised that quite a few Germans lived in Britain, but they were mostly patriotic about their homeland. We were worried that if we had to share a camp with such people, our lives might be short lived as, in their eyes, we were traitors to Hitler and Germany. The policemen were very sorry and apologetic, but said they had to do their duty.

We took the cases out of storage, where they had been gathering dust for the past 18 months. If there is a God, why, oh why, did he allow some people to suffer so much trouble? Again, we packed the cases, choosing our clothes carefully as we now faced an uncertain future.

Two days later, the same two policemen came to see us. We hardly dared to breathe. What was their duty today? When they saw our anxious faces, they smiled happily at us. "We bring you good news! We have been enquiring amongst the local people, including the miners. They think you should be left on the farm and they'll look after you." We felt as if our chests would burst with emotion and I think each member of our family had tears in their eyes. Little had we realised that the kindness and help we had given to these people would be returned so many times over.

As the policemen were leaving, they noticed that the wireless was connected to the light bulb. They pointed out that we were not allowed to use one. Papa removed the plug from the light fitting and wrapped the wire round the box. He offered to carry it to the police car, but the policemen stopped him. "Leave it where it is, but do not reconnect it," they said. Papa gave his word that we would not do this. People often asked us if we were not tempted to reconnect it, but Papa would reply, "My word is my honour. Besides, there is no way we will risk this as breaking a promise will surely land us in an internment camp."

As soon as the policemen had left, Papa summoned us round the table to clarify the situation to us children. Up to then we had been aliens, but now we were aliens from an enemy country. We had to learn more than ever to blend into the surroundings and to "anglicise" ourselves and integrate. Papa laid down a few rules. Under no circumstances were we allowed to go out with friends to any place where the Forces boys would meet and relax. We were to keep out of the way and stay on the farm and work. Our friends, if they still wanted to visit us, would always be welcome as usual.

The next important visitors were the ARP men, who told us about the blackout and said they wanted to check ours. We showed them the big wooden shutters which covered the window, but just a tiny chink of light showed through the middle where the shutters met. They suggested that we should buy blackout material and make curtains.

Papa and Kurt worked out how many yards we needed to cover those high windows for the six main rooms as well as the kitchen and bathroom windows and the window above the main entrance. The shopkeeper was delighted to sell us so many yards though he wondered whether we really needed so much material, but we could not afford to take the risk that the smallest light might show.

When the Home Office had granted us permission to stay in England, Mutti, Papa and Kurt had been issued with a Police Certificate Registration Book, stamped

18th July 1938. As I was under age, I would have to wait until I was 16. On 30th September 1939, these Registration books were signed by the police.

When Joan visited us again, she noticed that the wireless was disconnected. She suggested that we should have some music to relax to in the evening and so she brought over her gramophone and some records. In order for us to have more than three records and build up a small library, every time one of our friends visited us, they would bring along another record. Some were classical music, while others were big band records which had melodies for dancing on them.

Our general farm hand was called up, so this extra work had to be divided among the family. Mutti would now help with the milking, using the milking machine, and Papa would finish the milking process by hand. I would help in the dairy, filtering and cooling the milk, and then washing the equipment. After this, I would feed the chickens and collect the eggs, and then start on the housework. Because of this extra work load, I had to cancel some of my lessons at the Technical College. I was able to transfer the English and Literature classes to the evening, but as I was well ahead in German, I stopped these, along with the Physics and Chemistry lessons.

Papa and Kurt shared the work driving the tractor until late into the night. Two little lamps were fixed to the tractor with covers on them to comply with the blackout regulations. Kurt would prepare the field during the day and plough the first furrow, making sure that it was straight. Then in the dark, he would just follow the first furrow. He would carry on driving the tractor until he was practically falling asleep.

As more men joined up, our friends Tim, David and John came to say farewell. They had volunteered and they promised to keep in contact with us when they came home on leave. Frank too had left, having joined the Fleet Air Arm. When he came home on leave, he would take me out. He looked so splendid in his uniform and I was the proudest girl in the world walking next to him.

An official letter arrived asking us to attend a tribunal in Wakefield on 6th October 1939. As Mutti spoke little English and someone had to stay on the farm and look after the animals, Papa wrote a letter asking for permission for Mutti to stay at home. We were very nervous, wondering what the outcome of this interview would be. Arriving at the Guildhall, we were ushered into a waiting room full of Germans. Several of them were older people who had come to this country after World War I. We all sat in silence, waiting to be called and meet the committee. Papa was called first and after about half an hour, they called for Kurt and then me. I was so frightened, but the committee did not ask me many questions as I was still under age.

Then the committee conferred and, turning round and facing us, announced that we were allowed to go back to the farm and help to win the war by bringing in the harvest. As a parting comment, one member of the committee said that only ten Germans had been allowed to go home — we were three of them. When we arrived home, Mutti hugged us all in turn. She had been frightened in case we did not come home again. Our Registration books were stamped with the following words: "The holder of this certificate is exempt from internment until further orders and also exempted from special restrictions under the Alien Order 1920 as amended . . . Refugee from Nazi oppression. Signed . . ."

Every day, as soon as the newspaper was delivered, horrified we would read how the German army was pushing through the different countries. They marched through Germany, conquering France, Holland and Belgium while the British troops retreated. The song-writers composed songs for the Forces to sing, such as "We're going to hang out the washing on the Siegfried Line" or "Run, Adolf, run away, and throw your gun away". These helped to cover up the heavy mood everybody was feeling. Then suddenly there was unusual activity on the road. Army lorries in convoy. Then we read in the newspaper about Dunkirk and how the retreating troops were rescued from the Dunkirk beaches. We thought it was a miracle, how so many troops were rescued. Even the weather and the calm sea had helped in this evacuation. We prayed and prayed and hoped that Hitler would not send his troops to follow the retreating Forces.

The local miners would come and ask Papa whether Britain was going to lose the war. "God forbid," he would reply. "If they come to England, my family and I will be hanged from the nearest lamppost," as to them we were traitors to the Reich. We would not let that thought develop, and, with more confidence than he felt, Papa would reassure these miners, explaining that England was an island which had not been conquered for centuries. They would ask about Lord Haw Haw. To this Papa would honestly reply that he never listened to him as it was pure propaganda. Of course we did not listen to him because our wireless was disconnected.

By now our family had learned to live by our intuition again as we had done in Germany. If we sensed hostility towards us on the part of people we met, we would leave quickly.

Another official letter arrived, summoning us to a tribunal in Sheffield. This time they wanted references from friends who would take responsibility for our allegiance to England. Our friends were only too pleased to do this for us. Again Mutti stayed on the farm to look after the animals. We were all worried about what the outcome of this interview would be. We three, Papa, Kurt and I, prepared to leave with a heavy heart, but smiled reassuringly at Mutti, to give her a feeling of security. We said our goodbyes, hugging her for that extra minute as if in this way we could hang on to our lives. We walked out of the side gate and turned round to have a last look at our home. No one said a word, but we all wondered whether we would see it again. To give each other support, we held our heads high and walked to the trolleybus to take us into town where we would catch the bus to Sheffield. We sat in silence all the way, partly so as not to give way to our emotions, but also so that the other passengers could not hear that we were foreigners. I cannot remember which building we were to go to, but on arriving, we were shown into the waiting room. It was filled with Germans and again no one spoke a word. The atmosphere was very tense, everyone clearly apprehensive about what the outcome of this interview would be. It would determine our future.

Eventually, we were the last three people left. Only three others had walked out of the interview room and out through the waiting room. What had happened to the others? Then a loud booming voice called Papa's name. This stirred us out of the shell we had retreated into. We did not say a word and in silence hugged him. We just looked into each other's eyes. He nodded his head slightly and went through the door. My brother and I sat ever so still in this vast room and looked at the guard as we moved a little closer and held each other's hand. This was like being back in Germany when we had only each other to rely on. We watched the hands of the clock move on very slowly. Then Kurt's name was called and I was all alone. I couldn't run away, but just had to wait to see what fate would bring. Time seemed to stand still as I waited all alone. Then my name was called. There was no one to hug me so that I could face whatever awaited me. I opened the door and saw a red carpet, a runner leading to a big long table where the gentlemen sat. I was told to walk to the chair facing this table. My heart pounded so hard that I felt the heartbeat in my eyes. Walking towards the table I glanced sideways without moving my head and I could just glimpse Papa and Kurt sitting there. I took a deep breath and shut my eyes for a second. At least I was not alone any more and it gave me some comfort.

I was told, "Please sit down." Then they asked me questions about how I was getting on at school. I replied that I had left it as I had to work full time on the farm. They thought I was a lucky girl as many children left school at 14 years. The next question was "How do you like England?" I tried to explain that the little I knew, I liked. The people near our farm were very kind to us and helpful. Then came the accusation and it was like a bombshell: "So as a good German girl you denounced your father to the Nazis and he was transported to a labour camp." I was so upset. I was speechless. I opened my eyes to the full — they felt as if they were going to pop out of their sockets. Finally I managed to stammer, "No, no, no," and began to cry, repeating "No, no, no." One member of the committee said, "Be honest and admit it." In my feeling of shock and horror, I just did not know how to cope with this. This was the cruellest accusation and I turned round and looked at Papa. He stood up and, begging for their indulgence, asked if he could speak for me. He said that Kurt and I had been very caring children, and it was due to our behaviour and silence that he had been protected from a longer confinement.

There was a pause, silence, and then the interviewing committee had a discussion. They announced, "We are pleased to say that you may return to the farm and help to feed the British people. We wish you all the very best."

The Alien Registration books were endorsed saying that we were "Friendly enemy aliens" and refugees from Nazi oppression. The tribunals had to place enemy aliens into one of three categories:

A. Those to be interned
B. Those who were not interned but were still subject to restrictions
C. Those that could remain at liberty as being subject to Nazi oppression or those that had definitely thrown their lot in with the country.

Those who could produce evidence of character associations and loyal intent were placed in the C group. Before we left, Papa mentioned that we had a lorry and tractor on the farm, both used for working the land. The lorry carried manure into the fields and was used for bringing the corn from the fields to the farm yard. They granted Papa permission to use both. The only restrictions placed on us were that we had to be in our home between 10.30p.m. and 6.30a.m. Tending the cows in the cowshed was classified as being at home. If we wanted to stay away from the farm, we had to notify the police in Doncaster and they would endorse this in the Police Registration book.

Sitting on the bus on the way home, Papa, Kurt and I again travelled in silence as we were emotionally worn out by the horrendous ordeal. As we arrived back at the farm, Kurt and I rushed into the kitchen, calling "Mutti, Mutti, we're back, we're back!" We hugged and kissed her. Papa caught up with us and he just embraced us all.

CHAPTER EIGHT

Dunkirk and MI5

Up to the time of Dunkirk, people had viewed the war in a fairly relaxed way. It was after all so far away, but after Dunkirk the whole atmosphere changed. Factories introduced shift work, with three shifts covering 24 hours. Women started to work in the factories. Everybody was saying that we had to avenge Dunkirk. The soldiers who had been rescued from the beaches, after they had had a rest, were determined that they must prepare to fight back.

Many convoys drove along the main road. One morning, two soldiers on motorbikes rode into the farmyard and came to the kitchen door, saying that they noticed that we had cows and wondered if they could buy some milk as they were thirsty and tired from directing convoys all night. We were only too happy to help and absolutely would not let them pay for any food or drink. Mutti offered to cook them a breakfast. They introduced themselves as William and Peter. Both spoke some German, which pleased Mutti as she could join in with the conversation. While enjoying their breakfast, they were about to tell us about their work directing the convoys and where they were going to.

Papa stopped them immediately, saying that they were welcome any time, but under no circumstances must they bring up a subject involving military activity. Both soldiers were interested in our large old farmhouse and asked to have a look round as they were fascinated by the architecture of old buildings. Papa and Kurt had to go outside to work and Mutti and I gave them a guided tour. When we came to the spare bedroom furnished with one double bed, they wondered if they could rest for a few moments. They had not slept in a bed for weeks. They too had been evacuated from Dunkirk. They leapt onto it, and started stretching and rolling on it just like two mischievous schoolboys. They were amazed at the firmness of the bed. Mutti explained that the mattress was made from horsehair lying on a spiral sprung base. This seemed of special interest to them as in their home they slept on a mesh base that sagged in the middle when you slept on it. Mutti suggested that they roll the mattress back to have a good look at the base.

When we returned to the breakfast room, our long-case clock was chiming and they noticed the deep sound of the chime. They were curious about the clock's history as they had never seen one like it before. Was it an antique and did we wind it up with a key? Mutti explained that it was one of the few items we had managed to get out of Germany. The case was made specially for my parents' wedding in 1920. It was smoked oak, but the movement was made in England. It was a precision clock. Two large brass weights controlled the mechanism. One weight moved the pendulum and the other weight controlled the chime. The fact that Mutti could talk in German to these soldiers acted like a spring releasing her pent-up emotions. She could understand and take part in a conversation, and so she offered to take the brass dial and clock mechanism out of its casing, so that they could have a good look at it.

Papa and Kurt came into the kitchen to have a cup of tea before going into the fields. The soldiers asked Papa if they could visit us again and invited Kurt for a drink in the local pub as a thank you for our hospitality. Papa thanked them but declined the offer, saying that Kurt was not allowed to go to public places to have a drink.

Finally they said goodbye and asked if they could visit us again when they came this way. "Yes, of course, you are welcome at any time," Papa said, "as long as you don't mention anything connected with your duty."

About a week later, William rode into the yard and knocked on the door. He introduced his partner. William entered the house as if he owned it. I laughed and said to my mother, "I came, I saw, I conquered." This applied to William and I nicknamed him "Siegfried", which means "victory in peace". Mutti had made up the spare bed, in case they came again very tired and wanted five minutes' rest. If my heart had not belonged to Frank, who was by now a pilot in the Fleet Air Arm, I would have hero-worshipped William. It was wonderful when they came to visit us as for once I was not the kid sister, but was treated as a young lady in my own right.

On one of their visits, I told them about a man who had knocked at the kitchen door and said that he thought I collected stamps. I replied that I did. Years ago Papa had given me his collection and I had carried on. They were all old stamps, but this man wanted some present day ones from Germany or Russia, or better still, international ones from Spain or Switzerland. He would offer me a good price for them. I told him that I could not help him as we did not write to anyone abroad nor receive any letters. He tempted me again, saying that if I wanted more money, he would gladly pay and this would help us financially. "Sorry, I cannot help you," I said. "All my stamps are from before the war." He must have got the message because he never troubled us again.

A few weeks later, to our amazement, we did receive a letter from Germany — from Herr Schulz, who had shared his flat with us for a while. He offered his services, if he could be of any help to us should the Germans invade England, so that we should not be hanged as traitors. He offered to vouch for Mutti, Kurt and me, that we were good people and had only left Germany because of Papa's influence, to help him find employment and earn money for his family. Wishing us well, he signed himself "Robert Schulz".

He did not know our address so wrote on the envelope, "Family Spatz, England". It took three weeks to find us, via the Red Cross in Switzerland, Spain and England. I wonder if the modern post would find us, or whether it would be thrown into the wastepaper basket.

It was the darkest time of the war — and for us — and we hoped that this letter would not harm us. Thank God the Germans never came to England!

William and Peter had become regular visitors, but every so often they had another partner. They explained that they always had to travel in pairs for safety. While busy with the housework and farm work, I looked forward to Frank's letters, hoping that he would let me know when his next leave was due. Suddenly, they stopped coming. Every morning I would rush to the kitchen door to see if the postman had brought a letter for me. I think he felt sorry for me as he used to say, "Sorry, dear, not today." My thoughts ran round in circles. Was he all right? Yes, of course. He was at sea and could not write and post a letter to me.

When I went shopping to the corner shop, I would often stand aside and let other customers be served first. I did not mind waiting. When no other customer was in the shop, I would ask questions to learn more about English foods and the way they were served. One morning, while waiting, I overheard two women talking about the different local boys in the Forces. When they mentioned Frank's full name, I listened carefully. Each word was like a hammer blow striking me. One woman said, "Isn't it sad that such a fine young man should be shot down and drowned so early in the war. It must be terrible for his mother, her being a widow." I wanted to scream out, "What about me?" Tears blinded my eyes and I ran home as fast as I could, went upstairs to my room and wept uncontrollably. Now it was clear to me why there had been no letters for me. With just a few

142

words, my whole world had been shattered. This was the worst thing that had ever happened to me. My hero, my boyfriend. Dead. I would never see his dear face again or hold those hands or listen to him playing the violin or my favourite melody, *Clair de Lune*. There was no hope that he would come back. If only they had said "missing", there would have been some hope. Mutti was very concerned. This was not just an emotional outburst. I could not talk, but cried and cried.

Over the next six to nine months we had many visits from our soldier friends — we called them "our boys". One time, when our friend David was on leave, he told us that he had applied to be transferred to the Intelligence unit as he spoke fluent German and French. He had already been given a date for an interview. William and Peter just listened to David and wished him good luck. It was the last time that William and Peter visited us. We had called them "our boys" and we missed their happy, cheerful visits. We assumed they had been posted to a different area.

We had quite a few chickens and used to send the eggs to the Marketing Board. Depending on the number of eggs we had to send them, they would issue coupons for chicken food. If a person came to us and wanted to buy eggs, we were allowed under special circumstances (e.g. sickness or pregnancy) to sell one egg per week. A young Air Force man came to the door asking if he could please buy some eggs for his pregnant wife who was ill. He introduced himself as Jack Wood and made us laugh when he translated it into "Hans Holz". Of course he was disappointed that we could give him only one egg. He offered us extra money. We dared not break the rules and regulations. If we did, it would mean the Isle of Man for us, where the big German internment camp was. We gave him the one egg so that no question of black-market dealings would arise. He came several times for his one egg and then his visits suddenly stopped, so we never knew if and when the baby had arrived.

Two more incidents involving members of the Forces took place. A soldier called Albert came and asked if we would teach him more German. He spoke a little and wanted to improve his pronunciation. We explained that during the day he would have to put up with Mutti and me as both men were working in the field or milking and tending to the cows. He thought that it would be quite a happy arrangement. In conversation we mentioned that we did not go out, but our friends visited us and one of our relaxations was dancing, which we did at home. He very politely asked Mutti for a dance. I wound up the record player. He observed that the radio was disconnected from the light fitting. He laughed and suggested that it would be easy to reconnect it as Victor Sylvester's dance band would be playing. "It's one of the best bands. They play a good steady rhythm to dance to," he said. We explained that we were not allowed to reconnect it to the electric power. Our friends had given us the record player and some records, and they would often bring us another record, so that we slowly built up a good collection of different bands. The next time Albert visited us, he brought a record to add to our collection. It was "Begin the Beguine". I had never heard it before and whenever I hear that melody played now, my thoughts flash back to the early days of the war and Dunkirk and the few visits Albert paid us. Another time he again suggested that we ought to reconnect the radio while he was with us — we would save on the needles for the gramophone. No way could he persuade us to do this. We had given our word to the policeman when war broke out and our word was our bond. Albert was a charmer. He danced with me and pretended to enjoy it. Even togged out in battledress and heavy army boots, he danced lightly on his feet. After several visits, however, he told us that this would be his last as he was going to be posted away.

Many times when the family sat by the fireplace, we would talk about the different personalities these boys had. We often wondered whether they ever gave a second thought to us and how we were surviving the war.

We — Mutti and I — had another visit from a soldier in battledress. This time we were very upset by this soldier's behaviour. Somehow his battledress looked just slightly different from the ones the other boys wore. He knocked at the door like the other boys did, but in a strange way of speaking, he asked if he could come in as he did not want the neighbours to see him and could we give him some food. All the other boys came openly and were friendly, and would wait till we invited them into our home. Mutti said to me that we had no bread or ready food in the house. The Egg Marketing Board had collected the eggs and it was our baking day. Mutti made our bread. She used 7 lb of flour and worked this into a dough, dividing the mixture into several loaves and a trayful of bread rolls to be ready for when Papa and Kurt came in for their second breakfast. The rolls were already baking. Mutti's reaction to the soldier seemed to be the same as mine. She had another look in the larder and noticed some left-over boiled potatoes from yesterday. She said to me that she could make some Bratkartoffel and I should run over to the stable and see if the hens had laid an egg. Never let it be said that we turned a hungry soldier away. When he heard Mutti saying "Brat", he said, "Ja, ja. Brat, schön." Mutti and I looked at each other and then looked more closely at the soldier. He had a gold tooth in the middle of his front teeth. We had never seen an English person with a gold tooth before. And there was his strange way of talking. English was our second language, but the ear is very attuned when it is not a dialect but a foreigner speaking. The tone is just slightly different. Mutti came close to me and whispered, "He is not English." I had come to the same conclusion myself. We were very frightened but, trying to brave it out, I asked where he came from. He took his military identity card out of his pocket. We had never seen one before so I did not know what to look for. Mutti laid a place for him at the kitchen table and he asked to sit at the other side, so that the neighbours could not see him. That did it. I was 15 and a half years old and I remember clearly that I was wearing the first pullover I had knitted. With the wool that was left over, I had knitted a long scarf that I wore like a turban to

146

cover up my paper curlers. The set was a lovely blue-violet colour. I was proud that I looked a little more grown up. I gathered up all my teenage courage and fighting spirit. Fighting for Britain. I asked him to leave with me and go to the Police Station — "because you are not British". He objected and became nasty, warning me not to follow him. However frightened I was, I still got hold of his belt and said firmly, "Yes, you will come with me to the Police Station. If you are British, you have nothing to fear." As we got to the gate, a boy happened to cycle by and I asked him to ride over to the Police Station and tell them that I thought this soldier was a foreigner and to ask them to send a policeman to meet us. The boy raced off fast. The soldier still objected, but I held on to him as if my life depended on it. He finally stopped struggling. We had only gone about 25 metres when a policeman on a bike met us. He and the soldier seemed to exchange glances and then the policeman smiled and said, "Oh, he's a Welshman. It's all right. They are a strange breed." I pointed out what I had noticed, but the policeman said, "You are free to go, sir." As the soldier turned round to walk away, he spoke through his teeth: "Do not follow me." I ran quickly home and said to Mutti that I wanted to see where this mysterious soldier would go. It was like a game of hide-and-seek. I watched and then ran from one house entrance to the next. When he arrived at the neighbour's farm, he turned in. The farmer's wife was on her own. I waited a moment and then knocked at the door and told her our reaction to this man. She was amazed and said that he was a very friendly and polite person who spoke a very cultured English; he was enjoying a cup of tea. So I went home. Mutti and I were very puzzled why and how he could behave so differently with different people.

A few months later, David was on leave and we asked him how he had fared in his interview. Before he answered, he asked a question: "Have William and Peter visited you recently?"

"Come to think of it, not since your last leave, when you told them you were hoping for a transfer to another unit," we replied.

David laughed and said, "That makes sense." We could not see the funny side of this. David asked, "Guess who interviewed me about transferring to the Intelligence Corps?" None other than William and Peter. Both were high-ranking officers, but when they came to visit us, they wore ordinary battledress and did not even have a lance-corporal's stripe on.

David pointed out that they were from MI5. We did not know what this meant. David explained that this group checked people out. They also turned David's application down, the reason they gave being that he was too talkative. They also mentioned that they had asked to be taken off our case as their many official visits had turned into friendly visits.

Now when David explained about the MI5 connection, we worked out that each soldier and civilian had been testing us in different ways. William and Peter checked out if we had any hidden radios — hence the rolling about on the unused bed and their interest in the workings of the long-case clock. Did we get correspondence from abroad? Hence the interest in the stamp collection. Did we keep to the rules and regulations — one egg per person — or did we sell eggs on the black market? Did we connect the radio? And finally, how would we behave if a German soldier came to our door? Would we hide him and give him shelter? So, in the true British spirit, they found out the answers to all these questions, but without using Gestapo tactics.

CHAPTER
NINE

Interview at college

Fields flooded — Going to college — My call-up

Hitler's army was pushing its way through France and Belgium. If ever prayers could help to calm anguish and fear, we prayed and hoped that the Channel was wide enough to hold back that steamroller of a force. We had escaped from Germany, but if the German Forces came to Britain, that would surely be the end of our lives. The friendly policeman came to see us again, delivering a message from the Home Office, that we should pack four small suitcases. If we did not have these, we should buy them immediately. Should the German Army enter Britain, by parachute or by crossing the water, we must be ready to leave the farm at a moment's notice. There would be a place for us on the last ship leaving England. Oh God, had it really come to this? And what about the little money we had left? Neighbours came and asked Papa what he thought of the situation. Never did we let other people guess our fear and so Papa would reply, bravely, that Britain had not been conquered since the Normans came in 1066. Every morning we rushed to see the newspaper and read the latest news. Dunkirk was the headline. Dunkirk — the beach to which so many soldiers had retreated. Dunkirk — the place where the defeated British forces had gathered, hoping for a miracle. Dunkirk was a defeat, yet in another way it was a victory, showing how people pulled together: the medical staff, the Salvation Army offering tea, nurses ready to help wounded men into trains away from the harbour. Then came the call for help from fishermen in their trawlers, little and bigger boats used for pleasure and, of course, the big ships from the fleet to evacuate all these boys from the beaches and bring them back to England. The German air force was busy machine-gunning the boys on the beach and bombing the ships. Dunkirk — it was a name that aroused fear in us.

To start with, we did not understand why neighbours mentioned the place in hushed voices as the newspapers were not very explicit. Then when they printed the full story, the horror struck us. Would Hitler follow the retreating arm, while the gallant seafaring men were evacuating them or would he send bombers and then follow with parachutists? We lived from hour to hour, catching the latest news from people talking and then in the morning, rushing to buy the paper. Dunkirk was a defeat for our army in Europe, but the evacuation of the tens of thousands of soldiers was also a victory over defeat. Still, we couldn't help thinking of all the equipment, guns, lorries, ammunition and so on that was left behind on the beaches — not to mention the boys that didn't make it back home to England.

Overnight, the atmosphere changed. Up to then, people had taken the war in a fairly leisurely way. It was all happening on the other side of the Channel, but now that killing machine of the German army was facing our coast, our island. To be able to defend this land, we had to make new equipment in double quick time. People seemed to have a stronger sense of purpose. The civilian population was spurred into action, joining in with the battle and showing their fighting spirit. Now the wheels in the factories were turning at high speed as full 24-hour working was introduced, three shifts of eight hours. The men who had been rescued said that as soon as the army was fully equipped again, they would be ready to go back and fight.

Because of this, we had less help from casual workers and Mutti once more worked in the fields. Finally she had to stop as she had so much stomach pain. When the doctor visited us and examined her, she suggested that she needed an emergency operation. As the hospital was filled with the wounded troops, she had to go into a private nursing home. I had to meet Matron and discuss the cost of it all. She explained the terms, the fees for the surgeon and anaesthetist, and of course the bed and board for three weeks. Also covered were the theatre fees. At home, when I heard that the theatre was included, I asked Mutti whether I could go instead of her as she would not be able to understand what was being said on stage!

I took Mutti to the nursing home and saw her settled in and then hurried home using the trolleybus. I had just arrived home when a very agitated nursing sister arrived by taxi. They had been having trouble with Mutti and they wanted to rush me back in the same taxi as the operating team were standing by. The sister said that Mutti would not speak or open her mouth. The sister explained what the trouble was: as the nurses were preparing her for the operation, she asked Mutti whether her teeth were all her own. She replied "No." "Please take them out," said the sister. A very upset Mutti replied that she could not do this. Sister came, then Matron and they pointed out that the teeth had to be removed. "You cannot" — and after that last remark, Mutti bit her lips. As soon as Matron saw me, she said that the surgeon and her team were waiting to operate, but Mutti must remove her false teeth first. I too said, "She cannot do that." An exasperated Matron shook her head and mumbled to herself, "Never have I encountered such difficult people." She turned round and left the room. A few minutes later she returned with a set of false teeth and explained that under the anaesthetic she could choke on her teeth. Ah, now I understood the panic! But Mutti's teeth were fixed in her mouth with a gold crown. There was a sigh of relief all round and she was rushed away.

Each time I visited Mutti I asked her whether she had been to the theatre yet. "No, not yet," came the reply. On her last day I asked to see Matron and explained to her that Mutti did not want to go to the theatre and please could I have the ticket instead. This time the joke was on me as of course the theatre fee was for the operating theatre and not a theatre show.

My brother had enrolled for a course in engineering and I joined a night class learning to trace and make blueprints. The principal tried to find me a place for work experience, but no firm would have me as all blueprints were classified as secret documents. So we cancelled the lessons. At home, my parents discussed whatever could I do that was not under government control. Their idea was that I should have more education as I had finished school at 13 and a half years of age. Finally, Domestic Science and Teaching were decided on. Making enquiries about this training, I was told that the College of Housecraft in Leeds was the nearest, and so I applied to go there. A letter arrived inviting me for an interview with the principal, Miss Sutton. She asked what grades I had in the different subjects as all the girls had a school certificate. They had passed five subjects. I had not sat for a single subject and was advised to take classes that would help me. As far as Teaching was concerned, that was out of the question as my English pronunciation was too foreign, but I could join an Institutional Management course the following September. The course covered many subjects: cookery, housekeeping, laundry work, needlework, and bookkeeping and accountancy. I hoped by the following year to have sat for a City and Guilds exam in Cookery. Miss Sutton smiled benignly and offered me a chance as she remembered her two happy years studying in Heidelberg where, to start with, she had had great difficulties with the German language. She pointed out that I would be the bottom of the class, but to justify her action of giving me a place, I would have to work hard and reach about tenth place in a class of sixteen. Then I would be able to stay on and complete the course. I had one term to make the grade! I promised to do my best . . . She would allocate a suitable place for me. I had ten months to prepare for this, borrowing suitable books from the Technical College to help me.

My parents were pleased with the outcome of this interview. Then the problem of accommodation arose. Only the Teaching students lived in Hall. The Institutional students either lived at home or in digs. Now we had to work out the finances. Teaching students had a grant so that their training was free, but the Institutional ones had to pay college fees and for the accommodation, fares, books and other expenses.

The war came closer to us. German bombers dropped bombs on the Doncaster railway. It was a main junction with work sheds for repairing the engines. There was also an ammunition factory in the town. After that, the German bombers flew over Doncaster on to Sheffield. The blitz was terrible. We could see the dark sky lit up and glowing from all the flames. A couple of landmines fell on our land. When the sirens sounded, Papa and Kurt would check the stables, making sure all the doors were closed, and then we would go into our air raid shelter. We built it in the centre of the house with some bunk beds. As the walls of the house were so solid and thick, only a direct hit would kill us. The air raid warden was shown where it was, just as a precaution. David came on leave again and, when the sirens were blaring out their soul-destroying sound, I started to cry. David took pity on me and kissed me on my mouth. My emotions were in turmoil. To be kissed on the mouth. Didn't he realise the consequences of this? He had kissed me on the mouth. He laughed and said that I looked as if the earth had just collapsed around me.

One evening after attending the nightclass, soon after the bombing of Doncaster, I sat in the back row of the trolleybus to go home. Several people in the bus knew me by sight, not personally, but as the "Jerry from the farm". As the trolleybus was leaving, a slightly drunk soldier jumped on. He bought a cheaper ticket than I had, so he wasn't going so far. I was relieved as he was swearing because the sirens were howling. He was saying that he was on leave and had been rescued from Dunkirk, but now "those bloody Germans" seemed to be following him. "If I ever meet one, I'll kill him. I'll break his bloody neck!" — he shouted. The people who knew about me turned round and looked at me. All I could think of was, "Thank God, he will be getting off before I will" — but he did not. There were only a few people left in the bus when it reached my stop. I got off, the soldier followed me. I tried to run, but he caught up with me and asked me what the hurry was. I replied that my parents were waiting for me. All I thought about was how I could get past the park entrance which was pitch black because of the blackout. With the few words I had spoken, he realised that I was not English and he wanted to know where I came from. So I braved it out and said, "I am one of those bloody Germans you swore about on the bus."

He laughed at this. "No bloody German would be walking about free." Here was my cue. "If you don't believe me, the police station is only two minutes' walk from here. You take me there and you will find out that I haven't told a lie." He said he didn't want any trouble and would take me home. I was terrified because that meant going past the park. So I tried another angle. "My parents don't allow me to speak to soldiers and I will get into terrible trouble." So we stood near the bus stop under a street light and talked. He wanted to know why we were in England and what I was doing out on my own. I begged him to let me go before my father came to look for me. He gave me a searching glance and frowned. "If there are more bloody Germans like you, why are we fighting them?" We shook hands and I crossed the road and ran past the park as if my life depended on it.

Some days later Mutti remarked on the fact that I was eating very little and she was worried because I was beginning to look pale and ill. She wanted to take me to the doctor. This was not necessary, I said. I was just not feeling too well, but would feel better in a few days. It was during the second breakfast, at about 10.30a.m, that Mutti said she had made a doctor's appointment for me. I started to cry and said that I knew what was wrong with me. Since my periods started, they had always been irregular and I had been kissed on the mouth about 12 weeks ago. So I blurted out, "I am pregnant. Pregnant, yes, pregnant." Deathly silence was the response to this announcement. My brother was the first to recover from this shock and asked who the father was. Without hesitation I replied, "David."

"When did this happen?"

"During the blitz on Sheffield."

My brother threatened David, saying, "He will get a surprise when he comes home on leave again."

Sure enough as usual, David came home on leave. My brother opened the kitchen door to him and punched him hard on his chin, saying, "You dirty dog, taking advantage of my sister when we offered you so much hospitality." David was dumbfounded and wondered what he had done. He declared that he was innocent, he had not touched me. He wanted to know when it had happened.

"During the blitz on Sheffield."

David denied it. So Kurt asked me gently to say exactly what had happened.

"He kissed me on my lips."

"What then?" asked Kurt.

"He kissed me on my mouth."

Now my brother exploded, hitting the table with this fist. He turned to Mutti. "Haven't you told her any of the facts of life?"

Mutti replied, "Yes, I told her that when two parts of the body make contact, that will create a baby."

My brother was really angry, saying, "No one is leaving the table till Mutti has started telling Trudi the facts of life. In a few months she will be going to Leeds and will not have the protection of the family. She must be told."

158

So Mutti started, telling me that a kiss is the beginning of love-making, followed by lots and lots of cuddles. This is when the men left the table and Kurt thought that Mutti would carry on with the lesson. As soon as they had gone, Mutti said that it was the touching of the lower parts of the body that makes the babies.

Papa had bought the best seed corn. "If you want a good harvest, you must sow good seeds," he would say. As he walked the cows back to the meadows, he would check the fields and coming home he told us that the first green shoots were showing and there was a faint green hue over the fields. He was happy.

Unfortunately, bad luck was soon to take its toll and it was not of our making. The tragedy happened when the dyke of the river Don broke and water flooded the meadows and cornfields as well as the orchard. Luckily, the flood water did not reach the outbuildings or our house. In double quick time, the cows were fetched from the meadows and driven into the cowshed. The neighbours who had given us the goose eggs rushed over to our house, frantic and desperate. Our neighbour's fields, stables and house were all flooded. Could we help out? Of course, Papa and Kurt rushed round and helped to herd the cows through the water along the road to our farm. We had just enough stalls for them. Then Papa drove the lorry to the other farm, lifting the pigs onto it. Then came the difficult task of catching the chickens and geese. They were put into boxes and loaded onto the lorry. Then they were brought to our farm and put into the spare stables. Once the animals were safe, Papa and Kurt returned to the other farm and helped to carry furniture, some upstairs and some onto the lorry. They worked all night. Mutti and I made pots of tea for the men each time they came home with more animals or some furniture, which was stored in our spare bedroom.

The farmer's wife had collapsed. All she kept saying was, "We've worked hard all our life to make a living and in one night it's all wiped out and everything's destroyed." She sat huddled in an armchair. Mutti suggested that she should go and lie down on our spare bed. No, she was going to wait for her husband.

All these extra animals made the working routine difficult. We had to milk the cows, but also keep the milk from the neighbour's cows separate. Feeding the animals was also hard as the men had to fetch the hay from the top of the haystack which was in the flooded orchard. This hay was intended to feed the cows in the late winter. Papa was very worried and upset. The young corn shoots would rot away after being covered with flood water. All our hard work and the future income from these fields had been washed away. Every day Papa and Kurt would wade through the knee-high water to check the fields and see whether the water was subsiding. Soldiers helped with the emergency repairs, using sandbags to fill the gap and build the dyke wall a little higher, but water still seeped through the makeshift defence. All we could do was wait till all the water had seeped into the ground, which was saturated.

Finally, the water sank into the earth and Papa went to check the meadows. He was horrified to see all the rubbish and litter left behind. As soon as the ground was firm enough, Papa drove the tractor over the meadows, harrowing it carefully to collect the worst rubbish. After this, Papa called for help — anyone who was willing was given a large rake to make sure that all the glass, tins and nails were removed, and especially to look out for any branches or twigs from yew trees. These were highly poisonous to the cows. The cost of hours and hours and labour to clear the waterlogged fields used up practically all our money. This flood had a major impact on our finances. There was no compensation or insurance money. Finally, Papa thought he would let the cows out and drove them into the orchard, which had been carefully checked and raked. As the cows walked out of the cowshed and saw the daylight, they started to jump about like mad March hares. It was a funny sight to see these big clumsy beasts leaping around, but we did not laugh, just hoped and prayed that none of them would break a leg. When they had calmed down, Papa and Kurt took them to the first meadow, making sure that they did not stop on their way past the park as this had not been checked for rubbish.

Soon after, early one morning, our two dogs came to the house, barking frantically. Papa and Kurt dressed hurriedly to investigate the dogs' strange behaviour. As soon as the two dogs saw them, they ran towards the meadow. Papa and Kurt followed, trying to keep up with them. All seemed well as the cows were waiting by the gate. The dogs ran round three of the cows and barked and barked. Panic gripped the two men as they ran to two of the cows that seemed still to be resting. They looked strangely still. They were dead. The third cow was lying on her back and kicking all her legs in the air. Papa could not see the reason for this, except that her tongue was hanging out. We rang for the vet. When he saw the poor cow, he had no choice but to shoot her. Her tongue had been cut to pieces and then the vet found stuck in her throat the top of a glass bottle with a porcelain stopper and a metal clip that held it in place. Apart from having her tongue cut, the poor cow was also slowly choking to death. The vet examined the other two cows and said that they had been poisoned by pieces of yew tree. The loss of these three cows had a major impact on our finances. The cows were our capital and of course there was also the loss of the milk. We sold the dead cows to a firm which used the hide to make leather, while most of the carcasses were manufactured into soap. The manager paid us a pittance. His explanation was that he had to use a special lorry to haul the beasts away.

Once more the meadow was raked. We saw our money dwindling away. We still had to pay Arthur, buy new seed and feed for the animals as well as fuel for the tractor to harrow the fields ready for sowing. How were we going to keep afloat and find the money to live on? Some vegetables in the orchard had survived, and as we could not afford to buy meat, Papa killed the oldest hens. Once again I had to do the shopping and it was the same as in Germany before the war. Should I buy a quarter pound of tea or some flour? Of course we bought our rations of butter, cheese and sugar. I stopped going to the night classes: that would save a penny ha'penny each way for the fare. The saved money would be spent on far more important items, food.

Papa sat very quiet and finally he thought he had found a solution. He would try and see if the team-master of the threshing machine would employ him. Yes, but it was the dirtiest and dustiest job. He had to work where the chaff came out of the threshing machine and see to it that it was filled into large sacks. Papa accepted. The dusty work and long hours were well paid. It would pay for Arthur's wages and be enough for housekeeping if we were very careful. When this job came to an end, however, we would be back to square one. Mutti made a suggestion that she should ask a couple for help. They were brother and sister, both Quakers. They had adopted a Jewish girl. She visited us a few times and made fun of me because I had to work so hard. She suggested that I should apply to be adopted or fostered by a Quaker family. Mutti thought if she visited them, she could ask if they would lend us some money till the next summer's harvest. They were very generous and gave Mutti fifty pounds.

Now my brother acted and once again applied to join the Forces. He was told he would cause more problems being a Jerry fighting with British Forces against the Jerries. He was not accepted, but they came up with an alternative. By now Kurt had gained his Higher National Certificate in Engineering and so the Labour Exchange offered him a job in the Pilkington factory making tank wheels. It was excellent pay. He had to work an eight-hour shift, changing every fortnight from early morning to the midday shift, and then onto the night shift. Shift work was well paid because of the unsocial hours. He had to live near the factory as with the late shift and early morning one, there would be no bus service running at these times. After paying for his digs and food, he gave the rest of the money to Mutti. This kept us going in housekeeping money and paid for Arthur and for fuel for the tractor. As tank wheels were so badly needed, workers could do overtime and Kurt worked one and a half shifts per day. Some of the extra money was set aside for more seed.

One day during milking time, six boys, evacuees from London, came to the farm and walked across the yard, straight to the cowshed. When Papa stopped them and asked what they wanted, they answered, very sure of themselves, "Please, mister, we want to see the bull." We were the only farmers in the neighbourhood with one. The bull was always kept in a separate stall during milking time. This was a precaution since the incident when he was peacefully grazing in the orchard and boys had used him as a target with their catapults and paperclips. The rest of the day he spent with the herd. He was also the cows' protector as no one would dare go near them with the bull around.

The milking was timed very carefully so that the milk could be filtered, cooled and put into churns, which were then taken to the collection point, so Papa could not take time off to show the boys the bull in the other shed. Instead he chose one of the cows. The boys wanted to know how they could recognise him (her!). Papa explained that he (she) was bigger than all the cows, had the longest horns and a bushy tail. The boys had a good look at the beast and left, quite content. A few days later, one of the original boys brought some other friends. Again, without permission, they went straight to the cowshed and he pointed out the cow to the other boys, telling them that it was the bull. Unfortunately, my brother was busy milking her! Still, the boys were quite happy and left. The following Saturday, when Papa visited the cattle market, several farmers smiled at him in a friendly way, and some of them even doffed their caps. Papa was very puzzled by this unusual behaviour. Finally they said that they had to salute the farmer who can milk a bull! The boys had clearly told this to the families they lived with and assured them that they had seen it with their own eyes. Also, they bragged about it at school and this sort of news travels fast and quickly reached some of the farmers. It took several weeks for this story to die down.

Spring had come and the waterlogged fields were finally workable. It was too late to sow spring corn, but Papa thought that if we sowed carrot seed, it would earn us some money quickly and we would not have to wait till late summer for the money coming in from other crops such as sugar beet. As the seed grew into young carrots, the weeds grew as fast as the carrots, if not faster. Mutti went out into the field again with a couple of other women, raking and hoeing the weeds. Then came the big day. Papa decided to check on the size of the young carrots to see whether they were big enough to pull and make into bunches. He pulled a couple and stared at them. Then he ran into the field and pulled a few more, and again just stared at them. They were riddled with wire worm. He pulled some more, quicker and quicker as if he could outrun the wire worms. He just stared and stared, not uttering a single word. Finally, he looked up at us and said that not all the carrots should be wasted. He would send the cows into the field. They could use some of the crop as food and save the cost of other feeding stuff.

Soon afterwards, a Health Inspector from the Ministry of Agriculture and Fisheries paid us a visit as the dairy we supplied with had reported that our milk was tinged pink. He wanted to inspect the cows to see whether they were suffering from mastitis — inflammation of the udder — and whether the milk contained blood. Papa said that all the cows were healthy and if one was ill, he would not add its milk to the milk from the others. The Inspector checked them all over carefully and found that the udders were completely healthy. He took out some small phials and took three samples from each churn. One sample would be analysed, the second one would be kept in reserve in case Papa wanted to challenge the result of the investigation and the third phial was given to Papa. A few days later, the Inspector returned and wanted to know what we fed the cows. Papa told him the usual feeding stuff apart from the fact that the cows had had a couple of days on the carrot field. The Inspector laughed heartily about this simple explanation. He congratulated Papa, saying it was the creamiest milk they had ever tested and the richest in Vitamin A — of course, it was the carotene that coloured the milk pink! The Inspector added that if it were peacetime, Papa would have won the first prize for his milk.

A letter arrived from the Yorkshire College of Housecraft informing us of what I had to bring with me. All my clothes had to have a name-tape sewn into them. I was getting more and more excited, but at the same time frightened. How would I cope on my own away from the family? But I did not want to let them know how anxious I was. Again, one of our German cases was packed with my clothes and, in order to save money, I was told that I could not come home till half-term. I was given some money for a taxi in Leeds to my digs. I felt like crying, but bit my lips to control my emotions, especially as money was so scarce, but my parents intended that I should catch up with my education (full-time). We said our goodbyes and then my parents gave me some last-minute advice: "Don't go with strangers or even speak to them. At college, be friendly and kind to the other girls. Study hard. Remember you must be halfway up the form by the end of term."

A last hug and Kurt took me to the station. We sat silently on the trolleybus. Then onto the train and a farewell wave as the train left Doncaster station. The train was not crowded as it was Sunday. I felt so lonely. The train passed our meadows and tears were rolling down my cheeks. If the train had slowed at the signals,

I would have jumped out. It would be six weeks before I saw my home again.

When I arrived in Leeds, as far as I was concerned it could have been the other side of the world. Boarding the taxi, I gave the address to the driver. We passed the City Square, with the nearly naked statues of women, then took the main road out to Headingley. I was surprised to see that many houses were detached and modern, standing in their own gardens. As the taxi stopped, a young couple came out of the house to welcome me and suggested that we have a cup of tea so as to get to know each other. They had been informed about my nationality and had no objection to it. It was a lovely house, and to complete the picture, two young boys, about 2 and 4 years of age, joined us for tea. I thought I was lucky to be living with such a nice family. Mrs Huggett explained their routine and how best I would fit in, sharing the bathroom and breakfast. During the week, I would have breakfast and join the family for high tea. That was a cooked dish: macaroni cheese, cauliflower cheese or potato and egg pie. This consisted of a layer of sliced, cooked potatoes, covered in white sauce, then two hard boiled eggs, sliced and covered with the rest of sauce, the whole finished off with sliced potatoes. Two eggs fed the three adults and two children. Remember that the ration was just one egg per person per week. Finally, before I went to bed, Mrs Huggett would make a hot drink for me. At the weekend I would also share luncheon with the family. I could join the family in the lounge, but had to do my college homework in my bedroom.

This was a happy beginning and on the first Monday morning, I got ready to meet the other girls. From the moment I was introduced to the girls from my form, I had a very cold reception. The group was thirteen girls, and I made it up to fourteen. The girls looked at me — no, through me. As far as they were concerned, I did not exist. They ostracised me, never spoke a word to me, and when I asked them if they could help me and tell me where the next lesson would be, they shrugged their shoulders and walked away. Three girls seemed to be the leaders of this group, with one in particular, Mary, being the instigator of any action. She was beautiful and looked like Elizabeth Taylor, the actress.

Luncheon was in the large dining room and the principal would say grace. Then two students from each table fetched the food served up in silver dishes. We helped ourselves, passing the dishes along the table and as I was pushed to the end of the table, I was the last one to get the food. Sometimes the dishes were empty and the girls had nasty grins on their faces.

The biggest revelation was how little English I had learned at the Technical College in Doncaster. There, when the teacher dictated notes and I had forgotten the sentence, I would look up and the teacher would repeat what she had said, so I could keep up with taking notes. Now I could look up as often as I liked, but no sentence was repeated. I left big spaces in my notes, hoping that perhaps one of the girls would lend me her notes, but the only reaction I got from them was, "If you can't keep up, then you shouldn't be here taking this course." Oh, those girls were cruel. How I looked forward to half-term, when I could go home for one week.

After living with the Huggett family for a week, I realised that this was not a happy home. Mr Huggett worked in a bank and twice a week he had night duty, firewatching in case the Germans used incendiary bombs. Now that I was living with the family, Mrs Huggett suggested that I should babysit for the two boys and she would go to work in the Forces canteen run by the WVS. Mrs Huggett came home well after midnight and would sometimes bring home a soldier who stayed until the early hours of the morning. On top of these two nights, she worked a further two nights at the canteen, but then Mr Huggett was the child minder. On those evenings he would play the piano — music Mutti had played — and just like her, he would sometimes rest his hands on the piano keys and then slowly start to play again. Did playing help him too to find the answers to his problems? Did he realise that Mrs Huggett was bringing these different soldiers home? I was finding it difficult to cope with the tension in this house as well as the trouble at college. To unburden myself, I wrote a long letter home. A reply came by return post. It was written in German. It was quite short on the subject and then carried on with news from the farm. The short message was, "Mind your own business and stay in your room when either Mr or Mrs Huggett is on their own at night. As to the college girls, remember they may have a brother, father or even a boyfriend in the Forces and you come from the nation they have to fight. So just put up with it and keep calm." I cried myself to sleep.

One evening when Mr Huggett was playing the piano, I mentioned that I enjoyed listening to it. Many melodies were ones I recognised from my childhood days when my mother used to play them. Now he played for about one hour every evening. I listened to the music in my room. Music from Lehar, Schumann, Verdi and many others. When I sat quietly in my room, the music made me feel very emotional and I wanted to run away back home, but remembering that my parents had already paid for the course and the sacrifices they and my brother had made for me, I had to stay and face the heartless treatment the girls dished out.

I counted the days till half-term, when I could spend a whole week at home. It would be a treat to help and work in the old routine.

Mr Huggett mentioned that there was a very good bus service to Doncaster. I found the bus station and was informed that buses to Doncaster ran every hour and a return journey was less than half price. I decided to try this journey out as I could not save money more quickly than that.

To help with the different subjects I had to learn about, I borrowed the necessary books. There were so many new words for each subject, but there was one subject in which I outshone all the girls, needlework. We had to learn how to use a sewing machine. The girls had difficulty with sewing a straight seam. Mutti had taught me this and for years I helped her, mending and patching and altering some of her dresses to fit me, or we would buy a remnant and then work out how best to put the dress pattern on it and cut it out. I also used to make blouses or aprons from worn-out shirts. The men wore them out at the places where their braces rubbed against the material. Once we had conquered the "Make-do-and-Mend" lesson, we started on cutting out petticoats and French knickers. The teacher, Miss North, was very observant and one day she asked me to stay after class. I was worried about this. When we were on our own, she asked me whether the girls always behaved in the same way to me, giving me the silent treatment or being very spiteful, or was this behaviour only in her class? I assured her that they behaved like this every day, every hour. She gave me a friendly smile and asked if I missed my home. She thought she would give me a break and invited me to accompany her to theatre to see a Shakespeare play, *The Merchant of Venice*. What a lovely surprise! I told her that I had never been to a theatre. My spirits soared up into the sky. At last someone did not hate me. We met outside the theatre for the afternoon performance. I was lost in the beauty of the play. The words and acting were wonderful. Above all, I felt that at last I had a friend and ally.

The last day came and half-term started. We finished early and I literally ran all the way to the bus station. I had taken my case with me and put all my notes into it. I jumped on to the homeward bound bus. People often don't value their family enough and I was like a sponge, soaking up all the love given and storing it for the next few weeks back in Leeds.

I had to check to see whether all the cows and calves still looked the same. I fed the chickens and offered to clean the big Yorkshire Range in the kitchen. Mutti laughed and said that she never thought that I would miss the chores. Ah, but it made me feel that I belonged here. Kurt wanted to see my college notes and asked whether I understood what I had written. The answer was a simple "no". He then explained the notes on biology and physiology, and dietetics, nowadays called nutrition. He then took the trouble to explain the next steps in these subjects. It would help me with the next lessons.

All too soon it was time to go back to Leeds. On the first day back at college, nothing had changed. Still the silent treatment. Then the three girls, the ringleaders of the group, came and stood round me and invited the other girls to come over. Mary came close to me, pulled my nose, my ear and then my hair, and said, "Fancy that! They're all stuck on her face, just like ours." She gave my hair an extra hard tug and laughed, "Girls, it's not a wig!" Then she pinched my cheek. Again Mary spoke, "I wonder if she feels pain, like we do," and as I flinched, she laughed again. "So she is human and not a monster!" Now all the girls laughed. I didn't know which was worse, the silent treatment or being ridiculed, but at least after five weeks, they were the first words spoken to me and after this, they always left some food in the dishes at lunch time.

About a week later, Mary came and hooked her arm through mine. I held my breath. "What is she up to now?" I thought.

"You know, you are not so bad after all. And we're not really as nasty as we have been to you. Shall we try and be friends?"

This shattered my self-control and tears started streaming down my cheek. I suppose she realised that I had not reported their behaviour to the principal. Several other girls came and patted me on the shoulder. Now we were a group of fourteen girls and not, as before, thirteen girls and one odd one out. I still had to face some occasional difficult moments, but now that the girls were friendly, I could deal with any other traumas.

Housewifery. In these lessons we were taught how to clean and run a home. For this, we went to the college hall where the teaching students lived and the teacher allocated our duties to us, from parlourmaid up to the housekeeper, with one girl as hostess. Every week the rota was changed. The hostess had to keep a diary and work out the cost of the meal the cook prepared for the group and two guests. It was the hostess's privilege to invite the guests of her choice, usually her favourite teachers or a student from the second year.

On this day it was not my fellow students who caused me trouble, but the teacher, Miss Wells, who took the Housewifery class. She was a very tall woman with broad shoulders, and had a very forceful manner. After demonstrating how to replace the filament in an electric iron, using the ironing board as a table, and leaving the hammer and screwdriver on it, she informed us of the menu for that day. My duty was to act as cook. Listening carefully, yes, the soup and sweet were easy, but the main course puzzled me. "Toad in the Hole." I looked over to the store table to see the ingredients, but could not see any frogs' legs anywhere. Quickly I checked the word in my German-English dictionary. "Toad" was a sort of "frog". Correct, but if there were no frogs' legs, how was I to cook them "in a hole"? I put my hands up and asked where the frogs' legs were and how was I supposed to cook them in a hole. Miss Wells thought that I wanted to be the clown or comedian of the class and asked me to come to the front of the class and stand by the ironing board. Once more she said that the main course was "Toad in the Hole" and again I replied that I could not see any frogs' legs on the store table, only sausages and eggs. She picked up the hammer and repeated, "Toad in the Hole" and with each word she hit me on the top of the head with the hammer. She then asked if I had worked out what to do.

"No, there aren't any frogs' legs and anyway, I can't cook them in a hole."

Again down came the hammer on my head and each word was spoken slowly as if she was spelling them. "Toad in the Hole." The more times she hit me on the head, the more confused I became and for a third time the hammer hit me. This happened in a training college, which my parents had paid a lot of money for me to attend. It felt more like a reform school than a training college.

Finally, Mary came to my rescue and pointed out that I was not English.

"Ah, well, let the student acting as parlourmaid help her," Miss Wells replied.

I never thought that life away from home as a student would be fraught with so much trouble. After this, the other girls realised that something that was a simple thing to them, such as Toad in the Hole, was difficult for me.

Now as I walked and talked with the girls, I realised that the three leaders of the group could also be spiteful and malicious to the other girls. There was one girl in particular, nicknamed "Poppy Pupa". For the laundry lesson, we had to bring some underwear to wash, made, if possible, of different materials, such as silk, cotton or celanese. Remembering that we needed clothing coupons to buy new underwear, most of the girls brought their school bloomers or celanese panties, generally known as "passion killers". We were the Cinderellas of the class. Poppy Pupa brought the most delicate silk and lace underwear. Her father owned a textile factory that made underwear and since the beginning of the war he had had to produce underwear for the women's army and only a small percentage for the civilian market. Poppy Pupa wanted to hit back when the girls teased her about her pretty underwear and said that we were "Simple Simons" and would never attract any of the opposite sex in our "passion killers". A sharp reply came back, "We attract boys by our good looks. We don't have to show off our underwear first!" This kind of bickering went on all the time. The girls were so immature; they had been sheltered from the rigours of life. I was only a year older, but felt the difference was more like ten years. My nickname was "Granny" or "Prof" (professor), depending whether they wanted to hurt me or not.

I was always thinking how I could save a little money. The easiest way was to walk home to my digs. It saved a penny ha'penny. On Fridays, I stayed behind to use the laundry room to wash and dry my white overalls as I could not afford to send them to a laundry.

On my way back to my digs, I used to pass a row of detached houses and would often notice a family sitting round a table having a meal. One day as I neared this house, a lady came out of the house and down the drive to the garden gate and spoke to me. "Are you at college with my daughter?" Not knowing who her daughter was, I worded my reply carefully. The lady then introduced herself as Mrs Bushell and asked if I would like to join them for tea on Sunday afternoon. My spirit rose, my heart beat faster. At last, someone was being friendly towards me. She must have known about my being a "Jerry" as all the students knew about me and knew me by sight. By now I knew how to spend my savings, so I bought a small bunch of flowers for Mrs Bushell. It was a lovely day — a real Indian Summer day. We had tea in the lounge. It was served in beautiful bone china cups, with very dainty sandwiches and home-baked cakes. I delighted in being looked after so well. Margaret, the daughter, was a year younger than I was, but she was already in the form above me and would be leaving the college at Easter. When I mentioned the difficulty I had with note-taking, Margaret offered to lend me her first-year file. This was a lifeline. Not only could I keep up, but I could also read about the next lectures. Before I left, Mr and Mrs Bushell invited me for lunch the following Sunday, and also to stay for tea. What luxury! We had lunch in the dining room, which was furnished with an antique mahogany dining suite and a crystal chandelier hanging over the dining table. It was gentle and gracious living, and one day, when I had my own home, I thought, I would like it to look like this.

We all liked and respected each other. After several visits, they told me that Mrs Bushell had a very weak heart and because of this they had only one child. As I seemed to be so sensible and responsible, they thought that I could be like an older sister to Margaret. After lunch, Mr Bushell, Margaret and I washed up while Mrs Bushell rested. The three of us went for a long walk to help settle that tasty lunch. We walked to the Hollies, a very nice park, and took the long way home. I think it lasted about two and a half hours. We were to become lifelong friends, separated only by Margaret's death.

When Margaret suggested cycling, I laughed heartily. To imagine me on a bicycle was a hilarious thought. For a very short time in 1930, my family had to move from Hamburg to a small village in the Lüneberger Heide. The doctor had ordered this change of rhythm from city life for my mother's health. I was only six years old and everybody cycled, so I had to learn how to do it too. I remember the shaking of the handlebars, till I copied and managed to hold it steady. I had not been near a bicycle since that time and now Margaret was suggesting that I should try as she wanted to show me the countryside around Headingley. She held the bicycle while I tried to find my balance. Suddenly I could do it. As they say, "Once learned, never forgotten". During the fine weather we were off. It was a freedom I had not experienced before. The first day Margaret took me on a ride, it seemed to me we cycled a hundred miles, but it was only fifteen, and when I got off the bike, I walked as if I was still cycling. The world looked beautiful, especially in the early spring days when the hedgerows and trees were covered with a faint hue of green.

Margaret encouraged me to join the Youth Club, where we would have interesting discussions and meetings. In the spring, we had an outing to Knaresborough. Groups of four or six young people hired boats and we rowed along the river until we came to a small island. We thought that this would be an ideal place to have our picnic lunch. No sooner had we settled and unwrapped our sandwiches than an angry and ferocious swan attacked us, his wings spread out, and chased us off the island! We ran as fast as we could back to our boats, leaving our sandwiches behind. As we hurried to the boats, we glimpsed another swan sitting on a nest. It must have been the instinct of the swan to protect the eggs that its partner was brooding.

At the end of term, I hurried home for Christmas. I loved every minute, especially the feeling of being in my own home again. The hardships we had faced together welded us together. I still had to report to the police when I changed my address and curfew hour was still 10.30p.m.

The holiday passed too quickly and a few weeks into the spring term, Mrs Huggett told me that she was not feeling too well and therefore asked me to find other digs. I think it was more that she was nervous in case I told her husband about the visitors that turned up when he was on night duty.

A girl in Margaret's class, Pam, lived in digs and was leaving them at the end of term. She had been very happy there, so one day after college, I accompanied Pam back to her digs. Her landlady, Mrs Phyer, was pleased to know that she would have another girl from our college living with her. She was a middle-aged lady, about 50 years old, with silvery grey hair. She suggested that I listen to her house rules and then make up my mind if I still wanted to move in. The most important one for her was that I shouldn't play music from the radio too loud in my room. I had no radio, so that was easily solved. The other rule was not to stay out late — not later than 10.30 to 11p.m. Again, this caused no problem as my police curfew was 10.30p.m. I would share the living room with her, but my college homework had to be done in my own room. As we talked, I thought how sad she looked, when in conversation she mentioned that only four weeks previously she had lost her husband. To ensure that I would come back to her after the Easter vacation, she suggested that I brought some of my things.

After Easter, I returned to my new digs and rang the bell. I was horrified to see Mrs Phyer. She looked so lonely and lost, and as if she had been crying a lot. She seemed to have coped with her husband's death, so why now this helpless, hopeless behaviour?

She suggested that I should find some other digs as she could not cope with life at that moment. She went to the sideboard and picked up a telegram and handed it to me. It informed her that her only son had been killed in India by the Japanese. To her life had no purpose any longer. She had lost her husband and then her son only ten weeks apart. While talking to me, she collapsed. I rang for the doctor. His verdict was: a nervous breakdown. He wondered if I could cope and look after her with the help of a district nurse who would check her out during the day while I was at college.

My mind went back to when Mutti had had her nervous breakdown in Germany, and I said that I would look after her. As she improved, she wanted to check my homework and made suggestions about how I could alter and improve it. Mrs Phyer seemed to adopt me. I think that I somehow filled the empty space left by her son. She became stricter than my own mother was.

One day, Pam paid us a visit with her boyfriend, Philip. He was in the Canadian Air Force and on sick leave. We all sat round the large fire, the glowing coals piled up in the hearth. It was very cosy. Pam picked up her boyfriend's cap and threw it over to me asking me to look inside it. On the leather rim were the names of many towns. These were places he had bombed and among them was the word "Hamburg". Pam asked, "Isn't that where you used to live?"

"Yes," I replied.

Philip had a strange reaction to this. Apparently, that had been his last mission. Seeing his strange reaction, I tried to keep the conversation on an even keel, and said, "I think you have done too many flying missions. Could you not take a break?"

"No," he replied. The doctors had tried to change his feelings about this raid, but they could not help. They had suggested that perhaps a friend could talk to him. This was why Pam had brought him to us.

He looked at the glowing fire and pointing to it, said, "When I flew over Hamburg, that is just what it looked like." He revealed the torments he had been suffering in his mind. "There must have been women and children down there who had nothing to do with the war. I am a murderer. A murderer." The doctors hadn't been able to help him. They called it "mental fatigue". I suggested that Mrs Phyer and Pam went to bed, while I tried to put my point of view to him. I tried to explain how he also saved lives. He would have saved the lives of many fighting soldiers as this bombing and others would shorten the war. Also, he would be helping to save lives in Britain as the Germans were bombing us. I tried to impress my views on his mind, hoping that what I was saying would have an impact on him, especially as I came from Hamburg. I talked and talked, trying to convince him of my view. I talked until the early hours of the morning. I must have got through to that conscious mind of his as suddenly he keeled over and fell fast asleep.

Pam had mentioned that he had not slept for days. Perhaps my outlook on life and the war was the key that unlocked the door to his troubles. He was sitting on the settee and I could turn him round and put his legs up. I covered him with a warm blanket. He was in such a deep sleep he never noticed this action. His face looked relaxed. When he woke up, he looked round the room and spoke. "I think my nightmare has gone. I can sleep again." In contrast, I could not sleep as I was emotionally worn out.

It was nearing the end-of-year examination and I spent many hours revising. I remembered the conditions that the Principal had made when I came for the interview: my grades had to be near to halfway up in the class. Then came the dreaded day when the Principal asked me to come and see her. My heart was pounding. Was it good or bad news? She said that I had not quite reached the grade of the eighth girl, but had achieved tenth position and she was pleased to offer me a place in the second year. Then she asked me a crucial question: "Are you a man or a mouse?" I replied, in a timid voice, "Mouse".

"Well, by the time you leave here next year, we will have changed you from mouse to man!"

Knowing the financial crises at home, I had been thinking of stopping the course and I wanted to asked whether I could return to complete my training once the family had conquered its current troubles. Fate decided for me. A letter arrived from the Ministry of

Labour. It was my call-up papers. The Ministry could interrupt my training as I was nearly 18 years old when I had started. This was a blessing for me. Now I could resign without having to mention the money trouble. Nor would I make my parents feel inadequate about not being able to raise the money for the second year. Because of my call-up, the Principal arranged that I should spend the last few days in the institutional kitchen so that at least I would know how to use large-scale equipment. I was glowing with pride and had an indescribable feeling of exhilaration: I had achieved my goal.

The letter from the Ministry of Labour was short. "Report to the Ministry in Doncaster immediately." The Principal assured me that, because of my good work and exam results, a place would be available for me as soon as the war was over. With very mixed-up emotions, I faced the unknown future. After the war, I found out that I was the only girl called up from this college as the rest of the girls had started their training straight after leaving school and so were a year younger than me. In a way I was glad that this happened. Apart from releasing my parents from the financial burden, it showed that the Home Office treated me and recognised me as any other British citizen.

CHAPTER
TEN

Bevin Boys' hostel

Transfer to Roue Abbey School

I said my goodbyes to everyone at the college and reported to the Doncaster Ministry of Labour. From there I was directed to work in a Bevin Boys' hostel. Every tenth man who was called up was conscripted to work in the mines and these were known as "Bevin Boys", after Ernest Bevin, the Minister of Labour and National Service. I was lucky as I could go home during my off-duty time. Yet I tried to persuade the person dealing with me that I would prefer to join the Forces. It was a definite "No", however. In the Forces I would become a liability, not an asset.

Humbly, I made my way to the hostel. The accommodation was made of prefabricated huts. I reported to the warden. Short and sharp, he explained my duty. The split shift. It sounded very complicated to me. The Bevin Boys worked three shifts and in turn, and at different times, they each needed breakfast, lunch and an evening meal. We would serve breakfast to the boys going out on duty while the ones coming from their shift would get their evening meal. I found it very confusing to start with. Then the warden called for the chef, Pedro. He was Spanish with greasy black hair. He appeared smaller than he really was as he had very broad shoulders and was heavily built. He stared at me and took me to the kitchen and told me my duties. After lunch I had a few hours free and then late duty. As we entered the kitchen, I was amazed at the size of it and the quantity of equipment. My year of training had not prepared me for this. The huge kitchen was spotlessly clean and had big boilers, steaming ovens, chip fryers and solid-top cookers and roasting ovens. Then there was a section with confectionery ovens, proving ovens for making bread and tables for working on. All the cakes, sweet pastries, puddings and bread were prepared and baked here.

A long row of hot and cold service counters separated the kitchen from the dining room. In the far end of the dining room, a section was marked off for social activities. Then Pedro took me to the large store-rooms and pointed out that everything leaving the stores had to be signed out. Finally, on to the refrigeration room. Here, the meat was prepared and made ready to cook. Prepared pastry from the bakery department was handed over to make steak and kidney pies or puddings. The chef told me that my duty was to look after the boilers for making stock, soup, custard and milk puddings. Also to boil potatoes and vegetables, and after the meal to clean these boilers. During serving time, I would be told what to serve and how. To add salt to the potatoes or vegetables, we used a large scoop like a bedpan, a scoopful equalling one teaspoon. Every item leaving the storeroom was weighed and once a week on Fridays was stocktaking.

When I went to clean the boilers, I noticed that the stockpot was one-third full with cooked meat and vegetables. Looking more closely, I could not believe my eyes at what I saw. Big, bright maggots were crawling everywhere. I was horrified and had to run to the toilets to be sick. I reported this to the chef and asked if the boiler man could remove this mess. In his broken English he shouted, "Mind your own business. Just fill it with water. It'll make delicious stock."

"But, chef, the maggots! That food base must be thrown out."

This remark seemed to unleash his temper. He shouted back at me, "I told you. It'll make delicious stock." Then he pointed out that while there was life in the maggots, no one would suffer food poisoning as the maggots ate any putrefied meat. "Anyway," he went on, "in some countries maggots are a delicacy. Where the Eskimos live, maggots are sometimes the only supply of protein. So be a good girl and get on with your work." I obeyed the order and turned the water tap on the boiler on. For weeks I could not eat or even taste the gravy or stews or soup.

Often, when the cook responsible for the stew had seasoned it and tasted it, he thought it very tasty. Then chef would check it out by putting his face over the boiler and smelling the steam coming off it. In his usual boorish manner, he would shout, "You insipid cook! Have you not learned how to handle seasoning yet?" and would demand the different seasoning containers

— salt, pepper, paprika — adding handfuls of these into the gravy and stew. Again, he would put his face over the boiler and sniff the air — like the Bisto kids — throwing more seasoning into it. Eventually, he would give a self-satisfied smile and say, "Just right. Now serve it." Weeks later, when I dared to take my first taste of the stew gravy, I had to admit that he was indeed a wizard with seasoning.

To stir the food, we used big wooden paddles. The women kept warning me about working with the chef in the refrigerator room, but they would not tell me why they were so frightened of him. I could not understand this. They were women between 30 and 50 years of age and I was the baby of the team. I would describe them as a tough variety, big and strong, and they swore like troopers. My knowledge of swear words had been very limited. I learned more English vocabulary in a week there than I had in a year at college!

My turn came. "Work in the refrigerator room. Cut up the meat for the steak and kidney pie." The bakery department had sent the pastry and I was rolling it out when chef came in and offered me a mugful of coffee. After one hour being chilled, I thanked him for his kindness. The kitchen was always very hot and because of this, we wore only bras and panties under our white linen overalls. Pedro came and pushed me against the preparation table and pulled at my overall. He became very forceful as I resisted his advances. I remember that I had started to roll out the pastry to fit the roasting tins. Chef started to shout that he would teach me what resisting him would mean. He picked up the rolling pin and hit me on my stomach and hip. I must have fainted because I woke up in the First Aid room, with one of the cooks putting a cold compress on my forehead. She told me then that when she had resisted his advances, once back in the kitchen, he had picked her up and sat her on the hot solid-top stove. Her overall was singed and her bottom was one large blister. Now I understood the fear those women had when ordered into the refrigerator room. My right side hurt and I felt sick, but I would not give chef the satisfaction of thinking he had won. Remember, I was only 18 years old and having to deal for the first time with colleagues and a paid job.

I went to see Pedro and said in a very deathly calm manner that I wanted a word in private with him. He looked surprised, but still had a derisive smile on his face. Once in his office, I said to him, "We are both foreigners. We both know the rules by which we are allowed to be free and work in England. One of them is not to hurt or harm any citizen. So, if you ever come near me again or touch me — whether in friendliness or anger — I shall report you to the Home Office and you will be interned." With that, I walked out of his office, holding my head up high, and not letting on that I was frightened — nay, terrified. This confrontation had an amazing effect. The other cooks wanted to know what I had said to him because from that day on, he did not touch any staff and instead of shouting at us, spoke to us in a civilised manner.

While serving meals to the Bevin Boys, I started to talk to some of them. It soon became apparent what a mixture of characters there was. Because of the call-up, many miners had left the collieries and joined the Forces. Suddenly, there were not enough miners to keep the supplies of coal coming. Mr Bevin had had the bright idea of replacing them through conscription. These Bevin Boys were a real mixed bag: some tough guys, some more refined and educated men. Some liked it as it saved them from fighting. Others would have preferred to be in the Forces. One thing that caused them to feel hurt and upset was that, because they had no uniform, when they were off duty other people would either ostracise them or call them hurtful names. Talking to some of them when off duty, they explained the differences in the collieries. In modern ones, the gangways where they worked the coal seams were supported by steel rods; in older mines, the roofs were supported by wooden beams. The difference was great. Steel might be modern, but had one major disadvantage. If a roof was going to cave in, the steel rods gave no warning, they would just snap and the miners had little chance of escaping. Wooden beams, on the other hand, would start to creak and groan from bearing the extra weight. This was a warning signal to run and get out of the tunnel. Some of the boys who liked animals were allowed to work with the pit ponies pulling the coal wagons. Man and pony became very attached to each other. One boy told me how once the roof caved in and he was partly buried under the fall. He despaired, thinking that perhaps no one would rescue him. The pony he worked with had finished his shift and was stabled. Suddenly the young miner heard the noise of something scraping at the debris, then the nose of his pit pony nuzzled him, pulled him out and thus saved his life. The pony dragged him to safety. These pit ponies spent most of their lives underground, which caused them to go blind. This one would have to go to a home when he retired. The young miner resolved to buy him and let him spend the rest of his life in a meadow.

Some young Bevin Boys were so frightened of going underground, especially after an accident, that they would apply time and again to be transferred to the Forces. Some of them would drop a large piece of coal on their hand or foot so that for a little while they would not have to go back underground. If it was found out that this was a self-inflicted wound, they would get into serious trouble.

I joined some of the boys in the section of the dining room set aside for social activities. I noticed that they felt very protective toward me, especially the rougher and tougher boys. We shared cups of tea and talked, trying to put the world to rights. I remember that a film with Ingrid Bergman and Gary Cooper was shown in town, *For Whom the Bell Tolls*. Ingrid Bergman had a hairstyle known as the "bubble cut", rather short and just curls brushed out. As my pronunciation was similar to Ingrid Bergman's, they started to call me Ingrid. One day as we sat and talked, one of the boys apologised, hoping that I would not be offended, but seeing they had renamed me, they had clubbed together and collected enough money so that I could have a perm and a bubble cut. It suited me, and it was my very first perm. It was also much easier to look after and care for my hair, instead of having to use those paper curlers every night.

Finally, I took courage and went to the Ministry of Labour in Doncaster and asked them if they could transfer me to an establishment where I could cook foods other than custard and stock, milk pudding, and could also serve food. Once you know the quantities necessary to fill a 30- or 40-gallon boiler — sometimes even larger — then anyone can use a paddle and stir the food.

Some time after I left the Bevin Boys hostel, I received a letter, dated 11 December 1944, from one of the men who had been transferred to another colliery and hostel. This is part of it:

"Today, thank God, I am ill: a common cold, but sufficient to keep me from work, to escape, at least for a short time, the horrors of a subterranean existence.

"I have taken private lodgings. The hostel was unmitigated hell, full of rowdy, ill-disciplined vulgar 'oiks' wishing to impress by their new-found manliness and freed from the restraining influences of their homes, who swore, drank and smoked as profusely as their meagre wages would allow. Windows were broken, doors were smashed. It became impossible to get to sleep before 12.30 at night and since one had to get up at 4.30 a.m., this was not exactly ideal. I only remained at this hostel for four days before I moved to these lodgings, with homely people.

"In the mine I am engaged in ripping. This is simply the widening and heightening of the underground roadway, which, due to the pressure and weight of the rock, has contracted and narrowed, the supporting steel arches being contorted and twisted into grotesque and fantastic shapes like fragile wire in the grasp of a giant. In such places you feel the immense power of the rock surrounding you; even the rock itself seems to cry out from the excruciating pressure of its neighbours. When one piece falls, you expect to see it suddenly expand as it is released from the roof, once again able to breathe and regain its natural size. The miners themselves seem gnome-like, swinging fairy lamps at their sides, dwarfed to insignificance by the presence of the soil around them. Everything is unreal, more like a nightmare: the obscuring overpowering darkness cut only the tiny twinkles of light. The splitting rock, anxious for freedom, strange foul smells and, when alone, deathly silence. You feel you must wake up screaming.

"I am especially glad that you find your new place enjoyable. Glad at least one of us is partially contented.

"Ever yours, Ken."

Waiting for a letter . . . how many times has my life been drastically changed by the arrival of a letter? The long-awaited missive came summoning me to the Ministry of Labour's office for an interview with a Miss Norton. I arrived at the appointed time. My heart was beating fast, wondering where the next move would take me. Oh, when and to where would I be re-directed? Just like being in the Forces, I would get 24 hours to report to the next place.

When I met Miss Norton, she assured me that my nationality was no obstacle for this post as assistant cook since it was at a public school and abbey. That meant cooking for 750 boys who lived there during term time and about 90 priests who lived in the monastery all year round. The Ministry of Labour issued me with a travel warrant to Reading. Miss Norton would meet the train from London and then we could travel by taxi to the school. I was excited at the prospect, but at the same time a little frightened at leaving Doncaster — nay, Yorkshire — where I had learned to a certain extent to blend into the background.

Now my parents began to worry about how I would find my way across London to change stations, not to mention the dangers of the V1 and V2 bombs. But I was young and had faced other troubled situations before. I assured them that I would be fine. Immediately, Mutti wrote to David, who had been invalided out of the army and lived in London, to ask him to make sure that I caught the right connecting train.

I said my farewell to the few friends I had made. In a way, I was glad be leaving the tough kitchen staff behind. Saying goodbye to my parents and brother was much more emotional as I did not know when I would see them again. My brother took me to the station and gave me a last hug before he bundled me onto the train. Once again, one of those cases from Germany held my belongings and would accompany on my next journey. The rhythm of the wheels worked its magic and awoke that spirit of adventure in me. I imagined that they were humming to me, "Going places, going places". As the train steamed its way through the countryside, past countless towns, I shrank into myself more and more, and sat huddled in my corner seat.

David was true to his word and met me at King's Cross station. We had just enough time for quick snack in the station buffet. I mentioned how strong the tea was and served in such thick white cups. He laughed at this. "It's good railway brew and will make your hair curl." Then he became serious and explained the way the V1 doodlebugs behaved. This kind of flying bomb had a motor that made it fly, with a special deep hum and a flame shooting out at the back. While you could hear it and see the flame, you were quite safe as it would fly on, but if both stopped, you had to find a wall or even just the edge of the curb, and lie down and protect yourself. The V1 was quite tricky. It would descend like a dive bomber or glide on for a while, but you had to be ready to act quickly. Another idiosyncrasy of the bomb was that while the motor and flame were still noticeable and you thought it had passed, it could reappear as the slightest warm air stream or wind could reignite it.

Then came another new experience, travelling for the first time on an English tube train to Paddington station to catch the train to Reading. To my amazement, it was crowded with soldiers, mostly Americans. As soon as David had found a seat for me and waved goodbye, I sat and pretended to sleep, putting my hands on my lap, in order to keep an eye on my watch and check the time without stirring.

When we reached Reading station, relieved, I jumped up, collected my case and looked for Miss Norton, who welcomed me with a friendly smile. She hailed a taxi and now I was on the last stretch of my journey to Roue Abbey and School. She used the time to explain the staffing of the school. Her post was that of housekeeper and so she was in charge of all the staff. I guessed that she was about 35 years of age, rather plump. Matron, about 55 years old, looked after the welfare of the boys, who were aged from 10 years old up to 18. Then there was the Linenkeeper who looked after the laundry and school uniform, and the maids, most of whom were Irish. They cleaned the school and made the boys' beds. The senior staff, Housekeeper, Matron, Linenkeeper and Cook, each had a bed-sitting room, but the maids slept in a dormitory. Now came the touchy point — there was no other bed-sitting room and I was not allowed to share the dormitory, but there was a room above the kitchen and it seemed sensible that I should live there.

196

The countryside we travelled through was beautiful, much greener than in Yorkshire. So many trees, bushes and hedges. The sun was shining and I was hopeful that it was a good omen. Then I saw the school. What a grand building! Somehow I felt a little intimidated as I had never been in such a beautiful building. Miss Norton invited me into her sitting room for a cup of tea. I gave a sigh of relief. The room was as beautiful as the building and very tastefully furnished. If my room was only half as comfortable, I should be very happy. Now more relaxed, I was looking forward to my new job. My salary was quite good; for a trained assistant cook it was £100 per annum with free board and lodgings.

Miss Norton gave me a guided tour, along the long corridors, past the many classrooms, then past the Bursar's office and a small school chapel, then through the dining room and finally we arrived at the kitchen. The Cook, Miss Perry, greeted me with hostile looks, but the two women who came in to work daily to help with the vegetables or wherever they were needed were much more friendly towards me. At a glance I realised that this was not a modern kitchen. No gas and hardly any equipment. A huge oak refectory table was our working area for preparing, cooking and serving the food. Two big Aga stoves stood back to back. The fuel was anthracite. There was an open fireplace on which the vegetables were cooked. Then in a corner, a small table for my benefit, to have my meals on.

Miss Perry, in her gruff voice with its Irish accent, said, "Be on time for preparing breakfast in the morning. You'd better start at 6 o'clock," and thus I was dismissed. Between the kitchen and the dining room was a large pantry with several large wooden sinks and cupboards to hold the china. Here the maids washed up the boys' plates, dishes and cutlery.

We had to cook for the priests, but we were not allowed to enter the pantry or their dining room. The cleaning and polishing of the dining room, laying the tables and washing up was done by two young men who had slight learning difficulties and so were not in the Forces. Miss Norton said that as I now had a general picture of the working of the school, she would take me to my room. I saw a staircase just outside the kitchen door. This led up to my bed-sitting room. A rude awakening awaited me as it was the bleakest, barest room I had ever seen. It consisted of one bed, one wardrobe, one chair, a washstand with a bowl and a jug of water, and a bucket. No armchair, no mirror. If I wanted a bath, I had to walk through the school to the female staff bathroom. The toilet for me was outside. For the evening or night, I had to use a potty. For a second I smiled. "A jerry for a Jerry!" Then it dawned on me that once the work in the kitchen was finished, I would be completely alone, cut off from the rest of the staff by the long corridors and classrooms.

I felt forlorn. I, with my fear of the dark and of being alone, was now completely alone. I tried to remember my parents' last piece of advice to me. "If you do not like it for any reason whatsoever, or have to work hard and for long hours, remember many a young man in the Forces would like to change places with you."

I hardly slept that first night, knowing that I was all alone in that part of the school. I think I would even have welcomed a mouse. Just before midnight, I heard footsteps coming towards my room. I jumped out of the bed and pushed the wash table in front of my door. I could not lock it as there was no key. Trembling and frightened, I sat on the edge of the bed. Then silence. I was just about to lie down when the same footsteps sounded going away from my room. About an hour later, the same happened, someone coming up to my room, then silence for a few seconds — it seemed more like 10 minutes — then they walked away. What was I to do next? I took one of my pillows, shook it and put it in the bed where I should have been sleeping and covered it with a blanket. The other blanket I put under the bed together with the second pillow. I used my coat to cover me and keep me warm and so I spent the first night sleeping under the bed. As a matter of fact, I slept in that fashion for three weeks.

My breakfast duty was to cook the porridge. It was a rushed job, especially when the Aga stove was not very hot. I decided that I would put the large iron saucepan on the night before and make the porridge. This worked well and the porridge tasted good. Depending When it was a fried breakfast, the bread was fried in the large square iron pans and the bacon was put on trays and baked in the oven. To make toast, we had large wire mesh holders and toasted the slices of bread in them on top of the Aga stove.

Once a week after breakfast, I had to clean the two Aga stoves. This was easy as I remembered all the corners of the flues that blocked easily on our own Aga at home. As the Aga did not give out as much heat as was needed, cleaning the flues was my first job, while the caretaker brought the anthracite.

During the morning I met the Bursar, Father Dunstan, a middle-aged fatherly figure, softly spoken. He officially welcomed me. I took this opportunity to ask whether he could arrange for me to be transferred to the maids' dormitory. My request was denied as Miss Norton was in charge of staff arrangements.

Miss Perry's antagonism resulted from her belief that at 19 years I was far too young to hold the position of Assistant Cook. She had worked her way up the ladder from "Tin Pan Alley" to become a cook at the age of about 50 years. Until she became a cook, she had to scrub the kitchen floor.

My other duty, straight after breakfast, was looking after the storeroom and issuing the ingredients for the day. While weighing out the food, a young priest came into the storeroom to help. What a man — no, what a priest! A tall figure with shining ginger hair and matching red eyebrows. The colour of his hair was emphasised by the black monk's habit. His eyes sparkled, he was so vibrant and full of life. He would have made a gallant Gaelic warrior!

He informed me that he would help me in looking after the stores, for example stock-taking and ordering food as he had to look after the accounts and the cost of the food. Now I could use my knowledge from the one year training in cooking the meals and doing some bookkeeping. I soon settled down to the long hours.

200

However hard I worked, the hostility from the cook increased, till one day she exploded and shouted that she would get me down on my knees scrubbing the floor. As I had some college training, I was appointed as assistant lady cook, and therefore did not scrub floors and also had help in clearing up after the preparation of the meal. Cook was a working cook and had to do the clearing up herself.

We started work at 6 a.m. and twice a week had days off duty starting at about 6 p.m. The next day started at 9 a.m. and we would work till 10 p.m. The late-shift duties were to prepare for breakfast and see that the Aga stoves were stoked and filled with anthracite. Several times when I was on early duty, I found that the Aga stoves were out. Pandemonium! Bedlam! No hot water for tea and no water for porridge. Lighting an Aga is quite easy, but it takes about an hour or two for the stoves to heat up. Father James helped me to rearrange the menu. Cereals, and bread and butter with jam. The boys enjoyed the change and were given milk to drink.

This made me think: why was there a cold Aga only when I was on early-morning duty and had had the night off? I began to check the Agas. They had not been stoked up and the fire had burned down, while the anthracite scuttles remained full. Cook could not make me scrub the floor, but in this way she could cause trouble for me. So I began to attend to the fires myself and the next morning, all would be ready to start the cooking. I wanted to explode to show that I too had a temper, but Mutti's training — "Always think before you act" — won. I bided my time, waiting till the next time I was on night duty on my own. I conveniently "accidentally on purpose" forgot to stoke the fire and fill the Agas with anthracite. Sleeping just above the kitchen I thought that I would be asked to get up and help. So that I did not have to tell a lie when I was asked to help, I made sure I had my excuse ready. I took a double dose of Epsom Salts and a double dose of castor oil, so that I truly did feel a sick woman. When Matron came to see me, she ordered that I should stay in bed the whole day and cook had to prepare some broth for me. Well, that cured the cold stoves!

One day, Father Aloysius, who was in charge of staff welfare asked me if I was ill as I looked so tired. Here was my chance to tell him about the mysterious footsteps and I told him about not being able to sleep. He was silent for a minute and then said, "It is not a person trying to get into your room. Nor is it a ghost. The footsteps you hear are the priests going along the cloister on their way to midnight mass. An hour later they return the same way."

The steps I was hearing were the echo of about 80 to 90 priests as the cloister corridor is about half way up my room. That night was the first night I slept in my bed!

Miss Norton realised that I was feeling very lonely and isolated, and was sorry she had no comfortable room to offer me. She invited me for tea again and suggested that I move in with her and share her bed. That way I would have the comfort I was hoping for. She indicated that in return she wanted some of the

202

ration coupons that I took out of the boys' ration books for their food. She could then buy extra tinned food and take it to her flat in London. Again, I wrote to my parents for advice and the reply came by return of post. Under no circumstances should I agree to either suggestion. Both would lead me away from the straightforward life and honesty that I had been brought up to. After telling Miss Norton that I preferred to stay in my room and that I needed the ration coupons to feed the boys, I never received another invitation for a cup of tea. I tried to make friends with the maids. They were lively and pretty, and I hoped their companionship would help me. The first question they asked me was whether I had a boyfriend, and if not, they would introduce me to some Yankees. All they talked about was how they spent their time with these Americans soldiers and compared the presents they had received for favours granted. Shyly I mentioned that because of my background I must not make a point of meeting soldiers. They gave me a blank look and thought that if I joined them, I would only cramp their style and spoil their fun.

Every day I looked forward to the short time when the "Gaelic Warrior", Father James, would come to the storeroom. While issuing the food, we talked on any subject. He said he was happy to discuss these various subjects with me, but never to argue. These short conversations became the highlight for me and they acted as a balance mentally. There was no animosity, no teasing or belittling. It made me feel like a normal human being. It gave me self-respect.

There were two women who helped to prepare the vegetables, and later cleared up and cleaned the large saucepans. One of them was the wife of the baker. All bread, cakes and pastries were prepared and baked in the bakery. The two women took great delight in teasing me about my English. I still had trouble with the V and W, and would ask them, "Please vash the salad in the vater vith salt in it and mix the dressing vith winegar." This had them in stitches.

Being teased was a new experience for me. Up to then, people had smiled at my pronunciation, saying it was attractive or fascinating, or else they would smile at my mistakes. But being teased, I felt hurt. Then one day as they were laughing at my mistakes, I suddenly saw the funny side and joined in and laughed with them. That was a breakthrough and the start of a new understanding between us.

Every so often, one of the brothers would bring me some honey and butter, and if I needed extra milk, I just had to let them know. The brothers looked after a farm belonging to the Abbey. They were not allowed to speak, however, and if I wanted something extra, I could ask them and they would reply by nodding or shaking their heads.

My father used to call my kitchen "the rich pots of Jericho" as I had written home about the extra allowances we had — even some eggs and, of course, plenty of home-grown vegetables. All these extras made catering so much easier. Sometimes the parents of the boys would send us hares or braces of partridges or pheasants. Cook would just put them on a shelf, saying that they had to ripen and to leave them for a week or even longer. They would smell very "high", but she would do nothing about it. One day Father James noticed the smell and checked it out. He exploded. Didn't we know that the birds should be hung and the hares paunched? Yes, I did know, but Cook said to leave them on the shelf. Now came the worst request or hidden order. It was my night on duty and I could not leave the kitchen till they were done. I started on the pheasants. Plucking the feathers was easy. The skin looked greenish and the feathers pulled out easily, but then I had to draw the innards out. The smell from the putrefied bowels and stomach was appalling. I was sick. Then I gave myself a talking-to. "Silly girl. At this rate, you will be here all night. Pull yourself together and just get on with it." The maggots in the stockpot at the Bevin Boys hostel was an easy job compared to this. Six pheasants, six partridges and three hares. I paunched these and then tried to visualise how Papa used to skin rabbits. First, cut round the feet, and then pull them through the skin. Then hang them up on a strong nail and pull the legs free from the skin and the rest of the body follows. By midnight I had completed the task. Father James came to see me before he went to midnight mass. He looked at my tired face and the blood-stained overall, and nodded his head, simply saying, "Well done! Good night." My tired spirits and sagging shoulders lifted. Oh yes, that was high praise indeed!

Once a week all the maids had the afternoon and evening off, so that they could go out together. Several priests would take their places, and wash up and dry the plates, cups and saucers, and cutlery that the boys had used for their evening meal. This particular evening the fathers seemed extra slow. It was nearly 10p.m. and the end of clearing up was not in sight. When I had finished my work in the kitchen, I went to the pantry to see why the work was taking so long. I noticed that one priest picked up a clean and dry plate, and then put it down again. He repeated the same action, picking up and putting down a plate. I realised that he had done this for the last two hours and this explained the lateness of completing the washing up. I could not fathom why the other priests had not stopped him. Smiling, I went over to him and in a friendly tone suggested, "Please, Father, help with the washing up or put the crockery onto a trolley. Please pull your weight as it is getting rather late." He looked perplexed and asked, "Is that how you see me? That I don't pull my weight and work hard enough?"

A simple "Yes" was my reply. "Ah well, I must do better than that then." He picked up a tea towel and dried up. All the other priests stopped in their tracks and stared at me. You could have heard a pin drop, all the other priests were so silent while we had this brief conversation. It was not until the Father had picked up a tea towel that they started to work again — and in complete silence. I puzzled about this, but could not see that I had done anything wrong. I had asked politely and I could not go off duty until all the work was done.

206

Next morning, when Father James came to help issue the stores, he was laughing and wondering if I knew who I had spoken to last night. "Yes, of course," I replied, "One of the priests." Again Father James nodded his head and then pointed out that no one ever spoke like that to the Abbot. No wonder that the other priests had downed their tools in astonishment while that conversation took place.

CHAPTER
ELEVEN

Meeting an RAF man

A new farm — Prisoners of war

The question of Christmas holidays came up. I asked if I might be permitted to go home to my family. Miss Perry, the cook, was quite happy to stay on. That meant ten days' leave. Home. That word had a special meaning for me now. I counted the days till I could travel home. Even standing in a crowded train from King's Cross to Doncaster could not dampen my spirits. Though these were sad times, the spirit of Christmas and goodwill could be felt everywhere. My parents and brother gave me such a warm welcome that the feeling of loneliness of the last months vanished instantly, and I cried and cried. These tears seemed to wash it all away. I could see more clearly how fortunate I was to work at Roue School. After a day at home, I soon picked up all the work I used to do and that helped Mutti to take things easier. Time passed so quickly and when I had spare time, I played my records over and over again. It did me the world of good to hum and sing along to those familiar melodies.

Remember, we could still not use our wireless — one of the restrictions on "aliens".

During the winter term I had not left the school once as I had to save every penny for the fare home and also to buy some presents. Joan and John invited us to their Christmas party as in previous years. This party was the highlight of the holiday and meeting old friends again was a happy event. They noticed how quiet I had become and realised that perhaps life had not been easy, and so they did not tease me or pull my leg. As in previous years, Joan's mother had made a delicious spread, and we played party games, finally sitting round the fire, roasting chestnuts and singing carols.

After the festive day, my parents asked Kurt and me to sit down for a talk, a conference. They explained that because of the flood and the loss of cows, and having to buy extra feed, they could no longer keep the 150-acre farm going. They had notified the Managing Director from the Colliery that they would be leaving in the spring. I thought that as there were no college fees or accommodation to be paid for me, and with Kurt's wages, they could keep afloat. Papa said that Kurt had done more than his share, putting in hours of overtime. It took several minutes for this news to sink in.

Papa had been looking through the *Farmer's Weekly* to find a smaller farm. One was advertised in Everton, about four miles from Bawtry. Papa wanted Kurt's advice and Mutti also had to like the farmhouse as she was on her own for most of the day. We caught a bus to Bawtry to get the connecting bus which ran every three hours. Because of the snow, however, we missed the connecting bus. Papa decided that we would walk the distance and then catch the return bus. After we passed the first village, we saw in the distance a farm on a hill, with an unmade road leading up to the house. Mutti wondered how ever those people managed to do the shopping and what would they do if they forgot an item, such as the yeast for making bread. The farm we actually went to view was not suitable. Sitting on the bus home, we came past the farm on the hill again. Mutti thought how lonely it must be to be so far from the road and the village. Little did we guess that day that in the coming spring, my parents would be moving to this very farm.

The Christmas leave passed too quickly, but this time I faced the return journey to London and then Reading, then on to the school, with more confidence, and I took changing trains and stations in my stride.

The work in the school became more routine and only the cook's festering jealousy of me for having achieved the same position as she had, but only so much younger, spoiled things.

One day the Bursar came and asked me for a favour, "Please will you come to my office after your evening duty — about 10.30p.m." This puzzled me. I did not know what to do nor what to make of it as the Bursar was a very private, reticent person. Should I go, or make some excuse next morning that I was too tired and forgot about it? My thoughts were going round in circles. My imagination ran riot as during the holiday friends had teased me, telling me fantastic stories about how priests would initiate young girls in the pleasures

210

of the flesh. My work that evening finished just after 10p.m. and I went to my room and changed from my white overalls into an ordinary dress. I made my way to his office. A record was playing, the "Meditation" from *Thais*. He spoke: "I apologise for involving you in my predicament, but I did not know who else to ask. Matron is much too old and the maids — well, they would embellish this and not use any discretion. Also, you are the only Protestant and therefore you do not have to go to confession." All the time he spoke, I became more and more concerned and worried. Whatever could he want? He changed the record for Tchaikovsky's Piano Concerto No. 1. Then he spoke again and asked me to agree to whatever he would be saying, and would I respond positively? I became more and more mystified. Finally he said, "You will soon see. It will happen before midnight." But what would happen? By now I had no fears. I was sure he was not going to seduce me.

Then there came a knock at the door. It opened and there stood the housekeeper in a silver-grey negligée. I could see her naked body through it. She entered, but stopped dead in her tracks when she saw me. The Bursar said that she was intruding as we were busy doing the costing of the food and cleaning materials. She gasped. "But you are having coffee and listening to music while you work?" He replied that I had had a long day and he did not think that we would be finished before midnight, after which he had to go to midnight Mass. She turned round and walked out, leaving the door open. As our glances followed her, she looked like a ghost floating along the cloister corridor. Now the Bursar told me that she had come every night for the last two weeks and whatever he said, she would take no notice of it. And how could he have explained this to me beforehand? He also asked me to come again for the next few nights, till the penny dropped with her that she had no chance of seducing him. I went for a further four nights. The last two were uneventful. The poor woman was so frustrated, living near so many handsome men that she could not control her emotions. The priests were all very well educated. Apart from their training for the priesthood, they all had extra university training for their roles as teachers, administrative staff, doctor, etc. The school was like a well-run estate. As a matter of fact, I enjoyed those few evenings, having a good conversation and listening to the music.

This episode was over and forgotten when the Bursar asked me again to call on him. This time he asked me if I had borrowed — or had heard of other people borrowing — some of the school's silver and crystal ware. This was only used on special occasions. I said that I never went to that part of the school and didn't even know where the silver and crystal were kept. Also as I lived apart from the rest of the staff, I did not hear any tittle-tattle.

It was not long before the police arrived and searched everybody's room. In the housekeeper's room they found a cupboard full of the stuff and two large cases were packed and ready to be taken away to a flat she had in London. She was instantly dismissed and the packing of her now empty suitcases was supervised. She was taken by car to the station and put on the train to London. A few hours later, a light was noticed in her room and checking it out, the Bursar found that she had returned. She was in bed and would not get dressed. The Bursar and Assistant Bursar dressed her and again took her to the station and put her on the train. Once more she returned, but this time she had hidden her clothes. She must have thought that her perseverance would win, but this time the police were brought in. They threw a monk's habit over her head and a police van took her away.

It was springtime — Easter would soon be upon us. Lent was, of course, a time of fasting for the boys and priests. The head boy had asked me several times if I would cook some continental food for them. I thought that I would introduce a special soup. With it being a time of fasting, I should not use any meat or stock, and this soup would be a change from the different vegetable soups. It was Griessuppe. The base of the soup was water flavoured with lemon juice and rind and thickened with semolina and only slightly sweetened. I cooked the usual quantity and the serving boy from each table would fetch the soup in a tureen for his table. These serving boys kept coming for more and more. I served every drop, even the staff's portions. I was pleased that they had enjoyed it. After the meal the head boy came to the kitchen and asked if it had all been eaten up. Then he confessed that if they had not done this, the boys at the tables that did not eat a second helping would have to do extra duty. "But why?" I asked. Well, since cook was having an off day and had accidentally watered down the milk pudding too much, it was their duty to see to it that no complaint reached the Bursar. They thought my delicious Griessuppe was watered-down milk pudding! My first attempt to introduce continental food was a failure. I decided that the next time I would inform the head boy first. My second attempt was Viennese steaks — now better known as beefburgers, the only difference being that the steaks are smaller, about 2 cm thick. These were thoroughly enjoyed by one and all.

For Easter we had to cook for the priests only and they were hoping for a feast cooked with the rations saved during Lent. The menu was:

* Consommé Royale
* Easter Sunday Roast
* Gateau with Cream

Cook was watching me carefully when I started to cook the soup. I used minced beef, but cooked it only for a short while. This way I could use the minced meat and make shepherd's pie with it. As eggs were rationed, I could not use any to clear the stock with, so I saved the eggshells from making the cake mixture for the gateau. These shells would act as a sieve and clear the consommé to a certain degree. Then I made the savoury egg mixture for the "royale" garnish. Miss Perry wanted to write the menu on the blackboard for the priests' dining room. She sent one of the handicapped men to ask me for the name of the soup and out of sheer devilment, I called it "Eggshell soup with custard". She wrote this on the blackboard. When Father James saw the menu, he wondered if I could serve an entrée as well. At such short notice, all I could offer was portions of corned beef covered with puff pastry, which I had previously made to be used for making into cream slices for tea. That idea was happily accepted. On Easter Sunday I started to work at 6 a.m. and it was about 3 p.m. when the Abbot came to the kitchen to thank us for the wonderful meal we had served. As a thank you, he presented us with a large bottle of their wine.

I had not eaten any breakfast nor had any lunch by that time. Apart from having an empty stomach, I am also allergic to yeast and grapes. Therefore, half a glass made me quite tipsy and I began to run around the Aga stoves in a crouched position, one hand at the back of my head with the fingers sticking up — supposedly feathers — and with the other hand I patted my mouth saying, "I'm a little Indian girl. Catch me if you can." The hunt was on, and as they tried to catch me, I enjoyed it to the full when I managed to evade them. Oh yes, they finally caught me and put me to bed.

Soon after Easter, cook told me that she was leaving. In a way I was happy, because it would mean the end of her hate relationship with me. Then I thought about it, hoping and wishing that I could be promoted to senior cook, with all the advantages it would bring, such as my own bed-sitting room. The Ministry of Labour took a different view, however, and sent a new cook, Miss Black. She was a friendly person but with no outstanding feature. She had not worked or cooked in a kitchen without gas or electric cookers, and needed advice and help with the menu planning. For example, we could not serve a roast and roast potatoes and a baked pudding or pie.

After the Abbot gave us the large bottle of Buckfast wine, he suggested that I should take a week's leave and go home. I could not imagine this at all, as my parents had left the farm near Doncaster and moved to the place we saw in the distance up a hill when we walked that wintry day.

As on previous journeys home from London to Doncaster, the train was packed and I had to stand in the corridor. This too was crowded with people and next to me stood an airman. I was still nervous and shy talking to people, so I faced the window, but in the twilight I could see the reflection of this airman. He was just a little taller than me and had very blonde curly hair. Suddenly a young boy pushed through the crowd holding up a toy plane and making a noise of a humming engine, "Brr, brr, brr" and then "bang bang bang", imitating a machine gun. I could feel the reaction of this airman, his body becoming rigid. When I saw his face in the reflection of the window, it looked startled. Instinctively I turned round and apologised for the thoughtless action of the boy. This seemed to break the spell and he smiled and said that it was just a boy showing off his plane.

As I had turned round to face him, I thought I might as well talk to him. He too was travelling as far as Doncaster to stay with his parents and during the week would travel on to Leeds to his new unit. It was amazing how quickly one could get to know a person in a crowded confined space. It also seemed that we shared similar interests. His eyes were blue and sparkled, and every so often, a smile would bring a gentleness and softness into them. I realised that this happened when I made a mistake or used the wrong word, but he was too polite to ask me where I came from. On Doncaster station platform, he asked me if we could meet again. Throwing all those many years of caution and self-control away, I mentioned that I had time to spare as the bus that would take me home only ran every three hours. We had a cup of tea in the station's cafeteria. It was dark brown, strong tea served in thick white cups. I enjoyed it and thought it was the nicest cup of tea I had had in my life. While sipping this magical tea, he asked me if we could meet again. My heart raced and I could feel it beating as I was getting excited. A man in the Forces wants to meet me, yes me, again. I must remember not to mention this meeting to my parents. How could I manage to arrange a meeting, living 12 miles from Doncaster and with that terrible bus service? I then had a brainwave. My parents still did some shopping in Doncaster and with careful scheming, I could plan a meeting on Friday. We arranged to meet at the bus station where my bus arrived.

Going home on this three-hourly bus, I had no idea where my bus stop was. The conductress stopped the bus by a sand track, which led to the house. I wondered what I would find at the end of it. Home? I ran the last few yards towards an enormous house, more like an estate house, hidden by huge chestnut trees. Home is the place that gives shelter and rest. I was so happy to see my parents again. But meeting them in this new farm, I sensed a strange tension between them. Both were very nervous. Papa was good at covering up his feelings, saying he would like to show me over the house and take me to my new bedroom. I noticed that there was no gas or electricity, but Aladdin lamps, and a Calor gas cylinder by the gas stove. In the lounge was also a blacked old-fashioned stove. Papa explained that they cooked on the stove as it heated the room at the same time.

The Calor gas was used on special occasions as this cylinder bottled gas was rationed to one bottle per month, and it was also used for lighting the lounge. At least it seemed that running water was laid on as in the corner over the sink was a water tap. When I pointed out this luxury, papa laughed. "Yes, we have running water. It is a big advantage . . . depending on the weather." He explained that in the distance was a windmill that would pump water into an underground water tank. If the weather was wind-still, then the windmill would not pump any water into the tank. To get the water into the house, we had an outside pump, and could pump the water to the top of the house and so have cold running water. This worked well for three seasons, but in the wintertime, the pump would freeze and we would have to make sure that there was enough water to thaw it.

218

I wondered why in this big house my parents did not use the kitchen. Papa explained that the house was divided and they shared it with a father and his two daughters. They needed accommodation as during the blitz on Sheffield they had lost their house and tragically the mother and baby sister were killed. They had also lost all their possessions. The farmhouse was easy to divide. When it was built, one part was intended for the family of the house while the other half contained the servants' quarters. This still did not explain the nervous tension. During tea Papa explained that he had applied for three land girls, but for each land girl, he had to employ two prisoners of war. My parents had to provide lunch and a pot of tea, and in the evening one lorry would collect the land girls and another lorry the prisoners of war. This seemed logical to me. Then came the punch line: the prisoners were German U-boat crew (submarine) and these were fanatical Nazis. Mutti then described how before they sat down for lunch, they would gather round the table, standing to attention, and would give the Hitler salute. Then, after the meal, they would sing a patriotic song before returning to work. My parents were frightened in case the prisoners of war realised that they were German refugees. The prisoners thought that my parents' speech was another Yorkshire dialect. When they had worked for the previous farmer, who spoke a broad Yorkshire, they could not understand him at all. Mutti and Papa were frightened for their lives, thinking that as fanatical U-boat Marines, the prisoners would think they had to do their duty and would hang them on the nearest tree.

My first task was to convince my father that he must speak to the camp commandant and ask for different prisoners, stating the reason for this request. The next Monday morning, six Italians came and after they sat down waiting for the lunch to be served, they sang. Both my parents left the room quickly as they were so relieved that they had both begun to shed some tears. So this problem, the cause of all the tension, was easily resolved.

It was wonderful to be at home and be part of the family for one week. Mutti was still the same disciplinarian as always, and I had to submit to an early morning cold bath. We filled the bath the night before, so that it would be at room temperature. In the morning, I used a sponge to soap myself and would then dip into the cold water counting to ten before rubbing myself dry. Mutti's argument was that this was a boost to the immune system. Also, it was an excellent cure for teenage problems as it "cooled the young people's hot blood". I thought that for one week I could suffer it in silence.

Friday was a lovely bright and sunny day. I managed to keep cool and calm. As we had arranged, Leslie was waiting for me at the bus station. Was it the early spring day, I wondered; I felt as if my emotions were ready to burst out and take flight. I wanted to sing. We walked to the local park and were the only people there. Leslie took hold of my hand. This acted like a spring as all those years of restrictions and fears came uppermost again. I protested fiercely, "Don't touch me! You do not know anything about my past." He stopped walking, put his hands on my shoulders and turned me to face him, saying, "I can tell from the way you are — so serious and with such a mature outlook on life — that you have not had an easy time. Your pronunciation gives you away. You are either German or Austrian. If you came from any other country, you would act with more confidence about who you are. So, jumping to conclusions, as you are free to travel about you must be classified by the Government as friendly enemy aliens." How simple it sounded, but I can't describe what a relief this was to me.

The hours we spent together that day seemed to carry me to an enchanted land. Finally we had a cup of tea in the Odeon cinema before I rushed off to do the shopping.

During the afternoon he wanted to tell me that he would be away on an experimental tour. I stopped him, "Please, Leslie, don't tell me anything about your job in the Forces. If we are still friends after the war, I shall be pleased to listen to all your tales and even ask some questions, but it will have to wait. You see, should anything go wrong, you would wonder whether your confiding in me might heve been the cause of it."

Time was flying by so quickly while I was wishing that it would stand still. When we said goodbye, he asked if I would write to him. "Letters from home make all the difference," he said. I asked him if he would write to me too, but what address should I give him? My parents must never know that I was corresponding with a man in the Forces and they would never forward any letters. The Ministry of Labour had warned me that I would be soon transferred to another place. Finally, I suggested that he could write care of my ex-landlady, living in Leeds. She was now also a friend and she would contact me and redirect the letter

Somehow I never thought that I would ever see or hear from him again. How wrong can one be! This friendship lasted some eight years or even longer. The holiday week passed too quickly and I returned to Roue School.

When I got back to the school, Miss Black was still having teething problems. Somehow she was not able to cope with the extra allowances of butter and honey provided for us from the farm. We use semi-skimmed milk for making milk pudding or custard, or to serve with porridge, and the cream thus obtained was made into butter. Her idea was to add extra fat to most mixtures and she thought these richer mixtures would improve the flavour and texture. I remember well when she served dumplings for the first time. They were very heavy and solid and greasy, so I asked carefully if she had forgotten to add baking powder. Without hesitation, she replied, "No, I did not use any as I used extra shredded suet. Like rich cakes, the extra fat aerates the dumplings." Using all my youthful tact, I suggested that she ought to use the Roue Abbey School recipes. She laughed at me, saying, "We senior cooks can teach you young ones a few working tricks." I did not know how to advise her without her losing face.

The senior pupils came to my aid, bringing us samples of results from a chemistry experiment they had done to do with balancing recipes. For dumplings, they tried four combinations:

1. flour, baking powder and a little fat
2. flour, no baking powder and a little fat
3. flour, baking powder and rich in fat
4. flour, no baking powder and rich in fat.

When she saw the results of this experiment using different flour recipes, she soon asked me whether I had a more suitable recipe. There were few other problems, which were not so easily rectified. However, after a short while, Miss Black adapted to life and things began to run smoothly.

Ever since I was old enough to think for myself, I had searched for my religion. I was brought up as a Lutheran, and the different Protestant religions I looked into seemed strange to me, and I found it difficult to fit into any of them. I went to services held by the Quakers, Methodists, Salvation Army and Church of England, but their ideas and services varied widely from the Lutheran ones I was used to. Each one had a different approach and I found a stumbling block with all of them.

Living at this Catholic public school, I was very impressed by the lifestyle of the monks and priests, and how they looked after the schoolboys. I made a point of asking the priest in charge of the staff at the school if he would give me instruction and teach me about

Catholicism. I was happy that at last I had found the answer and asked the priest if he would arrange for me to convert. His answer was direct. "No, while you live here at this school, you may not change your religion. Go back to life away from here. Live with your Protestant family and friends, and see how you can attune to Catholicism. I advise you to leave." In a way, this came as a relief for my own emotion as I seemed to live for the moments that the priest who helped to look after the stores would come to work with me. I do not know if he realised that I had strong feelings about him and lived for those moments when we worked together. The suggestion that I ought to leave was an easy way out and I went to the Ministry of Labour and asked for a transfer, quoting the priest's words.

CHAPTER
TWELVE

Englefield Green, Secretarial College

VE Day

The letter arrived in due course and gave me my new address in Englefield Green, Egham, telling me that I had to report to the bursar there. My new job was a promotion — Lady Cook in charge of the kitchen staff and cooking for 120 young ladies evacuated from Kensington Secretarial College. They had been bombed out and Lady Armhurst had offered the college her house, while she and her daughter-in-law moved into the cottage and, as far as I could see, made only one condition: that we provide lunch and tea for them. What a wonderful change from the sparse utility kitchens in Roue Abbey School. This time it was a modern kitchen with gas and electricity, and up-to-date labour-saving equipment. All the food I served had to be in small portions and arranged daintily on attractive plates and dishes. The dessert had to be served in crystal dishes — it was so different to the previous jobs

— feeding hungry Bevin boys or the growing lads at Roue School.

My job was easy: to plan meals for these young ladies. The small portions made life easier given the rationing allowance. Also, every morning, the gardener brought in fresh vegetables and delicacies. We had fruit out of season, for example strawberries, raspberries, peaches and grapes. All these were grown in large greenhouses, some of which were even heated.

My accommodation was also luxurious. I had my own bed-sitting room, furnished with Queen Anne furniture, and I had my own bathroom. I was hoping for a friendly atmosphere so that I would not feel so isolated and lonely as at Roue School, but I was in for a big disappointment. No, it was even worse, because the kitchen staff were "downstairs", while the young ladies were "upstairs". These young ladies were the daughters and nieces of diplomats, ambassadors and other statesmen. They had been brought up with this "upstairs/downstairs" divide, and in their world, the cook was not a particularly treasured person.

To get a change of scene, I used to go cycling in Windsor Great Park or go shopping in Windsor itself. Here, too, was a very haughty atmosphere. Also, I had never come across so many soldiers. They were the various royal guards.

Everywhere there was tension and excitement in the air as it was the last few days before the end of the war. Every day, everybody waited for the news to break that finally the war was over. Some of the young ladies did not wait for the momentous news, and as the term was nearing its end, some students left in order to be in London. Finally, the Warden left too. She locked up the college side of the building and made me responsible for the dining room, lounge and kitchen. I had to see to it that all was securely locked up and only had to look after the gardener and myself.

Then the long-awaited news was announced: Germany has surrendered. VE Day. People were jubilant. There was no special arrangement made to celebrate in Englefield Green nor in Windsor. The King and Queen had left the Castle to go to London and Buckingham Palace. I was alone in the house and so as not to spend this momentous hour by myself in my room, I ran into the streets and joined the masses. I ran towards people, whether civilians, soldiers, sailors or airmen. I hugged whoever was near me, tears streaming down my face. I pushed away all my previous feelings of fear. Victory! Blinded by tears, I tried to laugh and dance. People stopped me and tried to tell me that I did not need to cry. "But the killing and war is over," I said. They did not realise I was crying with happiness. Now that heavy cross that I had carried like a yoke dropped from my shoulders. Victory. Happiness. Freedom. No more fears of being branded a "bloody Jerry". I had always been fearful and shy as I could not carry a notice on my back stating that I was a refugee from Nazi oppression. VE Day was a blur to me. I saw crowds through the mist of my tears and all that registered in my brain was, "The war in Europe is over. Freedom from fear". The chains controlling my emotions broke. I was a person drunk from a beautiful word "freedom". What an exalted feeling! The pressure in my chest made me feel as if it was going to burst. VE Day meant victory and peace to follow. For me it was a special celebration, the defeat of Nazism and all the evil and horror it stood for. VE Day was the key for me to look forward to the future with hope

As it was nearly the end of term and the students had left and were not going to return to Englefield Green, it was decided that the house should be closed until September or October, and I packed everything carefully away. While I was clearing up and getting ready to shut the house, a letter arrived from Papa asking me to come home as Mutti needed a gall-bladder operation and would need care afterwards. The Ministry of Labour were quite happy about it and granted me leave of absence from my job, especially as they had no definite job for me. Also, as a farmer, Papa had the right to ask for permission for this kind of help, either from me or a land girl. The Ministry of Labour did not issue me with a travel warrant, so I used my saved money.

During the time I nursed Mutti, I received no pocket money and I spent a little on stockings and a sixpenny lipstick. As Mutti got better and stronger, she wanted to take over the reins again. As it happened, we had a difference of opinion on a particular subject and, true to her strict disciplinarian self, she said, "You are a child and will do as I tell you." I responded that I was older now and held down a responsible job and earned money. Well, that did it. She told me to pack my things and get out at once. I begged her to let me stay till the

Ministry of Labour redirected me to my new position, till the time of my leave of absence was over. Another thing was that I had hardly any money left. Her reply was, "I thought you earned money." She was overlooking the fact that I used some of it on the train fare home and also for the bus when I went shopping. It was no good running to the field were Papa was working. Since 1938, when he had come home, back to the family, he had left discipline to Mutti. Without her strong will, both in Germany and here in England, we would never have survived. I tried again and pleaded with her to let me stay till my next job was sorted out. I pointed out that when she needed me, I always came home. Mutti always said that home was a shelter from trouble, but my arguments were of no avail. Mutti's reply was, "Go and pack your things and see how well you fare away from home."

I walked down the sand path to the main road to catch the bus to Bawtry and then on to Doncaster. I stood in the High Street, looking in the window of a shoe shop. Tears were running down my cheeks. I had only a few shillings left and had no idea where I could go for the night without money. I thought of the Christmas parties, and Joan and her family. But no, my pride somehow would not let me and I wanted to shield Mutti from letting friends know that she could be so cruel and hard-hearted.

What was I to do? It must have been my guardian angel or fate lending a helping hand. An acquaintance passed me and noticed the state I was in. I told her of my predicament. After a brief silence, she suggested that I go with her, and stay with her and her husband. I pointed out that I could not pay for anything. She said that it was all right as both she and her husband were working, and her mother was looking after the baby. Granny was getting very tired, finding that a six-month-old baby was too much for her. Gwen suggested that I should look after the baby and give her mother a rest. She said that that would be worth more than any rent to her — she would be very grateful for my help. Gwen took me to her home and introduced me to granny and baby. Once I moved into that house, I not only looked after the baby, washing its nappies and so on, I also did some housework and in the evening, I would have a meal ready for us all. For a professional like me, cooking for four people and a baby was a piece of cake!

CHAPTER
THIRTEEN

Another boys' private school

Bunford — VJ Day

Eventually I heard from the Ministry of Labour. Once again I was directed to a boys' boarding school, in a small market town called Bunford. The school was situated nearly in the centre of the town and so was within easy reach for local boys to attend. There were 500 boys resident and about 100 day pupils, with 30 to 40 staff and visitors.

Again, it was a complete change from my previous jobs and I wondered what difficulties and troubles I would have to face this time. What puzzled and worried me was the very high salary the school offered. It was half as much again as I had received for my last job as Cook in charge. Seeing that finally the war with Germany was won, I hoped that the reaction of people towards me would be easier. Again I had a large bed-sitting room and bathroom. These were on the same floor as the maids' dormitories, that is, the kitchen staff and the school staff, the housemaids, who made the boys' beds and cleaned the dormitories and classrooms. These were young Irish girls. Those helping in the kitchen had to prepare the vegetables and wash up the dining room plates and dishes, along with the kitchen utensils. Matron and I were responsible for the welfare of these Irish girls.

I arrived a few days before term started and the headmaster's wife asked me to preserve some of her apple harvest, using the crab apples and turning them into jelly. Sugar was still rationed and I had to stretch it as far as I could. The result was a runny jelly. I boiled it a little longer, but the result was the same. Runny jelly. I tried to think how I could set the jelly without using more sugar or lemons. Then I remembered a lesson at college in 1942 when we had to use cream of tartar, and the result was wonderful. The jelly, when cold, had set so firmly that you could slice it with a knife.

The next thing was to preserve more of the many different types of apples. I peeled and peeled apples from morning to afternoon, dipping them into salted water to prevent oxidation and stop them from going brown. I cut them into rings and strung them up, hanging them in the cool oven to dry. This vacation work was easy and I did not have to work late.

At last I had to get the food in, ready for the boys' arrival. The headmaster's wife summoned me to pay her a visit at 10 a.m. to discuss that day's menu. She sat up in bed in an expensive-looking negligée. Her hair had a blue rinse and she was clearly trying to imitate the look of the film star. She requested that I should address her as Madam. This haughty snobbish attitude did not make me feel comfortable and I could foresee trouble. To show that I too had an opinion, I pointed out that, since I knew her name, it would be more courteous to address her by this, but the maids should address her as Madam. She then wanted to discuss the menu for that day and asked me what leftovers were kept in the refrigerator and larder, and how I could use these to supplement the menu. In my previous jobs, this was always the duty of the cook. Finally, after half-an-hour, she made up her mind and decided on the menu and food I had to cook for lunch and high tea. The boys should get a different menu from that of the top table, the headmaster and his wife, the teaching staff and visitors. The maids were allowed only vegetables and gravy. That was more than they would get in Ireland and their meat ration would go to the top table. Now this bedroom became a verbal battleground, a battle of wills.

I pointed out that discussing the pros and cons of the different menus until 10.30a.m. or later was altogether too long as I still had to ring the butcher and greengrocer to deliver the necessary ingredients. I stressed that I would not be able to produce a meal for 650 to 700 people by 12 o'clock. To save face, I pointed out that it took longer than one hour to produce a meal by midday — of course I could serve half-cooked meat and vegetables, if that is what she preferred. That would be fine with me! We were like two fighting cocks and I had to win to be ready to serve the meals. Eventually, I hit on a solution and suggested that I could see to the breakfast and then pay her a visit to discuss the next day's menu. I could then order the food in good time for it to be delivered. This idea appealed.

I hoped that she and the boys would enjoy the meals I would serve.

My next job was to work out carefully the rationing for every one. Up to that date all the good food was sent to the top table, including the big joints and also the game the parents sent for their boys. I paid a visit to the butcher and discussed with him what extra meat he could let me have in addition to the rations, such as sausages, liver, rabbits, and perhaps, for a special occasion, chickens, not to mention bones for stock. Several maids fainted while they were working and I realised that they were suffering from malnutrition. My next battle was to give the maids the ration allowance they were entitled to.

In one cupboard were several cookery books, but they were very worn. I even thought that most pages must have been eaten by something. At first I thought that it was caused by mice, but I never noticed any droppings. Soon, though, the puzzle was solved. One night I was not feeling well and thought a hot drink might help. I went to the kitchen. The red emergency light was on and therefore I did not switch on the main light. Horror of horrors. It was like a picture out of a science-fiction movie. The walls and cupboards were plastered with black oval shells, about two inches long. As the floor was dark, I could not see any. As I walked forward, they did not move, but I felt myself treading on something crunchy. I felt quite sick as I realised they were cockroaches. They did not move, but I moved

234

forward — crunch, crunch, crunch. I got a dustpan and brush and swept them up. Still no movement from the oval marks on the wall. There were not one or two, but hundreds, even thousands. The ones I scooped up, I emptied into the Aga. I don't know if they made any noise as they hit the fire, but all of a sudden, they moved very quickly and disappeared. They moved in such an orderly manner, no pushing or jostling, it was more like an orderly evacuation planned with military precision, by trained army soldiers.

This was my next battle. All "Madam" said was that there had always been beetles in the kitchen area and there was nothing she could do about it. But when I get a bee in my bonnet, I like to win. All the food was put into bins or tins and jars. Last thing at night not a crumb was left anywhere, only insect powder. The description on the box said that bigger insects would be knocked out for a while. This is when my midnight walks started. Masses of cockroaches would be lying about and I would sweep them up and burn them. I had to do this before the insects recovered. Within a month I had won. On my nightly visits I saw no more of the creatures.

I dreaded these morning sessions with Madam. We had such a different outlook on life and therefore our wills clashed. As I was becoming highly strung and nervous, I decided to report to the Ministry of Labour. During the term, the other victory day came. Victory over the Japanese. VJ Day. The school celebrated it with a large bonfire, accompanied by soup and rolls and sausage rolls. The person I saw at the Ministry suggested that I should see the term out and as the war was over, she thought that she could really release me from my call-up and let me find my own job. She pointed out that no other cook had stayed longer than four to five weeks. I had survived five months! This of course explained why they were offering such a high salary.

One day, Matron came to ask me about two maids, Kath and Elsie. They were my best workers, always willing to do an extra job. Kath was putting on some weight and I thought it was due to the extra protein and food they were getting. Matron looked after the linen and she pointed out that one set of sheets from these two maids looked as if a man had been sleeping in them. I did not even know what Matron was talking about. It seems there were signs of a man's semen. She asked if I knew whether these two girls smuggled a man into their room. I was not aware of this, so Matron asked me to accompany her one night to check on these two girls' behaviour. I was dumbfounded. Matron was right. "Elsie" was a man dressed up as a woman and Kath was pregnant! "Elsie" explained that the only way he could look after Kath was to come to England and both had applied for a residential job. This way he could work near her and that is when "Elsie" decided to dress like a woman. This way they could even live together. Matron reported them to the immigration office and, in one stroke, I lost my two best workers.

There was always something that needed looking into. Several senior boys came to see me and asked me whether I could spare some extra food for them. By the time it was bedtime, they were hungry again. They had written home about this, and their parents had sent biscuits, but these were rationed, and so were not enough to stave off the hunger pangs. I spent hours thinking about this and I came up with a suggestion that some boys should leave their shoe bags in the morning and I would fill them with some slices of bread, although I could not spare any butter, and in the evening, they could collect the bags. The boys were delighted about this as their parents would send some jam or honey. The boys left a message in the bags, thanking me and saying that they slept much better as hunger did not keep them awake.

Annexed to the school was a walled-in garden and a German prisoner of war looked after this. All "Madam" told me was that a maid was to take lunch to him and put it in the shed. One day, I noticed that the maid brought the plate back and the food was soaked by the rain. I questioned the girl how this could have happened and she replied, "Him being a German, he might want to kill us, and we just open the door to the garden and put it there by the door." I decided to go over to size up the situation. He was a quiet, middle-aged man and felt rather bewildered by the people's reaction. I promised that in future, the meals would be delivered properly. He then picked up a pair of scissors and started to snip at the edge of the lawn. I asked, "Why the scissors? Are you making fun?"

"No, the gardener thinks that with shears I have too strong a weapon to kill with, and a lawn mower would make the work too easy."

I shook my head and went to see the gardener to check this out. The reply I got shocked me: "Yes, let him crawl on his knees and keep the lawn tidy that way."

Was there no place of work without trouble? Would I be luckier now that I could find my own job, or should I just give up and ask to come home for good and help on the farm? Since the time when I had left home under those unhappy circumstances, I had written my usual one letter a week, to let them know where I was working. To start with, Papa had replied, but by now Mutti had also replied several times.

CHAPTER
FOURTEEN

Finding my own job

Getting to know Leslie

Being released from my call-up by the Ministry of Labour made me feel as if England was wide open for me to discover. Complete freedom was a heady feeling. Eventually calming down, I realised that I had no idea how or where to look for another job. So far I had been directed to jobs. The more I thought about it, the more I became frightened and panicky. What must I do to change my life and find a post that would be both congenial and friendly? Suddenly, I remembered the notice board at college that always displayed several job vacancies. I composed a letter to the Principal, explaining my situation, and asked for her advice and help. The reply came by return of post, suggesting that I should return to Leeds and, like some other students, apply for a position as assistant supervisor for school meals at the Education Offices. To speed up the process, she enclosed an application form and said she would be pleased to give me a reference as interviews were already being held. I needed a second reference. This was a difficult choice. "Madam" from Bunford

School would not give me a favourable one. The bursar from the secretarial college would most likely not remember me as I worked there for such a short time. So I decided that the years I worked at Roue School would serve me best and provide the source for a second reference.

Every morning, I checked to see whether a reply had come from Leeds. Time hung heavily. Eventually, the awaited letter arrived and, with trembling fingers, I opened it and read that I was invited to attend an interview before Christmas. The train journey seemed extra-long and all the time my thoughts were preoccupied with the questions that might be asked at the interview, turning them over time and again in my mind.

To make sure I was on time, I travelled the night before and as I could not afford the cost of a hotel, I booked a bed at the YWCA hostel. The warden showed me the dormitory in which my bed was. I was to share the dormitory with five other women. As the warden and I entered the room, the young woman already there looked flustered as she had been playing the violin. The house rule was not to make a noise and disturb the others.

As soon as we were on our own again, I suggested that she play some more as the little I had heard sounded very good and I enjoy listening to music. She, Sylvia, confided that she had an interview with the Philharmonic Orchestra and playing kept her nervousness at bay, so she played some more and then called it request time. It became a delightful musical evening.

When Sylvia walked, she limped and I wondered whether her leg hurt as she had to stand for a long time playing a violin. No, she had a big blister under her foot. I thought it an unusual place, but when she showed me her shoe, it had a large hole in the sole, larger than the size of an egg. The weather was cold and wet, and I wondered how we could mend the sole. I went to see the warden to ask if she had a cardboard box I could have. After she had found one for us, we outlined her shoe on the box and cut an inner sole to fix the hole, but that would not last long as the wet weather would soak the cardboard. The problem was not yet solved. I offered to cut up my bathing cap and lined the cardboard sole with it — that would keep her shoe dry. It was a magical repair. When I returned to the dormitory that evening, Sylvia hugged me and threw her arms around me. She was in high spirits and elated as she had been offered a job with the Philharmonic Orchestra. She attributed her excellent playing to warm feet! I made another suggestion. "Go to the Salvation Army and see if they will give you a pair of shoes — you can always make a donation once you have been paid." As a music student, she received a small scholarship grant and found it very difficult to make ends meet, even though she did earn a little extra money by playing at functions. After that evening, I never met her again, but I did see her playing in the orchestra.

The moment of my interview arrived and I faced a committee of six people who asked me about my work experience and the type of kitchens I had worked in.

They seemed especially interested in hearing about the very modern kitchen at the Bevin Boys hostel. Then came the stumbling block. The salary. It was very low as most assistant supervisors lived at home and therefore did not have to pay for rent or food. I was the first girl who had to pay her way and I tried to assure them that I would find accommodation somewhere that I could afford. Food was not so important as lunches and two breaks were included in the salary. The job depended on finding suitable accommodation and I should let the committee know when I would be in a position to accept the job they were offering me.

Lodgings. My next move was to visit Mrs Phyer who acted as my college mother in 1942. When we met, she was so pleased to see me and hugged me. She had not forgotten the weeks when I had looked after her when she had had her nervous breakdown after the deaths of her husband and her only son. I told her about my interview and how I was now looking for digs. Her first reaction was that she already had two students in the two spare bedrooms. Would any of her friends have a spare room? No such luck. She then wondered if I would be prepared to sleep on a camp bed in the front room? Yes, please, that would sort this problem out. She would only charge me what I could afford and she would provide lunch on Saturdays — fish and chips from the local shop — and on Sundays — the traditional roast lunch — as well as a nightcap of hot cocoa every night. Her cocoa was well-known as she balanced the proportions perfectly.

Apart from digs money, I needed the fare to get to work and a little money to spare, to buy the odd pair of stockings or allow myself the luxury of going to the early performance at the local pictures. On Saturdays, if you bought a ticket before 2:30p.m., entrance cost 6d. The film show ran continuously.

Life promised to be wonderful. Now I wrote to Leslie asking if we could meet on his next leave. He applied for 12 hours' compassionate leave, and when we met, he was very understanding that my emotions were in full flight. I was just happy to be with him and hold his hand as we made our way to the hotel for tea. What I really wanted was to be held in his arms. Where could we do this? He suggested Roundhay Park. It was a lovely winter's day. The sun was shining, and snow was on the ground and also covering the trees. The park looked like fairyland. As we made our way towards the end of the park, we walked under a large tree. Leslie pointed up and said, "Look, there's mistletoe growing up there."

I looked up and he kissed me on my lips. Up to then, it had been a peck on the cheek or forehead. It was the first kiss on my lips since the time when I thought a kiss on the lips would make you pregnant. My instant reaction was to flee, to run away. He was so surprised and chased after me. When he caught up with me, he got hold of my shoulders and asked me what had happened to cause this fierce reaction. I felt foolish and blushed, and tried to explain that it was a subconscious reaction, because in my teens I believed babies were created like this. He never laughed at this, but simply said that it was the way people kissed whenthey were in love. He then pulled me towards him, embraced me and kissed me tenderly full on my lips. My knees went weak, but he held me very tightly. The wind moved some branches of the trees and a dusting of snow came down. Through misty eyes, it looked to me as if hundreds of stars were tumbling to earth.

Back in my digs, I tried to remember the time in Roundhay Park and hold on to that moment of rapture. I told Leslie that he was my "dark secret" as I dared not tell my parents that I had been going out with an "aeroplane man". This time he did laugh heartily and corrected me: "Air Force man."

I started my new job. A letter informed me of the address of the kitchen and my duties. These were to assist the supervisor on the practical side of the kitchen work, making sure that 2500 meals were ready on time and packed into insulated containers. They then had to be labelled with the name of the school and the numbers of meals to be sent to each school. It was a modern kitchen, similar to the one in the Bevin Boys hostel. This explained the interest of the committee during the interview. The supervisor had worked for years for the education department and it was a promotion for her. The first thing to do was to try out the new equipment and at the same time teach the staff how to handle it. Then my main job was in the stores, checking the deliveries and weighing out ingredients, before putting them into galvanised baths, one mixing of pudding or pastry in each. I then had to enter this into the daily stock book and cost each daily expenditure. The supervisor transferred these figures into the weekly stock book. All this had to be in triplicate and the cost of five days had to be worked out. We had to be good at arithmetic — adding, subtracting, multiplying and dividing. We had no calculators and if we were two pence out in a costing in the week, we would spend hours trying to find a mistake. It could be in my daily accounts, or in the weekly one. Whichever, we had to find the difference. We were allowed fourpence ha'penny per meal.

We had to balance the more expensive course, a roast, with a cheaper sweet. On Fridays, the total of five days' worth of 2500 meals daily at fourpence ha'penny had to be correct. At the same time, the cost of the food had to balance with the money. We started this checking on Friday afternoon and on Saturday morning carried on with stocktaking.

At college we were taught nutrition. As part of this, we had to work out the protein and fat value of food. If there was too little protein, we had to add extra milk powder to the mashed potatoes, or soya bean or pea flour to the stews or gravy. Mutti was always amused when I told her what quantities I used. To add salt to the potatoes or vegetables, we use bedpan scoops. One scoop was equivalent to one teaspoonful in a private house.

I started work at 7:30a.m., but had half-an-hour travelling to work by bus first. I had to be punctual as it was my duty to open the doors and let the 23 women in. I was very careful when weighing out ingredients, and I weighed out flour for rolling out pastry. Cook would come with a large basin to collect this. On Saturday morning, I would check certain items and compare these with the weekly stock book. Every 10 to 12 weeks, an organiser from headquarters would come to check the stock. We never knew when she would turn up. On the last check, I had lost one hundredweight of sugar. Now the inquisition started. As I was responsible for control of the stock and always locked the storerooms, it was up to me to account for that one hundredweight of sugar: what had happened to it? The organiser checked and rechecked the books, even the recipes and quantities issued. They all tallied. As I was a new member of staff and responsible for the stores, the organiser pointed out that I would be suspended from my job. The questions were always the same: had I taken it out in small quantities to make up for the low salary and sold it on the black market? I was very worried and upset. Me — a Jerry — the thought of the black market aroused a terrible fear in me. The question remained: what had I done with that sugar? However much I assured her that I had not taken a grain of sugar out of the building, she still interrogated me: where was that one hundredweight of sugar? The question remained unanswered. The organiser had a last check to see if she had missed a bag or had even miscounted them — she even re-weighed the bin with the sugar in use. Just as the organiser was leaving the storeroom, cook came in and helped herself to a basinful of sugar. Fate had taken a hand in solving the problem. The organiser followed the cook to see what happened to the sugar. Cook put it on the table where the afternoon staff had their tea. The organiser asked cook how often she filled the basin with sugar. She replied: "Depends on the weather. In cold or wet weather, the staff drink an extra few cups of tea in the morning when they arrive for work." The organiser could not walk quickly enough to the stores where she weighed the sugar. She then calculated the amount used since the previous official stocktaking. It was well over one hundredweight. This extra weight allowed for the odd pound cook took out for the cups of tea drunk. The organiser was relieved as I was, now that the threat of suspension no longer hung over my head.

After this, I always locked the store doors when I was not working in it. I had a word with the cook, saying that she should have told me about her helping herself to sugar. She then told me that in the other kitchen, the supervisor allowed several pounds of sugar a day for tea. One lives and learns. I worked for about nine happy months in that kitchen. Working with an understanding supervisor and efficient staff made life very happy and contented for me, and slowly I started to unwind after all the years of hardship. I realised that my emotions and reactions were changing and I was starting to feel younger. I was no longer a person with an old head on my young shoulders.

Once, in conversation with the supervisor having our afternoon tea and a piece of pudding or pastry left over from lunch, I mentioned how much I appreciated this as it was my last food until next day at 11 a.m., when all the staff had a slice of toast. After this, the supervisor asked the cook to make a sandwich for me with the afternoon cup of tea. My salary was supposed to include food eaten on the premises. No food whatsoever was allowed to be taken out of the kitchen.

One Sunday, sitting by the fire, Mrs Phyer looked at me with a very gentle expression on her face. She started to say that I should no longer sleep on the camp bed. My first reaction was dismay. Where would I find other digs asking so little rent? She must have seen my face becoming thoughtful, at which point she said that she had decided that I could move into her son Toni's flat. It was a converted attic and since Toni was killed, she had treated it as a kind of shrine.

"You move into it. Toni would approve. When I needed care and help after losing both my husband and son, you cared for me. Now I shall do the same for you. I will only charge you as if you were sleeping on a camp bed."

It was a lovely flat: a bed-sitting room and, on the other side of the staircase, a kitchen. Towards the end of the month, when I had spent all my money, and if there was a good film on, I would asked Mrs Phyer if she would lend me 6d for the early performance till the first of the month, pay-day. She spoke beautiful English, but then she would say, "Pass ma bag."

The friendship I made with Margaret in 1942 when at college was still very happy. Her parents invited me often for lunch and tea on the Sunday. I treasured these days as they treated me like a second daughter. In a strange way, I felt more at home here than on the farm. The years away and the different lives we had led made us strangers and the strong family ties began to loosen.

I think that for me this was the happiest time since we came to England.

Change was in the air. A telephone call from the head office told me that they were going to transfer me to another, similar kitchen in Westfield. After I reported to my new supervisor, Mrs Gee, I was told my work schedule. This was the same as before and I settled down very quickly.

Mrs Gee soon reported that my work was satisfactory. The organiser paid us a visit, when she told me that I should deputise for Mrs Gee while she was in hospital. I was happy to do this and hoped that it might be the first step towards promotion. My pay was still very low and I still had to count my pennies very carefully. Every Friday morning, I had to travel into town to collect the wages for the women. I was allowed to use petty cash for the fare into town.

If I was very careful with my money, I could save two shillings and sixpence. With this I could buy stockings and stamps to write home and to Leslie. When he came on leave, my happiness was complete and, for a while, I would be on cloud nine. As the wartime regulations for foreigners were lifted, I was no longer tied down by that rule that I had to be at home by 10.30p.m. No more curfews. At last I felt like all the other people and, going out with Leslie to an evening performance, I could enjoy the end of the film and be in my digs by 11p.m. They were was the small things, these changes that made me feel so good. It was very important to me not to be different from other people in ways that most people just took for granted.

When Leslie came on leave and the weather was fine, we would have lunch somewhere and then take the tram to Roundhay Park. It became our special stamping ground — walking round the lake and sometimes even hiring a rowing boat for an hour, feeding the ducks, then the luxury of having tea and a film show. One lovely warm evening, with the stars twinkling, we decided to walk home to my digs in Headingley. No curfew. Exquisite luxury, not to have to rush and hurry. As we neared Watchhouse Moor, we saw the bright lights from the fair and heard fairground music playing modern music, songs from the war, and as we neared the fair, we saw the many roundabouts. We watched the fair from a distance. After the war years and the blackout, the sparkling lights looked beautiful. I just stood and stared, listening to the music as it drifted over to us. It was indescribable, wonderful. I noticed that Leslie was watching me and, with a cheeky grin and a mischievous wicked look in his eyes, he suggested that we join the fun. We held hands and walked towards it. I tried to remember when I had last visited a fair and had ridden on a carousel. I think it was when I was 10 years old, at a Christmas fair. We chose the carousel with wooden horses that went forwards and backwards, while the platform went round and round. We enjoyed the first ride immensely, so one ride became two, then three, then four. I was blissfully happy, but then my practical commonsense side won as I worked out the cost of the day. Lunch, tram fare, boat ride, tea, film show, and now the carousel. This day had cost Leslie more than I could save up in six to nine months — not even a year. Looking at the time, we had missed the last tram. We laughed happily. No curfew. No time to watch. It was a lovely clear evening, and I got hold of Leslie's arm, and we walked to my digs.

During our homeward walk, he explained and pointed out the different star formations — the Great Bear, the Haywain, the North Pole star. I hugged his arm and put my head on his shoulders. It was well after midnight and Mrs Phyer had locked up. I rang the doorbell. When she answered the door and saw Leslie, she spoke angrily. "How dare you stay out so late!" Only girls with a bad reputation, only tarts would do that, and she had a good mind not to let me in. I came down to earth with a bang. She had never spoken to me like that. She knew about Leslie but had never met him before. Leslie got hold of my arm and suggested that we walk back into town and stay at his hotel. Hearing this, Mrs Phyer became very abusive and pulled me into the hall, shutting the door. I was shattered. With a few angry words, a happy, innocent outing was ruined. Once up in my flat, I threw myself onto the bed and cried.

Neither of us ever mentioned this episode, but somehow the relaxed feeling that had existed between us was spoilt. Why could she not wait to be introduced to Leslie? All the time I had lived with her, it was the first time that I had stayed out after 10.30p.m. Was her reaction that she had worried about me, wondering where I was so late in the evening, or was it jealousy that she realised that there was another person in my life whom I loved? I would not have minded if she had told me off when we were indoors and on our own. On the Sunday morning I went out early, leaving a note saying that I would be out for lunch.

It was another fine day, and Leslie and I spent most of our time in Roundhay Park. All through the night, my thoughts had gone round in circles and I decided to bring up the subject of marriage. During the war, Leslie had said that he would not get married, because he did not want to leave a young widow behind. I had agreed with him, but not with his point of view. No, my reason for not getting married was that for him, marrying a German girl during the war could perhaps harm him, but now both points of view were out of date. He stopped walking and turned to face me, saying, "There's nothing I would like better than for the two of us to get married — but not yet. Where would we build our home? Let me get demobbed first and find a civilian job. Then we can settle down."

Yes, my sensible side understood his point of view. Soon he would be demobbed. Wishing and hoping helped the feeling along.

One day I had a surprise visitor. Mary. I did not even realise that she was demobbed from the WRNS and that she knew my address. Going back to 1942, and my first term at college, Mary and her friends were the big bullies, yet I always felt grateful to her because after half term, she broke the spell of ostracising me, by making fun of me and getting the other students from my class to laugh at me and become friendly. Because of this, I always had a soft spot for her.

252

When I was called up at the end of the first year, Mary also left. She volunteered for the WRNS as she realised that she would fail her examination to move on to the second year. The principal had promised that after the war she could retake the third term and, if she passed the exam, could complete the course. Here she was, now begging me to speak to Mrs P for her as she had been thrown out of her digs. She had taken a man up to her bedroom to stay the night, and now she had nowhere to go. I introduced her to Mrs P and said, quite upfront, "She's all clitter and clatter and noise. She will borrow your things and forget to return them." Because of her beauty and radiant smile, Mrs Phyer was willing to take a chance on Mary. We called Mrs Phyer just Mrs P.

Mary soon ingratiated herself with Mrs P. Mary was allowed to do anything. She had different "boys" (men) for tea in the front lounge, whereas I, having lived and nursed Mrs P for several years, was refused permission to invite Leslie for tea. As it was now early spring and a rainy season, I asked once more for permission and suggested that she ought to meet him and put behind her that midnight duel of words. I think she had been feeling guilty as I was now allowed to invite him for tea, instead of always going into a hotel lounge. I was so excited and baked some buns on Friday at college and made some sandwiches.

Leslie came for tea. We both sat close together on the settee. Suddenly the door opened and Mary made her entrance with a cup of tea, sprawling herself on the armchair opposite us. She wore a white dress with a floral pattern and a very low-cut horseshoe neckline. To save coupons, we made our own cami-knickers. The top was like a petticoat and as one could not pull down the knickers, they were buttoned up between the legs. Only Mary had not done this. My eyes nearly popped out of my head when I saw her genitals. I looked at Leslie. Not a muscle moved in his face. Mary said, "Ah — this is the mystery man you have been keeping hidden," and she laughed. Somehow I had to get her out of that chair. Having nearly finished my cup of tea, I deliberately spilt the rest and Mary came over to help me mop up the mess. Then I suggested that she ought to sit next to Leslie, in case I spilt any more tea and spoilt his uniform.

Turning round to Leslie, she bent forward and now he could see her breasts, something that in those days was regarded as quite immodest and indecent. She then took her forefinger and ran it up and down the crease of his trousers from knee to groin. His face remained a mask. She said, "I like men in smart uniforms." I ran out to Mrs P and demanded that she call Mary out, or I would slap her face hard.

Once we were on our own, he laughed and said, "What a minx. She would drive a younger, less experienced man to distraction!"

Somehow, though, our idyllic atmosphere had been tarnished.

CHAPTER
FIFTEEN

Leslie's demob

A job in New Zealand — Another kitchen

As the time for Leslie's demob drew nearer, I started to dream about our home, looking at furniture and curtains, and finding out which shops sold these items at a reasonable price. Leslie started to apply for positions and suddenly he came with the news that both a job and a home had come through. He would work for BOAC, and live with his brother and family in Windsor. It was early spring and he wondered if we could celebrate by going away for the weekend somewhere. Oh, dared I knock against convention and all the beliefs of my family? I mentioned it to Mrs P — she was for it and even suggested a place that would be just right for us. She was trying to compensate for the day she had spoilt for us that night I came home late. The place was in the Yorkshire moors called Reeth, near Richmond. Her friends looked after the village pub and she arranged it all for us. It would be the first time that I would see Leslie in civilian clothing. I was so excited and watched the clock constantly. Time passed so slowly.

Saturday morning finally arrived. I got up extra early to get to the kitchen by 7a.m. to make sure I had enough time to complete the bookkeeping and then rushed to the bus station for the arranged time. Leslie was already waiting. He looked as handsome out of uniform as in, perhaps even better, because the colour of his sports jacket showed up his golden blonde wavy hair. I ran towards him and, dropping my bag, hugged him. Then he did a full turn so that I could admire this new person.

We travelled on the bus to Richmond and then changed to a local one for Reeth. Travelling by bus had always had the effect on me that after 15 or 20 minutes, I would fall asleep, and this time, with the early morning rising, work and excitement, I think I fell asleep even more quickly. Every so often, I would open my eyes to see if all was well and then fall asleep again. Arriving in Richmond, Leslie was unusually quiet and I thought slightly upset. On to Reeth. The pub was in the centre of the village and we were welcomed and shown to our rooms. Mine was on the first floor and Leslie's on the second floor, at the opposite end of the building. Mrs P had clearly put in her chaperonely word.

It was a lovely evening and we told the landlord that we would enjoy that glorious sunset and walk along the moor. Just a friendly warning from him, "Don't go too far — on warm spring evenings, the mist often comes over the moor very quickly."

"Thank you, we will take care."

We walked hand in hand towards a glowing, golden red sky. The fields were fenced in by shoulder-high stone walls. After a companionable silent walk, Leslie broke the silence and asked, "Why did you not have the guts to say that you would be bored spending a weekend in the country?"

I could not believe what I heard as I had been so excited about it.

"You slept all the way to Richmond."

It took some explaining to convince him that I was happy to be with him anywhere and travelling on buses was like a sleeping drug to me.

Then we rested in a meadow. It was so colourful with primulas, daisies and violets. Leslie noticed the mist coming in over the horizon and suggested that we better make our way home. Then to our horror, a bull came out of the mist, charging towards us. We ran to the nearest stone wall. Leslie had no trouble climbing over it and he then helped to pull me on to the wall. Just seconds later, the bull caught up with us and he ran his head into the wall. We were shaken by this narrow escape, but when we realised we were safe, we laughed and this helped to relax the tension between us. In the mist, the bull looked terrible, black and steaming from his nostrils. We crossed the next field, trying to find the gate or a place where we could once more climb over the stone wall. Now the mist was more like a fog, and we had no idea in which direction we ought to walk. We held hands so as not to lose each other and I teased him, "Come on, aeroplane man, navigate us!"

"Yes," he said, "but there are no stars!"

Hours later, still climbing over walls, we spotted a moving light and we walked towards it. To our relief, it was the road, but now the question was, should we go to the right or left?

When hours later we eventually arrived back at the pub, it was in complete darkness. We had to knock loudly to wake the landlord. Finally, the staircase lights were switched on and the landlady looked through the round glass window in the door, screamed and ran away. The husband came and opened the door and explained why the door was locked. As we were not in the bar, they had taken it for granted that we had retired early. When his wife had seen my face in the window of the entrance door, with mist swirling around, she had thought that I was the ghost who haunted the old pub. When Mrs Tavern noticed that I was shivering with cold, she suggested that I have a hot bath. We explained the reason for our late return. Getting in the bath and relaxing made me feel good. Wrapped up in a large bath towel, I ran the water for Leslie to enjoy a warm bath. My room had wooden beams and I counted them and made a wish. "Oh, please, let me be happy with Leslie."

The door opened and Leslie, in his pyjamas, came in to find out whether I was all right. He went over to the window and looked into the misty distance. I suggested that while we were talking, he should come to bed to keep me and himself warm. He joined me and lay down, holding out his arm for me to snuggle close to him. With my head on his chest my forehead and nose cradled his chin. After a few minutes of blissful happiness, I asked him, "Don't you want to make love to me?"

He made a funny snorting laugh and put his other arm around me. He held me so tight that I could hardly breathe. "Make love to you, woman? I am in love with you. And that's why I won't make love to you. That's what happens on the honeymoon. Most men want to marry a virgin. Yes, men have sex with women, but the one we marry we want to be a virgin. Remember, I am in love with you and I can wait until we are married. If for any reason we should not get married, you would be 'second-hand goods'."

I asked him then just to stay a little longer, when in a gruff voice he replied, "Trudi, I am a man and only human. I can only muster so much self-control and discipline. Good night, and see you at breakfast." Kissing me on the cheek, he jumped out of bed as if the devil was behind him.

At last I could imagine us as husband and wife. I had waited for this moment for a couple of years — the moment when he would commit himself to our future as husband and wife together. I was so happy I could not sleep. I wanted to shout for joy and tell the whole world about it.

Sunday morning was another lovely spring day. We had a full English breakfast, but did not talk much as we were both dreaming about our future. This morning we had a last walk on the moor, keeping strictly to the road. With all the flowers blooming by the roadside, Leslie burst into song, "We'll gather lilacs in the spring again", but the second time round changed the word "lilacs" to "violets". It became our signature tune. A quick snack for lunch and then we caught the local bus to Richmond. We sat on the seats at the back of the bus so that I could see Reeth, the small village with its one pub, one church and about twenty houses, disappear from view. I never returned there again.

This time when I was falling asleep, Leslie offered me his shoulder, but then pinched my arm and I was fully awake. He had a wicked smile and said, "That'll soon cure you of your sleeping sickness."

Once more I was transferred to another kitchen. This was old fashioned, without a central boiler house. Here, each boiler was separately heated by gas. For food that would easily burn, like milk pudding and custard, we used a double-jacket boiler. This meant that water was in the double jacket and this stopped the food from getting burnt.

My new supervisor was a dour Scot aged about 55 years. She was a very experienced caterer who had trained before the First World War at Athol Crescent in Edinburgh, where a certain Lady X and Miss Perry had opened up the Naafi. During lunch hour she would tell fantastic stories about how the two women had tried to train 12 other volunteers and move into the men's domain. This caused confusion and difficulties as the campus was built for men only. Wash houses, lavatories, and so-on were designed only for men. Different suggestions were made to ease the situation, such as using small enamelled bowls for washing and introducing a timeshare for the lavatories. Miss Perry was a good storyteller. She used some funny expressions — for example, an angry person looked like "corned beef tartan", while tough or hard people were described as "hard-boiled turnips".

She was the best supervisor I ever had and she instructed me well. She taught me a very important lesson that I never forgot. On one occasion the senior cook had handled her work badly and I told her off in front of the other staff. Miss Perry stood by and then ordered me into the office. Here she gave me a sharp ticking-off.

"Never tell cook or any other staff member off in front of the other staff; you do that in the office. As the person in charge of staff (25 women), you never use that tone to any other member of staff. If you think you're about to lose your temper, remember this: if you are in the wrong, you cannot afford to lose your temper, but if you are in the right, you can afford to keep it."

I have lived by these three points all my life and if ever I felt as if I was about to lose my temper and shout, I would hear Miss Perry's voice.

During one of our lunch hours, I mentioned that I had been called up and that the Ministry of Labour had directed me to my various jobs, so that I would release a chef who could then join the Forces. Because of my call-up, I had not been able to complete my training. I could not afford it and my parents had thought that as I was holding down a good position, they would not pay for the completion of my course.

Miss Perry was thoughtful for a moment and then made the suggestion that I should apply for a government grant as all the people who were called up and either joined the Forces or worked in munitions factories were entitled to a grant. She said she would help me with the application. I saw no point in this as hopefully I would soon be getting married and leaving Leeds where my college was. Miss Perry thought that I should apply anyway, and should I be offered a grant and decided I no longer wanted it, I could always cancel it.

Life is strange. Just when all my hopes and dreams seemed as if they were about to be fulfilled, the first shadow of unhappiness reared its ugly head. The letters from Leslie became more and more despondent and I wondered what the trouble was. Had he met another woman and did not know how to tell me? Finally, he wrote that he could not settle in his job as he had to train young men from university in various technical skills and radar. Once they completed their training, they were promoted. Leslie brought this to the attention of the supervisor and wondered why he did not get promoted. Here, the senior staff member pointed out that he had no degree. Yet he was teaching and instructing the university-trained members of staff. How could he have a degree as he had gone straight from grammar school into the RAF? That training was his degree. Yes, they agreed with him, but "RAF degree" was not something he could write on an application form.

This was the final straw. He inquired about rejoining the RAF. Yes, but he would lose one promotion. More than ever, disappointment set in. One of his ex-pals from the RAF suggested that he should try and join the New Zealand Air Force. They would welcome him and they would promote him one level up from his demob status. A letter full of enthusiasm arrived. He had the chance to fly to New Zealand or go by boat, so he had booked himself — and me — onto the liner. The sailing time to New Zealand would be our honeymoon.

I read and re-read that letter. I was plunged into turmoil. Should I follow my heart and go with Leslie to New Zealand? Could I leave behind me the new life I had made in England? My parents had had such a hard time making my brother and me safe in England. Could I desert them now? I was brought up with the Fourth Commandment from the Old Testament: "To love and honour thy parents." They might need me when they were older. I realised I could not join Leslie.

My parents had asked me to come home as Mutti had had another operation and needed nursing. As a dutiful daughter, I asked the organiser at the Education Office for a one month's leave of absence from work. This was granted and so I travelled back home.

Then a telegram arrived at home telling me the time of departure of the ship. I would at least see Leslie off and wish him well in his new life. I rushed to my room and started to pack. In two days, Leslie would sail. I had one day to travel down to Southampton and then we could spend a whole day together. My mother gave me a strange look. She offered to polish my shoes and took them down to the kitchen. Soon she returned and pointed out that she would not give me permission to see Leslie off.

Her reasons were, "All the years that you have gone out, you have lived for the day you would get married, and so we had no trouble, no sex, but now, spending a night and day in each other's company, not knowing if and when you will meet again, emotions will run high. Leslie will be New Zealand and you here, perhaps expecting his baby."

An unmarried woman with a baby was the biggest scandal. Mutti would not listen to what I had to say, but walked out and locked the door. I thought I would climb out of my bedroom window, using the sheets from the bed to let myself down. Then I realised that Mutti had deliberately taken away my shoes. The farm was about three-quarters of a mile uphill. We had no telephone so I could not call for a taxi. When the hopeless situation dawned on me, I started banging at the door. I called for someone to let me out and pounded on the door till the sides of my hands were sore and bleeding. I begged and pleaded, "Please let me go." To no avail. I slid down by the door and sobbed my heart out. Finally, cold and shivering, I went to bed and stared into the night. With all my emotion and physical energy spent, I fell asleep. I dreamt that I was standing at the quay and waving goodbye as the ship sailed away. In the morning it was too late to rush out and try to catch up with the ship and I could not swim after it. It was not like a train where if you missed one, you could just catch the next one.

In the morning Mutti opened the door. Desolate, numbed, no thoughts, no emotions, just feeling lost, I started the housework and cooked breakfast. I felt as if

264

I was in another sphere. My mother tried to tell me that in years to come, I would see that her actions were for my own good. Nothing made any sense to me, I was like a soulless person, but years of discipline made me do my work for one day. On the second day, I went and finished the packing I had started before and just said that I would be returning to my job 10 days before the end of my leave of absence. My brother stepped forward and said, "Spätzchen, I will take you to Doncaster in the car. Work can wait."

With a few words I said my goodbyes to my parents. After we had travelled a few miles, I asked my brother why he did not open the door so that I could have gone to Southampton. His reply did not surprise me, knowing how strict my mother could be. She had said to him that if he opened the door, he too could go and leave home. As he did not get paid for working on the farm, he had no money of his own and so could not afford to help. Since Papa had come home from the labour camp, he had left all the disciplining to Mutti. To be fair to her, without her strong beliefs and strict discipline, we would never have survived, either in Germany or here in England.

The first letter I received from Leslie told me that he had had a similar reaction to mine, one of disbelief and disappointment, but still with the hope that I would come. As the ship sailed, he stayed on deck till he could no longer see land. He asked if I could imagine his feelings, being alone in a cabin for two — the honeymoon cabin.

CHAPTER
SIXTEEN

Taking up training again

Derek — Latham Hall

Life went on. Because of the many years of self-discipline, I performed my daily work like a robot — nothing mattered any more.

How does the saying go? Time is a healer. When one is emotionally shattered, one does not believe it, but in order to live on, one slowly puts these memories into a mental box and so shuts them away. That is until some incident happens — it may be a word, a melody, or even a familiar smell — and, like Pandora's box, it opens up and the memories come flooding back and it takes a while to close it again.

One day a letter from the Ministry arrived, notifying me that I was to be given a grant so that I could complete my training. My supervisor, Miss Perry, pointed out how wise I had been to apply for it. Reading the letter carefully, I learnt that the grant covered all expenses as well as a generous allowance for pocket money. I received the same grant as women who worked in munitions factories or were in the Forces. The pocket money was nearly as much as I was earning and I did not have to pay for my digs. It felt like untold wealth to me. This lifted my spirits and I started to look forward to the future again. All I could think of was September, when I could return to college. I asked the Education Authority if I could work until the 15th September, a day before the course started, and applied for leave of absence for 11 months.

Finally the day arrived and as I entered the college building, I met several members of staff who knew me and welcomed me back, hoping that I would enjoy the time there. What a difference from the days when I started my training in 1941. With anticipation I entered the classroom. We were a group of 14 students, six mature ones who had served in the Forces and seven others who came straight from school. I was the only student to join the course in the second year. As the staff greeted me in such a friendly way, the rest of the group accepted me and there were none of the hostile feelings that I had previously experienced. I spent some time revising my notes from the first year, and this time I had no trouble with taking notes from the lectures. All fears of the war were now passed and for the first time in my life, I had enough money so that I could buy a new dress or join in with social functions. It was a different world that I was now in.

Our college dances were well-known and as we were a women's college, we sent open invitations to the different departments of the University — the Medical and Dental Schools, the Engineering Department, and so on — as well as to the men's halls. Many male students accepted the invitation and came to the dances. Food was still rationed, of course, and as we were a domestic and catering college, we were renowned for our tasty buffet food. Of course we realised that many of the male students came for the "nosh" and not for our dazzling beauty. They were at least polite enough to ask us for a dance — a "duty dance" I used to call it.

Once I was sharing a table with some other girls and they had all been asked to dance. Sitting on my own, I felt very self-conscious and decided to help out with the buffet when a young man, who looked like a mature student, came over to me and asked me for a dance. We danced in silence, but I notice that he kept looking at me. After the dance, he escorted me towards my table but suggested that we should sit on our own. We passed by the buffet tables and picked up some snacks and some of our famous fruit punch. As soon as we sat down, he apologised for being so forward, but said he had to ask something: "I must ask you — as you speak with a foreign accent, are you German? It was your blonde hair and blue eyes that attracted me."

The answer was obviously "yes". In the 1940s, women with blonde hair were generally natural blondes as the toning and bleaching you see today was unheard of. He got most excited and carried on the conversation:

"Even during the war, when I was in the Royal Engineers, I told my parents that I wanted to marry a German girl. My parents were horrified. What luck that I met you. My dream can come true."

I laughed and asked if he had had too much fruit punch to drink, but thanked him for his compliment. The music played, but he got a pipe out of his pocket, stuffed it with tobacco and lit it. Puffing away, he started to talk again. The war years had wasted so many years of our lives and now he was going to catch up on time and tell me all about himself. He went on boldly, "I hope that you will like what you hear and like what you see, because I'm going to marry you."

I liked what I saw. He looked like Paul Newman and had a certain magnetism. I just smiled, however, and thought, "He's feeling freedom, now he's away from the discipline of the army, and this is making him talk so wildly." I did not tell him where I lived and simply regarded it as a pleasant evening interlude.

Two days later, the Principal sent for me. Entering her office, I saw this young man. Miss Smith was the new principal. She opened the conversation, saying that this young man, an engineering student, had been trying to find me, and had thought it would not be too difficult to trace me via the college. There could not be too many German girls doing the training. Miss Smith made a formal introduction and said that I would be excused from lectures for that day. My mind was in a spin! I could not believe what was happening to me. We went out together and quickly a whirlwind friendship developed. By Christmas, it had blossomed into romance.

It was all too fast. After the loss of Leslie, my emotions had been in limbo, but Derek got hold of me and aroused the sensation that I was alive again. I was under a spell — it was magical.

During a conversation he mentioned that he had been released from the army to oversee some production in a factory in Coventry and for this he had been made a freeman of the city. In a way this made him a slightly arrogant and he thought he could pass his exams without revising or swotting.

As Christmas drew nearer, I wondered what I could give him as a present. We were talking about sports and he mentioned that he enjoyed playing cricket. So far he had not got a white pullover. So this was my cue. Hour by hour, when not swotting or meeting Derek, I would knit a white cricket pullover, with the neckband in the colours of Leeds University.

Life was so exciting. I was going to the Grand Ball at the University, and it would be a long-dress occasion — the first since the war. I made a beautiful pale blue dress. The needlework teacher fitted it and I would twirl about to get the feel of wearing a long dress. When it was finished, I would try it on again in my room, humming a waltz and swaying to and fro. I felt so glamorous and when on the evening of the dance a gardenia arrived, I was in dreamland. Derek had been singing the song "The girl I shall marry will have to wear a gardenia in her hair."

After the reception Derek gave me his Christmas present. I was amazed. Never before in my life had I ever been given such a precious gift, a large topaz shaped like a dewdrop. I still have this jewel but wear it only on rare occasions. What was happening to me? I

270

was enchanted, bewitched. Only in fairy stories or dreamland did this sort of thing happen. Every so often I would ponder and compare this relationship with the one I had hadwith Leslie. That had been so much steadier and the feelings were so much deeper. I told my parents about this whirlwind romance. They warned me: it is too quick, you are blinded by romance and can see no faults. You are in love with being in love.

The next big event was the weekend after New Year's Eve. Mr Bushell, the father of my best friend, Margaret, worked for the *Yorkshire Post* newspaper and every year the firm held a prestigious ball. Both Derek and I were invited. Derek had arranged for a taxi to pick us both up before the dance and after the dance to take me back to my digs and Derek to his hall. We were a party of nine. Mr Bushell was an extra man. For this dance, Derek presented me with an orchid. We were all in a happy party mood, and Mr Bushell asked me for a dance — a waltz, my favourite — and we danced round and round. At this point I was so happy I could have danced all night. When we returned to our table, Derek was missing. Ah well, he must have asked someone else for dance, but he did not reappear for several dances. When he returned, he told me that he had been dancing with a woman who was on her own. She was separated from her husband and as he had given her the ticket before they parted, she thought she would use it. The tickets were only available to staff working at the *Yorkshire Post* or by special invitation.

When the time was nearing midnight, Derek said, "I'm afraid we have to walk home — you don't mind,

271

do you?" I certainly did mind! Three miles to Headingley in a long dress and wearing dancing sandals with snow on the ground! The reason we had to walk was that he had offered this woman our taxi as she had been unable to pre-book one and had left a young child alone in the house. Angrily, I suggested that he might as well see this woman home and I would share a taxi with the Bushells — Margaret and her father — who also lived in Headingley. A chink had appeared in my enchanted evening. A happy fairy-tale had developed cold icicles. My thoughts went round in circles. Somehow my feelings could not come to terms with his behaviour. I had never been treated like this. Often I wondered if he had in fact seen that woman home — and stayed the night. I never asked him as I could not face up to his answer.

The next big social event was the Valentine's Day dance in his hall. Since I had worn my evening dress for several occasions, I asked Derek if he liked off-the-shoulder dresses as this would save material and, therefore, cloth coupons. Definitely not! He did not like the idea that other men could see his partner's skin and shoulders. So I chose a pattern with a rounded yoke and made this in net material. No coupons were needed for net and it covered my shoulders.

Still seeing the world through rose-tinted spectacles and looking forward to Valentine's Day, I rushed to the hall and signed in at the Porter's Lodge. Our party consisted of 10 people and we all enjoyed dancing, and would change partners for some dances. After midnight, someone suggested that we go to Eddie's room for a drink. Eddie's girl was wearing a very revealing dress, with a low-cut neckline and very low back and no sleeves. My Derek, who had insisted that I showed no bare flesh, sat next to Eddie's girl and kept touching her and running his hands up and down her back and arms, saying "What beautiful shoulders, what beautiful skin!" Eddie and I just looked at each other, not knowing what to say to this behaviour. This was a rude awakening for me. If Derek could behave like this, ignoring his partner at such an early stage of courting days, how would he behave as a husband after a few years of marriage?

I felt miserable, but common sense had to prevail. After this dance, I made 101 excuses for not being able to meet him. I had to catch up with my studies. He called me a "sparrow brain" — "people who have to study and swot should not be on a college or university course." I pointed out that I was still learning many new words in English and had to cope with the subject in a second language. Feeling hurt and let down, I said to him, "I hope you fail your exam. You are far too arrogant and it might make you into a normal human being."

When the exam results came out, I, the sparrow brain, had a first-class pass, while Derek had failed. He came round to see me and told me that in his mind he heard my voice all the time saying "I hope you fail". As it was his second year finals, he could not resit the exam till the next year and he would have to retake the third term as well as the exam. His grant was stopped and if he wanted to complete his training, he had to earn enough money to see him through the last term of the second year.

Some time later, one Friday morning when I was back at work, I was going into Leeds to collect the wages for the women when I met Derek by chance on the bus. He was a different person, not so bombastic, and he explained that in order to earn enough money for one term's expenses, he had worked as a coal miner underground. After that he realised that life is not always a bowl of cherries and can be very hard if you are short of money. We parted on friendly terms and I wished him well, saying that I was sure he would pass the exam this time, now that he realised how essential hard work and revision were.

My year of luxury was coming to its end. The grant had been generous and for the first time in my life I had been able buy new clothes and join in any activities I wanted to — the odd theatre show or dance. Then I looked at my bank statement and was horrified to see that I had spent all the money. Going back to my job and knowing that the salary I earned barely paid for the living expenses and that we got paid monthly, I worried about how on earth I was going to manage without ending up in debt or, if I did, how would I pay it back?

On the college notice board was a letter from the NUS (National Union of Students) asking for students to help with getting the harvest in or to help run an international camp for students helping with the harvest. The pay for working and running the camp was good and did not depend on the weather for the harvesting of the crops. If I did not spend any of the

274

money I earned, I would have just enough. I was too proud to ask for help from my parents, who after all these years were finally winning through their own money troubles.

I applied for a cook's job and the NUS informed me that because of my catering experience, they were allocating me to Lathom Hall, Ormskirk, near Liverpool, cooking for 200 international students. I left my good clothes with Mrs Phyer and just took overalls and suitable gear for working. While travelling by train to Ormskirk, I tried to imagine Lathom Hall — it sounded so grand.

At the station the ticket collector told me that a bus passed by the Hall. Full of excitement I waited for the bus driver to tell me when I had to get off. It was right in the country, no houses near by and when I got off, I faced an imposing arched gate and a long drive leading up to the Hall. It looked just like a castle. I walked along the drive and as I got nearer, I realised that it was a ghostly burned-out shell of a building. I hesitated and wondered if I should turn round and walk away. As I was trying to weigh up the situation, a lorry sped towards me with lots of young people sitting in the back of it. As they spotted me, they waved and shouted a welcome, and, thus encouraged, I walked past the Hall and on into the grounds. Here, I saw many, many tents and two large marquees, together with several smaller ones. Looking around, I noticed a prefabricated hut with a notice on the door saying "Office". Wondering what to expect, I knocked at the door and met the organiser and assistant organiser for the camp.

They explained the layout of the camp. On one side were tents for the men, three or four to a tent. The women's tents were separated from them by two large marquees. Everybody was issued with palliasses and blankets. The students brought their own sleeping bags made of cotton, nothing so luxurious as the padded ones available nowadays.

The staff tents were by the side of the Hall. We had the luxury of camp beds and only two girls per tent. There were two smaller marquees, one each for the male and female toilets and wash houses. The large marquees were for the meals and social activities. The staff used the toilets in the Hall as their washroom. This part of the Hall still had a roof, so we passed the storerooms, used for blankets and food, and went on to the kitchen. Here was the familiar sight of an Aga stove and a couple of tables. Hugh, the organiser, explained how he ran the camp, pointing to a list and a timetable for the students as a voluntary help in the kitchen. Four of them would help with the preparation of food, washing up utensils used, cleaning down the tables in the large marquee and keeping it tidy. The floor was a lawn! The students working in the kitchen would lose a day's earnings, and often they would try to swap their kitchen duty with a student suffering from backache from picking up potatoes — they would then share the earnings between them. Students earned at different rates, depending on how fast they could fill a sack of potatoes. Each sack was weighed and at the end of the day, each student was paid according to the total amount they had weighed in.

After the evening meal, four of the volunteer students would prepare and make sandwiches for the next day's packed lunches to be taken into the fields. For two hundred students, each getting two double sandwiches meant eight hundred slices of bread. Up to then, I had never valued sliced bread, but now I could see the benefits. The sandwiches were stored on large trays and next morning each student would collect their sandwiches and keep them in a sandwich tin. There was no refrigeration, but the storeroom in the Hall was quite cold. However, this made it difficult to think up fillings in hot weather.

To pay for their food and accommodation (the use of tents and blankets), the students had to pay out of what they earned by picking peas or potatoes. Hugh pointed out that the previous week they had overspent and run the account into debt. I had to try and make a profit, and to balance the books I had to find simple and cheap recipes.

Breakfast was at 7a.m. As previously, when I had to cook using Aga stoves, I would cook the porridge overnight and also heat the water urns. They would be nearly boiling when we started to cook at 6a.m. The menu was porridge, something fried, toast and marmalade. My assistants would make the toast, grilled on top of the stove.

Anyone used to modern high standards of hygiene would be shocked to see how the students washed their plates and dishes. Two large zinc baths filled with hot water were put out. One was for washing utensils and had washing soda added to it; the other was for rinsing in. When the water was dirty, it was replaced with fresh hot water.

The first morning the Aga stove was barely hot, so my next task was to clean all the flues. Eventually I got the Aga into full working order and was able to produce good quality food for the students. After the third evening meal, some strong male students picked me up and paraded me up and down the marquee, chanting "At last, edible food."

Hugh kept strict control and ran the camp with military discipline. Anybody who did not adhere to his rules would be asked to leave the camp. Sometimes there were about 15 different nationalities. These foreign students came to England as part of their experience in a foreign country. It was often a requirement of their course if they wanted to gain a degree in their home country. Most students stayed for two or three weeks and then moved on to another camp.

Saturday night was the highlight. An impromptu concert held in the large marquee. Students performed dances, played instruments and sang songs, all with the theme of their own homeland. This was 1948, and we were amazed at the different cultures. Nowadays, with television and global travel, people are quite used to experiencing other cultures, but for us, it was an eye opener.

When I applied for this post, I never, never thought that some of the students might be Germans. So when I came face-to-face with them, I found it very difficult to know how to handle my emotions. At dinner time I

278

gave the serving spoon to one of the volunteer helpers and walked away. I ran to my tent, where I gave way to my emotions — for the first time in my life, I cried and kicked and beat the air. Here were people from Germany, the very people that caused me so much pain and heartbreak in my childhood, the people who had forced me to leave Germany and journey into the unknown.

When I recovered from my first fierce reaction, I decided to be cold and indifferent to them, never to let them know of my background. After about a fortnight, the day came when two of the kitchen volunteers were German students — I would have to work with them all day. I remember them clearly, a boy and girl. They worked well and after lunch they approached me asking whether they had done something wrong because they were aware of my cold indifference. It was the first time that I looked at them as people and not as Germans — the "nasties" — and I realised that they were younger than I was and therefore had been small children when the trouble in my life started. For the rest of the day I tried hard to smile and talk to them as I would to anyone else. As a matter of fact, when the assistant cook left, and no replacement was sent, the girl, Gisela, volunteered for this job. During the time I spent at the camp when I met so many Germans, my bitterness and dislike — no, hatred and loathing — ebbed away and I could listen to the German students singing folksongs and enjoy them. This often caused my thoughts to fly back to the past and awakened memories associated with happier days.

Meeting these different Germans, I found that most of them were kind and friendly, but then a new batch of students arrived, slightly older than me whose attitude was, "We may have lost the war, but by no means are we defeated." When they came up for their meal or sandwiches, I wanted to shout at them, "Don't expect the kid-glove treatment. No, I feel like throwing stones at you, pulling your hair and kicking you as you are the type that did this to me when I was 10 years old." Having lived in England these many years, I have learned moderation and compassion.

If a student wanted to work extra long hours and therefore needed their evening meal at about 9p.m., they had to notify me so that I could keep a meal for them. Any surplus food was given out as second helpings. Two of these new German students came to the camp late one evening, well after 9p.m. and wanted some food. They had not signed for a late meal and so no food had been saved for them. I offered to sauté some potatoes and fry an egg for them. Remember, I had been on duty since 6a.m. and by now it was well after 9 o'clock in the evening. As an alternative to the sautéed potatoes, I offered some sandwiches. This did not seem to be to their liking as they demanded that I should give them more attention and they started swearing. Well, my moderate good-natured bubble burst and I spoke to them in German, telling them that their manners were uncouth and offensive, and before I got any food ready for them, they had better apologise. Rules were made in order to have a smooth-running camp and if they did not like these regulations, it would be advisable for them to transfer to another camp. They were very surprised that I could understand them speak German. I laughed at that and pointed out that some students in England studied foreign languages. These two students later requested that they be moved to another camp.

Every Saturday night there was an impromptu concert, lasting well past midnight. It was another world. So much culture was new to us. I too wanted to watch these concerts and would stay up, giving myself only a few hours' sleep. I soon got into a state of sleepwalking. Someone suggested that I ought to try and smoke and that this would help me stay awake. This did seem to work and within a week I was a chain-smoker. Then it dawned on me that I was working seven days a week and anything between 14 and 16 hours a day, killing myself to earn enough money to see me through the first month of my employment. Instead, I was puffing all that hard-earned money straight into the air. What a foolish act. I asked for some time off and slept for 24 hours. It cured my smoking habit and I never touched another cigarette in my life.

One night, when there was a full moon, I retired to my tent and took myself to bed. The storm lantern was burning low. The other girl I shared the tent with had not yet come in. Suddenly a woman entered the tent. She had sheets wrapped round her like a Grecian lady. It was rather mystical, and I kept saying, "Jenny, stop messing around." This apparition walked past me and out of the tent, straight through the tent wall. Then

Jenny came into the tent and faithfully promised that she had not played a trick on me. Exactly the same thing happened the following night. This time I told Hugh, the organiser, about it and he replied that I was the first person to see the lady of the manor. On the estate was a small chapel, still in use, and I talked to the priest about it. He said that I had described "her Ladyship". Every full moon, she walks from the burnt-out shell of the Hall to the tree from which she hanged herself. The priest told me the sad story and concluded that my tent must be in the path to that tree. The story goes as follows: the Lord of the Manor and his friends were riding away for a lustful night in an inn, where his Lordship was to meet his mistress. His wife could no longer take this way of life and she set fire to the Hall. Once it was burning fiercely, she walked to the tree and hanged herself. When his Lordship saw the bright light in the sky, he realised that the Hall was burning. He jumped on his horse and rode as fast as he could homewards, calling out his wife's name. He galloped into the burning Hall to rescue her. Both master and horse burned to death. Apparently, if you slept in the Hall on the night of a full moon, you could hear the master calling and the horse galloping. Strangely, no one ever volunteered to spend those crucial nights inside the Hall. My bed and tent must have been in her path. I moved both a couple of yards and I never saw the ghostly apparition again.

My friend Margaret (whom I met at college in 1942) showed an interest in how these camps were run, so I invited her to come and work as a pea-picker. For weeks I had not had any time off apart from those 24 hours for sleeping, and I asked Hugh whether I could have the following Monday off as we were planning a trip to the Lake District, being on that side of England. The plan was to walk, take a bus or even hitch-hike, but not once did we put out a thumb to ask for a lift. We found that wearing a college blazer and carrying a rucksack, drivers would stop and ask us if we wanted a lift. Two Norwegian students and I had formed a friendship and so the four of us set off together. We also decided that if the four of us could not get a lift together, then we would go in twos, one boy and one girl, and meet at the Youth Hostel. First we took a bus to see us on our way into the country and then Per, one of the Norwegian boys, thought we should try for a lift. Margaret and I laughed and suggested that the boys could do this if they liked. Fine! Per saw a car coming. He took his student cap off in salute and made a continental bow, and only then did he put out his thumb. Like magic, even though the car had passed us slightly, it stopped, reversed and the driver asked us where we were heading for. Most drivers were ex-Forces chaps, many of whom were now working as travelling reps. They looked forward to having some company and also liked to do something in return for the many lifts they had had during the war. He offered all four of us a lift, if we could squeeze in. The rep enjoyed our lively company so much that he offered to take us to a café and buy us afternoon tea. In the end he took us two thirds of the way to the Lake District. Having thanked him for his hospitality, we waved goodbye. The next car came. The same routine: cap off, bow, then the thumb. No trouble at all. The car stopped and again the driver was happy to give all four of us a lift. We arrived much earlier in Windermere than we had expected. The boys were thrilled with the landscape as it reminded them of home. The Sunday return journey was similar, and we were delivered to right outside Lathom Hall. I asked the boys, "Why the routine with taking the cap off and so on?" They explained their actions like this. "You don't say, 'Hey, give me a lift', but you ask courteously for a lift by your actions: Cap off — 'How do you do?' The bow — 'please would you . . . ' — the thumb — ' . . . give me a lift?'."

Helping to run the camp was a great experience and meeting so many students of different nationalities taught me that each nation has its own culture and pride in it.

CHAPTER
SEVENTEEN

In charge of
my own kitchen

Soon my time at Lathom Hall came to an end. I left it gladly, happy to return to civilisation and the luxury of a bath, but I also had a feeling of satisfaction and achievement as I had earned enough money to see me through the first month at work until my first pay cheque arrived. Miss Perry and her staff were pleased to see me again. Nothing had really changed. It was like a dream that I had been absent for a year, a year filled with many new and happy moments to be stored in my memory for those later times when I might be old and alone. In order to have my diploma endorsed, I had to work under senior supervision. The years prior to that year's training did not count.

As much as I enjoyed my work, I was wishing and hoping to manage a kitchen of my own. It would be a smaller one than cooking for 2500 children. After 10 months, my wish was granted. I was appointed to manage and control the canteen of a girls' high school, cooking for 500, with meals in two sittings, and generally seeing to the smooth running of the dining room. This was relatively easy for me as I had had plenty of experience of school kitchens during the war. Two teachers were always on duty to direct the girls to their tables and to ensure general discipline.

Watching the staff carefully to understand their working methods, I decided that it would be to my advantage if I worked with each cook so that they handled the food as I wanted, starting with the senior cook, then the meat cook, and finally the sweet (dessert) cook. Vegetables, gravy and custard were the duty of the extra cook, who also acted as relief if one of the others was absent from work or if one of the cooks was running late with serving the food. It worked well, and just looking out of my office window facing the kitchen, I could always see how the preparation and cooking were progressing. My staff had to collect plates and cutlery, and wash these up, and also wipe down the dining room tables.

To work out how many staff I was allowed was based on a certain number of working hours per hundred meals and I had to calculate how to allocate these. The time was based on minimum or maximum allowance, and having worked in several different kitchens, I learnt the effect it could have on staff if several members were absent. Using the minimum hour scheme had the advantage that if one member of staff was absent, I could ring head office for emergency help. The women could not understand why I had no trouble in requesting extra staff.

Sometimes after lunch, some schoolgirls would come to see me and a friendly relationship developed between us. Every so often a funny incident would happen that amused me. For example, checking on the girls' table manners, I noticed that one pretty girl would eat her peas by scooping them up with a knife which she then lifted above her mouth so that the peas rolled neatly into it. Very delicately executed. So as not to make the girl feel embarrassed when correcting this habit, I suggested that she should be careful not to cut her tongue. She smiled sweetly and replied that only those people who did not use the knife correctly would cut or damage their tongue. How on earth do you answer a reply like that?

One day I read an advertisement in a newspaper asking for volunteers to train as catering instructors. Before the war, chefs were mostly French and this caused a great shortage of people with catering experience. I always want to teach and I thought that now my ultimate dream could be fulfilled. The advertisement stated that person applying should have qualifications in the subject and, if accepted, would be taught teaching methods for Further Education. I applied.

Now I had to prepare myself in case I was invited for an interview. When in 1942 I had applied to train as a domestic science teacher, the principal offered me a catering course instead as my pronunciation was still so foreign. Now I decided to arrange elocution lessons to prepare myself. I was lucky to arrange private lessons at the College of Drama where the tutor was a war correspondent now working with the BBC. Unfortunately, I have no aptitude in mimicking other people's speech.

My teacher used to walk up and down the room, his hands hitting his head in frustration at the difficulty of getting me to change the way I spoke. He complained, "With your German, and now a slightly Yorkshire accent, how on earth can I change movement of your tongue?" I loved the story of *Pygmalion*, but there the heroine was able to adapt easily, yet I persevered and never gave up.

Work ran smoothly, but two events stick out, taking their place in my box of memories.

The meat cook, Mrs Luke, told me that her party, the Labour Party, had invited 40 German children for three weeks. They were either orphans or had lost their homes during the war. They were very young children, between the age of 4 and 8 years. I offered to help so that the children would settle, but the people who offered a home to them thought that they would manage better with sign language as none of the children spoke English and the hosts could not speak German.

It was a very generous gesture as food including bread, was still rationed in 1948, , and the hosts were not getting extra allowances or coupons. They planned a Christmas party for the children, hoping to show them how English people celebrated this festive season. Mrs Luke wondered if I would like to come to the party. I asked the members of my staff if they could donate something towards it and they did me proud, bringing in a jelly square, blancmange powder, a little butter and sugar, and even some sweets, and the odd dried egg to make a cake. Mrs Luke was delighted with these gifts and other party members had also collected food. On the great day I met these young children with their pale faces and enormous frightened eyes. They looked at the table with all this party food and, even though they were invited by gesture to sit down and tuck in, they just stared at the food but would not touch it. I explained, in German, that it was specially made for them to enjoy, but the oldest child whispered to me that it was poisoned. Puzzled, I asked what gave them this idea. They explained that they had been shown pictures of Father Christmas and told that he brings gifts. Now I understood the reason for their fear as the word "Gift" in German means poison. They still doubted that the food was edible, so I suggested that they point out which of the foods I should taste. The hosts looked on in disbelief, when they saw me munching and sampling the foods, so I quickly explained the reason for this. Again, the eldest children pointed out that they were in England, the enemy country that had destroyed their homes and killed their parents. I had to choose my words carefully, to reassure them that we were friends and not foes. At last, they showed signs that they trusted me and the feast, and tucked in, enjoying sausage rolls and mince pies which they had never eaten before.

One child whispered to another that we were fattening them up before the kill, like in the fairy stories, such as Hansel in the story of "Hansel and Gretel". At that moment Father Christmas came into the room carrying a big sack over his shoulders. He sat down by the Christmas tree, opened his sack, and one by one the children had to go to him to collect a present. They hugged the teddy bears and dolls, the toy engines and cars. By now everybody was happy and as the children had enjoyed the food and presents, there was a happy ending to their visit to this country. I mentioned that it would be very nice if they could show their appreciation for the weeks in England and the party by singing a Christmas carol. They were very emotional and just nodded their heads in agreement. The older ones were so shy and the younger ones had not been taught to sing carols. In despair I mentioned "O Tannenbaum" ("Oh Christmas tree, how green are your leaves"). Several of the children knew this, so I started it and slowly, one by one, the others joined in. Then a loud roar went up from the hosts as they clapped and cheered. Like frightened little mice, the children ran to the nearest corner of the room, or hid under the table, whispering, "They're going to hurt us now." I too had been taken by surprise by this loud cheering. It took a little while to calm down and so I asked Mrs Luke for an explanation. Simple, she said. Unknowingly we had chosen the Labour Party anthem. I often wondered whether any of these children remembered their English Christmas and if they ever visited England again.

The other occasion did not have such a happy outcome. The staff were happy working for me and knew that they could come to me with any problems and that we would discuss them. When it came to holidays, staff had to tell me when they would be absent and I also had to plan the time each member of staff had to come in to do a thorough spring-clean. Certain conditions were laid down by the Education

Authority. During holidays, for example, the staff received retainer payments but had to return before the term started in order to clean the ovens and get the equipment ready to start working again. If they did not adhere to this, they would forfeit the holiday payment — 3 to 4 weeks at Christmas, 3 to 4 weeks at Easter, and then the long 8 to 10 weeks' holiday in the summer. Weeks before each holiday, I would discuss the times and how they would fit in with each staff member's plans. I would then send a timetable to the head office. Changing the day with another staff member caused difficulty with the insurance cover.

The day before the Easter holiday started, I overheard Mrs Luke making arrangements with another woman to come in, in her place, so that Mrs Luke could have some extra days' holiday. The person was going to sign in for her. Mr Luke, it seems, had booked a family holiday in Jersey and she would not be back in time. I was a little put out as I had spent hours trying to accommodate everybody's wishes and fit their holiday time in. I asked Mrs Luke to see me in the office as I was puzzled why she had not come to see me as soon as she realised that she could not keep up with the timetable. Immediately she went on the defensive and pointed out that her husband had booked the holiday and there was nothing I could do about it. Her attitude was very offensive as she pointed out that I could do nothing to stop her. Fair enough, but if she took those two days off, she would forfeit her retainer pay. Immediately she started shouting at me, "How dare you tell me what I can do. You are a bloody

German. My husband is a policeman and he will tell you what you can do. No Jerry is controlling our holiday", followed by more swear words and verbal abuse. I was speechless, stunned, shocked, and thought how thin the veneer of harmony at work was, if a woman complaining had to involve her husband in this way. Her action was so aggressive that the other women heard her shouting at me and repeating, "How dare you tell me what to do."

At first I was going to speak to her angrily, but then in my subconscious mind, I heard my last supervisor's voice telling me, "If you are in the wrong, you cannot afford to lose your temper, and if you are in the right, you can afford to keep it." Bearing this in mind, I rang the Head Office and the organiser there explained clearly the conditions that applied if you wanted to keep your 3½ weeks retainer pay — which amounted to half your salary. This seemed to irritate her even more, and with another volley of verbal abuse, she turned round and walked out. It was difficult to take in this abuse; not even during the war had I ever been accused like this.

All the women had stopped work and stood silently. My thoughts were, "We must get the meal cooked", and so I rearranged the work Mrs Luke did as meat cook. The rest of the day the staff stayed silent — it was as if a spell had been cast over the kitchen. Next morning, her husband rang up to find out the cause of the trouble. I pointed out that as a policeman, he would understand that rules and regulations have to be adhered to and that his wife had lost her decorum and had been very abusive towards me. Immediately he interrupted me and apologised for his wife's behaviour, remarking that he knew only too well that his wife suffered from an uncontrolled temper. "Please don't dismiss her as she really likes working for you. I shall make sure that she returns to work as arranged."

There was a certain amount of tension the day Mrs Luke returned to work, but after a few days, the normal happy atmosphere returned.

The next important event occurred when a letter from the government arrived. I looked at it, turned it over, wondering what news it contained. Would it change my life and my work?

CHAPTER
EIGHTEEN

1950–51 London

Teacher training — Meeting the king and queen — Appointment in Cambridge

During my life, I had learned to wait, but this time I was very impatient and found it more difficult than ever before. Waiting, just waiting for this letter from London that could change my life and fulfil my dream of becoming a teacher. In 1941, when I applied to the college in Leeds for teacher training, the Principal told me that I had no chance as my English was not good enough. Now, nine years later, I tried again as there was a shortage of technical teachers and had been invited to sit a one-day examination and interview. This letter would tell me whether I had passed the examination. If I had passed, it would open the doors for me. If I had failed, that would mean the destruction of my dreams, my ambition, for ever.

The examination had been a strange one. For the first three-quarters of an hour we had an IQ test. Until then, I had never seen one like it. We had to work out shapes and designs and find the odd one out. At first, I just sat and stared at the pages, but then suddenly it clicked and I hurried to make up for lost time. As for the next paper, I could see no correlation with this examination. The paper consisted of 100 names. We had to state their profession and our reaction to that person. The list contained authors, actors, chefs, scientists, politicians. Again we had to beat the clock and so I picked the names that I found easiest — Einstein, Emstein, Epstein. I remember that we discussed this at lunch time and the others laughed at me when I told them about my reaction to Ingrid Bergman. It was the time when she had caused a scandal, leaving her husband and children and going to live with the lover, the father of her unborn child. The way I remembered her best was in the film, *Escape to Happiness*, and so I put this. Adolf Hitler was also mentioned. I wrote: "Dictator." I had no second thoughts and condemned him for his brutal regime.

Then came an English test for half an hour. After lunch we were divided into groups of ten people and were given a subject to discuss. An HMI sat with each group and took notes. The subject was: "Is it important and necessary for the teacher to be an expert in the subject he wants to teach?" After a while the HMI suggested that we have a break and decide whether any of us wanted to change our minds. All but three of us suggested that a good knowledge is better than being an expert. As we were leaving the room, the HMI remarked that she agreed with the majority. The other two changed their minds, but I stuck to my decision. Then the question came as to why I insisted on my opinion. I gave Beethoven as an example. An expert in playing the piano, he simply could not teach scales to a beginner. He was well beyond this point, while a person with a sound knowledge of the subject, able to impart the basics, would make a better teacher.

Finally, in July, the long-awaited letter arrived. I looked at the envelope, turning it this way and that, hoping that it would give me a hint of the news it held. At last I took a deep breath and opened it with trembling fingers, knowing that my future depended on it. Unfolding it, I read the first sentence, which informed me that the Authority was pleased to offer me a place at the North Western Polytechnic. My heart raced — I jumped up and down like a schoolgirl, I was so happy and delighted. Then reality flashed through my happiness as I wondered whether I could afford it. I had saved every penny I could during the last year, but would it be enough? I read on and it gave details of the course. As I had stated that I would prefer to live in, it informed me that I would share a large house just off Primrose Hill, near the entrance to Regent's Park Zoo. "Report at 9a.m., 17th September 1950, at the college". To break my emotional tension, I laughed. Reading on, the government grant being offered did not seem sufficient, but then it went into details, stating that accommodation and food were included and any extra expenses, such as travelling to visit places necessary for the course, textbooks, etc., would be reimbursed. So the actual money was pocket money. This worked out to more money than I was earning. I was so excited that my dream of becoming a teacher might become reality. Reading on, certain conditions were laid down and we had to sign these to qualify for the grant:

1. If we did not complete the course, or if we were expelled because of ill discipline, we would have to pay back every penny the course had cost the government up to that point
Exception: if ill health prevented the completion of the course.
2. We had to seek teaching employment for three years not in schools, but in colleges only in the subject we were going to be trained for.

I could not see that these rules would cause a problem and I signed the contract gladly.

Now came the time to sort out my bits and pieces that I had collected over the years and I asked my parents if they would store these till I finished my course.

During those last few months up to September, my emotions were in turmoil. One moment I was up in the clouds and the next I was fearful, wondering whether I was doing the right thing, quitting a good, secure job and leaving Leeds, where I had blended in and felt at home. Also, my parents were worried that I was throwing away all I had achieved. These thoughts and doubts kept creeping up on me. Finally, the moment arrived when I said goodbye to friends and colleagues, and to my parents. "London, here I come!" It was the first time that I had travelled from Leeds to King's Cross station since the war. It was a very different

London from the one I remembered. The station was not crowded with men and women in the Forces; there were no blackout restrictions. It was a sparkling and shining London. 1950. It was Festival Year. Even the tube stations were shiny clean. New tiles on the walls. Remembering the tube lines, I boarded a train for Baker Street and then on to Swiss Cottage. From there I walked to the address.

It was a large villa, slightly war damaged, and my room-mate had already arrived and claimed the bed nearest the window. Valerie came from Manchester and, while chatting to see whether we had anything in common, we realised that we both had the same catering qualification. We were a foil for each other. She was tall and slender, with lovely dark eyes and hair. Talking about the years between our training and up to that point, I discovered that she had been in the WRNS. We were to become firm friends.

The house was so big that we were ten women sharing it, always two women to a bedroom. It was most interesting that the other girls had studied different subjects to us — secretarial training, dress design and dressmaking, English, dramatic art. Our room had two desks in it and bookcases as well as a wardrobe, dressing table and wash basin. We all had to share the bathroom.

We went to another house for our meals. Matron showed us over this. A large dining room and lounge downstairs and upstairs a dormitory, the sick bay and Matron's own flat. Then she explained that there were forty seats in the dining room as the complex was composed of two houses for the women and two for the men. After dinner, we assembled in the lounge for coffee and this was when Matron gave us the house rules.

Next morning, equipped with a small map, we walked to Camden Town and assembled in the lecture hall. We were greeted by different members of staff. The Principal made a welcome speech and pointed out that we were guests at the college as the one for us had not been completed in time. We were 100 students, chosen out of 1000 who had applied for the course.

Timetables were handed out and then we split up into groups according to our specialist subject. Mine was catering. Others were printers, solicitors, engineers, business studies. General subjects, such as teaching techniques, educational history, psychology, etc., we shared in the main lecture hall.

My group consisted of three chefs and nine women. Most of the women had an institutional bias to their catering skills. It was very interesting to find out about the different catering background the chefs had. They were apprenticed and worked for hotels. Their skills were better and they were quicker at chopping and slicing vegetables, but they lacked the knowledge about nutrition, cooking theory, bookkeeping, etc. that we had. When they gave a morning demonstration, though, we all sat up and admired their working technique. Cooking is cooking, and involves using the same recipes, but there was no way we could compete with their practical skills and experience. Valerie and I discussed this and joined an evening class for hotel cooking. As we settled in, some of us tried to find our way about London, seeing some of the sights I had heard about — Buckingham Palace, the Thames, famous art galleries, and so on. After one dinner, sitting relaxing in the lounge and drinking coffee, I suggested that we could form a group to see these sights, helping each other to find our way about in London. There was a silence and one of the 20 men in Hall laughed and made a joke: "The Jerries lost the war, but it looks as if they want to take over here in London."

It felt like a slap in my face. I had expected that during the war, but this was 1950. After my suggestion, they arranged group outings, but I never joined any of them.

Fortunately, I had met a day student, Nigel, who was in the printers' section. Another girl, also a day student from my catering group, showed a keen interest in him, so I backed off. This aroused his interest and he wanted to know the reason for it. He wondered if he had said something to upset me. My answer was a simple one. No, but I didn't want to rush in where angels fear to tread, and I mentioned how the students in the Hall made sure that I was put in my place. After this, he made a point of looking out for me in the lecture room, and so began a friendship and romance.

After half-term, I revealed to Nigel that I thought that I might have to leave the course as I was finding it very hard to cope with the educational psychology. There were too many new words and I could not manage to keep up with the note-taking. The result was that I did not know how to write the weekly essays. I had very low marks for them and I felt that if I stayed any longer, I would have to pay back too much money to the Authority. His advice was, "Give yourself a chance and I'll help you." He offered to lend me his rough notes the next day and at break time, he would explain any words I did not understand. He even let me read his homework so that I could see what was expected. Oh, what a lifeline that proved to be. Without his help, I would never have passed the course.

Nigel and I started to meet at the weekends, sometimes during Saturdays and if the study time allowed, we would also meet on Sundays. Nigel was a Londoner and he showed the city to me. So that there would be no embarrassment about money, we agreed that each of us would pay our own share. Only on special occasions would we treat each other. I started to love London and felt that it started to belong to me too. At night, when I remembered our outings, or even when I was sitting next to him during a lecture, I would visualise his face. Dark curly hair and very dark eyes. When he looked at me, I felt he could read my thoughts. He was just a little taller than I was. Being near him, I felt warm and secure. Yet right at the beginning of our friendship, he said something rather strange to me. "Don't become too fond of me, it will cause you heartache." Why did he warn me? I tried to puzzle it out, but could not find an answer to this. He was not married.

We went out every Saturday to an afternoon performance and, on rare occasions, also on Friday night. On Saturday mornings we would queue for that day's performance at the theatre, to see an opera at Covent Garden, or a ballet. It became my "Festival Year". It was the most wonderful year of my life, a year that shaped my future, a year that I never forgot. It was wonderful to share all this beauty, all the bright lights and gorgeous costumes — the theatre sparkled and shone, making each performance very special.

We loved to walk along the Thames Embankment and would stop by Cleopatra's Needle, leaning on the wall. The way we expressed our affection for each other would, in modern days, be smiled upon as rather tame, but watching the Thames flow by and listening to the military band playing in the background, we would hold hands or have arms and shoulders touching. We were in our own emotional world . . .

We would walk through the different parks and on Hampstead Heath, where we exchanged our first kiss. It was heaven on earth. I felt as if I could embrace the world!

Sometimes we travelled to Wendover and walked in the beech woods. His mother was very kind and would pack a tasty picnic for us. Life was wonderful.

Certain theatre performances stand out, such as the ballet in the New Festival Hall, with Margot Fonteyn in *Swan Lake, Sleeping Beauty* and many others too numerous to mention, but I soon realised that I preferred classical ballet to the modern style. I think *Checkmate* was one of the few modern ballets I enjoyed. We would queue for hours for tickets in the gods, sitting on benches with so little leg room that at the interval all we wanted to do was to stand up and

302

stretch. Festival year. Every performer did more than their best. It was Britain's big festival and for us at the weekends, it was music, music. Music held us enthralled.

Going to Covent Garden and watching the operas. So many of them. But after seeing and hearing them on that large stage with the wonderful acoustic, provincial productions seemed amateurish! Even up in the gods on our cramped benches, our hearts and emotions were stirred, and I would shed a few tears.

One particular performance stands out more vividly than all the others. I had booked tickets for Wagner's *Ring* Cycle. We had seen the first three operas in the cycle, but not the last one, *Götterdämmerung*. We realised that we could not go to this performance as a special lecture was laid on. So as not to waste the money (those seats cost 2s 6d — a lot of money for us), I went to the box office and asked if they would sell the tickets for me. The answer was "No", but they suggested that if I came on the day, I would find many people wanting to buy them. This was impossible, because of the lecture. A man standing near me overheard the conversation. He was keen to buy or exchange them — his tickets were for a week later. It was a special extra performance. I thought that it would be nice, but my tickets were the cheapest in the house, while his were in the circle which we could not afford. Amazingly, the gentleman was happy just to exchange them.

We arrived early for this performance as we wanted to savour sitting in those plush seats. The opera was magical, performed as Wagner intended it, with legendary figures from Germanic mythology. The Rhine maidens were mermaids. There was Wotan, the dragon and the Valkyries. Walhalla was heaven. At the end of *Götterdämmerung*, Walhalla collapses and falls burning into the Rhine. That's not how it is usually performed nowadays. Walhalla may be a factory, with Wotan as the factory manager, the Rhine as the running factory machinery, and so on.

Something was special about this evening's performance. We overheard that Kirsten Flagstad had requested the extra evening. The audience, everybody, was more vibrant than ever before and when the performance ended, people went mad, cheering and clapping. The stage was by now covered with flowers and more and more were being thrown onto the stage. Finally, Kirsten Flagstad spoke, telling us that this was her farewell performance with Covent Garden. She would give the odd recital, but this was her last appearance on its stage. It was fitting that her last performance should be in Covent Garden as her first performance in Britain had been here too. She sang several arias as a farewell. Everybody's emotions were flying high. I don't think there was a dry eye in the house, neither in the audience nor among the singers and players. Shortly before midnight, she said her final "goodbye" and the curtain came down. As we left the Opera House, it was very quiet. Hardly anyone spoke. Everyone was choked with deep emotions as it truly was the end of an era.

As it was after midnight, there were no buses or tube trains to take me back to Primrose Hill. We had to walk about three miles, but we didn't notice the distance as our thoughts were still floating high in the clouds. It was quite safe to walk along the roads of St John's Wood, even though the houses were empty, dark skeletons — bombed houses, a reminder of the Blitz on London. We held hands as we walked. When saying good night to Nigel, I felt sorry for him as he lived on the other side of London, so he had to walk all the way back into town and then out again to his home. It never entered our heads that he could have slept on the settee in our lounge as it was a house full of women. It was just not the done thing.

The end of term and Christmas came quite quickly. I was to go and visit my parents. Nigel wanted us to celebrate the festive season together and he invited me to a special meal, saying he would treat me. He chose a restaurant just behind Tottenham Court Road. From the outside, it did not look very impressive. It had a small entrance door with a striped canopy over it and at the side of the door just one small window. As we opened the door and went in, a vision of sheer luxury and splendour greeted us. My reaction was to ask Nigel whether he could really afford this type of setting, but before he could reply, a waiter ushered us to a secluded table and lit a candle — something quite special in those days. The waiter handed us the menu and I couldn't help noticing that there were no prices on it. With some help from the waiter, we chose from the menu and small, delicious portions of food were served. We felt more like millionaires than the poor students we actually were. After savouring these dainty courses and putting our napkins on the table, the bill arrived. Nigel looked at it thoughtfully, taking a few minutes to study it. I asked if it was reasonable. He looked up and his face was very pale. He said that he did not have that much money on him. I laughed, thinking he was teasing me. I suggested that we could always offer to wash up. His reaction was very serious. He asked if I could help out. We pooled our funds and found we had just enough between us. I remember that I had sixpence left. We thought that if we left this "generous" tip, the waiter would feel insulted. We walked home. Fortunately, I had already bought the rail ticket to Yorkshire back to my family home. Next morning, I could not carry my luggage from Primrose Hill to King's Cross station, so I had to ask Matron to lend me the taxi fare till the next term.

The Christmas holiday passed uneventfully. I helped Mutti, to ease her work load. Then I had to accompany Papa and Kurt to the new building, which my brother had spent hours designing to incorporate all the latest features. We used to call it the "Hotel Piggery". Kurt had also supervised its building and then I had to go inside to admire the latest arrivals. All the little piglets were in their separate "creep corner", with sun-ray lamps over them to keep them warm. It looked a happy piggy nursery. The sow was also happy as the creep corner meant she could not accidentally lie on a piglet and crush it. Those twelve little piglets looked as if they were made out of marzipan. Papa said that pigs were clean animals. If they were dirty, it was because of the farmer's lack of care.

In any spare moments I would bring out my notes and revise. I felt happy to return to London as I felt confident that I had assimilated and mentally digested the previous term's work — and had survived.

Back at the hall, during meal times, some of the men would keep on getting at me with innuendo and jokes at my expense, making me feel that I did not belong to the group. I never found out why they behaved like this. I once mentioned it to the teacher who taught us psychology. His opinion was that they felt that I had an advantage over them because of my college training, and so they were trying to make me insecure. His advice was to ignore their remarks in a way that would make them feel small and mean.

During the spring term came our most testing time — how would we adapt to teaching and applying all the techniques we had been taught?

To start with, we had to demonstrate to our group. I felt very nervous standing in front of the class. I said a little prayer that I would not let myself down. The hours spent on planning and timing helped enormously. Then we were informed and told the name of the college where we would practise teaching — mine was Croydon Technical College. It was a nightmare travelling to Waterloo and then on to Croydon. Every day thousands of people would come into London to work and as the stream of commuters came off the train, I had to battle my way through them all, pushing against the crowd. They knocked me and pushed me backwards. At times it was a struggle to keep upright. Pushing my way against the tide of people made me quite dizzy. That put me at a disadvantage for my first day of teaching. I arrived at the college and the head of department introduced me to the students. They were day-release, modern housemaids. The Croydon authority decided that they should benefit from further education in English, arithmetic and cookery. As I faced these girls, I realised that I had never encountered this type of girl before. From the first moment, I was frightened of them and this rather inhibited my natural enthusiasm. In the evening my room-mate and I talked about our students and I described them as my "See me more" girls. Remember, it was 1951 and "modern" standards of dress were more modest than nowadays. These girls looked very provocative in their blouses, with necklines that were cut very low, either round-necked or scooped out. Their blouses were of very thin material and loosely cut, so that when they bent forward, you could see down the front and see their breasts. Their skirts were so tight that that they had a Marilyn Monroe wriggle. At that time, Veronica Lake was the sex kitten and her hairstyle was imitated — longish blonde hair, combed across the forehead so that it covered one side of their face. As I checked their preparation of food, they had a knack of bending their head forward and swinging their hair back, so that it would cut across my face like a whiplash. The longer I taught them, the more nervous I became. After ten days, the HMI came to check my progress. After observing me for an hour, she suggested that the class worked on while she had a word with me. She wanted to know what was happening here. I explained my reaction to the girls. The HMI asked me to wait for her in the kitchen while she did some telephoning. I could see my dream of being a teacher evaporating. Smiling, she returned and said that on Monday morning, I was to report to the Finchley and Acton Polytechnic, teaching nursery nurses. "Tell your present students that tomorrow will be your last day with them." As I told them the news that I was being transferred to a different college, to my amazement, several girls started to cry and a few others said that their ladies were so pleased with their improvement in cooking and cleaning up, that they were going to invite me for tea. It was then that the floodgates opened and they blurted out that I was the only teacher who treated them correctly and with respect. The male teachers always made sexual innuendoes or were so strict that the girls felt as if they had come to a prison. Had I realised this, I would have been a better teacher for them.

This farewell put new wind in my sails. The Finchley Polytechnic was just a bus ride from my lodgings and the nursery nurses were a delight to teach, eager to learn and full of young, innocent enthusiasm. The subjects I was to teach were cookery and housewifery, and in this I had to include "care of babies". After a few weeks, the girls approached me and asked if I could tell them how babies were created and born. In 1951, sex education was non-existent, nor could you talk about it informally or else parents might complain. However, I wondered how I could deal with this. The next lesson was preparation and cooking of herrings. This was a lesson teachers dreaded as it always finished late because of the clearing up, with fish scales everywhere. I suggested that if everything was cleared up and there was some spare time, we could touch on the subject. I felt confident that there would not be a minute to spare to talk about this difficult topic. I demonstrated how to remove the scales from the herring without them flying all over the work surface. A good half hour before the end of the lesson, they all sat at their tables — every utensil was sparkling clean and I could not find a single scale! So, how to tell them the facts of life without breaking the rules? On my table were two roes left. A soft roe and a hard roe. One was of many eggs and the other the sperm. Putting one on top of the other, I said that this was how fertilisation takes place.

"Yes, but how does it get into the woman?" they asked.

I used the cockerel and the hen as an example. When the cockerel jumps on top of the hen, he makes love to the hen, just like the man makes love to the woman. Then came the next question:

"How does the baby grow and get born?"

I drew a sketch of an egg on the blackboard and compared it a woman's womb. The white of an egg is the water, while the yolk is the food for the chicken. In a woman, it is blood, and when the baby is born, that is the afterbirth. When the chicken is fully grown, it bursts the eggshell and the chicken is born. Next question:

"Is it the navel where the baby is born?"

"No, that is where the baby receives the food from the mother."

I kept looking at the clock, wishing that the bell would ring and end this lesson.

"How is a baby born?"

To this I asked whether anyone had watched while kittens were being born. Nearly all the girls had seen this. "Where does this happen?"

"At the back, near the bottom."

"Yes, human babies are born like that, too."

I was saved from any further questions by the bell. After I had closed the register and checked the money for this lesson, I went back to the staff room for my break. I was welcomed by a lot of laughter. The other members of staff were saying, "You poor soul — you fell for it." The full-time teachers all had their excuses ready to evade this subject. It was a good lesson for me, too. Never jump into such a pitfall with both feet, but stop and think about excuses!

When the HMI came to see me, she was pleased with my improvement. Baby care was another subject that caused much amusement in the class. I read up how to handle a baby. I had never actually held a baby in my arms, so with the help of volunteers — girls who had had practical experience of looking after a little brother or sister — we bathed the doll, dried it, powdered it and dressed it.

It was the last six weeks and our final exam was nearing. Ever since I started having my periods, they had been irregular. 6 to 8 weeks late — or even 10 weeks. But this time I was 16 weeks overdue. My whole body felt bloated and the final exam was only days away. Suffering like this made clear thinking very

311

difficult. My breasts were so sore and heavy that moving my arms was extremely uncomfortable. Finally, I went to the doctor who looked after us. He was about 35 years of age and he looked very thoughtfully at me and asked bluntly: "Have you been a naughty girl?"

Definitely not. Talking to him, he said he could give me an injection which would help to bring my period on as long as I was not pregnant. It would not help with an abortion. Once more I assured him that I had not had any sex and that I was just late with my period. He gave me the injection, advising me to carry on with my normal routine, but preparing me for a heavy period.

A few days later, we had a group outing to visit a butterfly and silk moth farm. I always loved the beauty of the different species and was thrilled now to be able to see such rare ones. How wonderful! We were taken to a special glass house, which was carefully controlled for heat and humidity. As we entered it, we saw special trees and bushes which the butterflies needed to live on — the nectar from the flowers, the leaves for laying eggs on and for the caterpillars to eat. A guide explained the cycle and how they pupated. The silkworm pupae had to be watched more carefully because the silkworm cocoons would be spoiled if the silk thread was broken and therefore useless. The cocoon is put into a large container filled with water and a mixture to kill the insect. Some chrysalises would be allowed the full cycle so that the emerging moth would lay eggs. Then we were taken to another room where the silk thread was spun and then wound onto a spindle, ready to be transferred to the loom.

As it was the final term, we started to fill in application forms for teaching positions. When we went to interviews, the appointment always depended on the outcome of the examinations. References would open the doors for interviews, but the examination result would seal the contract. After finishing teaching practice, I still had to prepare a project to show. I chose cocoa. I spent many hours collecting information on the planting of cocoa and how it is made into chocolate. I contacted various manufacturers — Rowntree's, Cadbury's and Fry's — and they sent plenty of literature. Nigel painted a large cocoa pod for me. I felt that my exhibition would not be complete without an actual cocoa pod, but no museum or chocolate firm could lend me one. Then we were issued with a special ticket to the Commonwealth Exhibition at Olympia. The quest for this pod culminated in the greatest thrill of my young life. Arriving at Olympia, I realised that I had chosen the day when it was to be opened by royalty. The red carpet was rolled out and the first person to arrive was Queen Mary. Although now elderly, when she arrived she insisted on walking past the people waiting to see the royals while her wheelchair was brought up behind her. She was so regal that it felt right to curtsey as she passed us. Then the Duchesses of Kent and Gloucester and their sons arrived, and finally the king, George VI, and his beloved wife, Queen Elizabeth. I was entranced by the beauty of the queen with her beautiful complexion and the serenity of her pale blue eyes. As it happened, I was wearing my navy camel-hair coat and a white beret in

313

the continental way, with a spray of violets adorning the lapel. Looking smart and confident, I approached the commissionaire, who just glanced at my special ticket and let me into the exhibition. I just wanted a cocoa pod! When I saw one of the royal party coming towards me along one of the paths, I would quickly enter a stall and walk out the other side and this is how I walked straight into the king and queen's party, with all her ladies-in-waiting. The queen was only a few feet away from me. I was surprised by the cheerful, happy family atmosphere that surrounded the royal couple, not easily seen in those days in TV coverage. Then for a moment my heart stood still. Here I was, a gatecrasher in the royal party. I was only a few feet away from the king and queen themselves. If the detective questioned me, I could be in trouble as I was still a German subject, even though I could be counted as one of their most loyal subjects. Then as now, I absolutely worshipped the King and Queen. For me they symbolised liberty and democracy, precious freedom from dictatorship.

We were passing a stall displaying underwear made of the new type of materials — chiffon nylon. It was so delicate that you could see right through it. Several dummies were wearing beautiful negligées made from this material and the queen admired one in particular. The manager made his excuses and disappeared for a few moments. Eventually, he reappeared carrying a cardboard box with acres of tissue paper and presented this to the queen. She was so excited and picked the negligée up. Holding it against herself, she turned to

314

face the king and asked, "Do you think this would suit me?"

The king, in his slow halting voice, replied, "Not now, my dear, not now!"

Witnessing this private exchange between the king and queen moved me enormously. At that moment they were not only the adored figureheads of the nation, but were also, quite simply, two human beings deeply in love and clearly devoted to each other. With tears pricking in my eyes, I felt overwhelmed with emotion about being able to live through such an intimate moment. For me, this was the highlight of my Festival Year.

The manager took this delicate garment and carefully put it back into its box, before handing it over to a lady-in-waiting. As the party moved on, the detective asked me to move on with them. He must have thought that I was a member of the party as the viewing was strictly reserved for the royal family and their entourage. The moment I was near a stall with a side entrance, I made a hasty escape.

Eventually I found the Africa stall and asked them if they would lend me a cocoa pod. There were very strict regulations about the import and export of these and they had to be returned intact. The Customs Office controlled the number supplied for the Exhibition and exactly the same number had to be returned. I promised that I would return it to the Customs Office. This day was the crowning glory for my Festival Year. Now I had to face the final examination. My cocoa project and presentation was a great success.

I was rather sad that the college year was coming to an end as I did not know what would happen to my friendship with Nigel — or should I say "romance"? We decided to have a farewell picnic. Once more his mother had packed a delicious picnic. As we were eating it and feeling at ease in each other's company, I asked him why he had never introduced me to his parents. For a minute he sat very still, then came close to me, putting one arm round my shoulder. With the other hand he took hold of mine. He was quiet and just looked at me. He looked shattered as if his world had collapsed. Finally he spoke, weighing his words very carefully.

"You know — or can guess — my feelings for you. You are the person I would love to share my life with. I do not mind what I do as long as I know that you are safe — like the time I walked half the night back to my house. Do you remember, right in the early days, I said, 'Don't get too fond of me as you will get hurt'? Well, it was then that I knew what you would come to mean to me. I told my parents about you. I'm 33 years old and for the first time, I know with whom I want to share my life. But instead of being happy for me, my parents said that they would never accept you as you are of German stock. I had a bitter argument with them and told them about your past, but their reaction was the same: 'We are Jewish and she is German.'"

My mind went blank. Once again I had come up against my past. Would it always haunt me? At last, I

316

asked, "Why didn't you finish the friendship in the early days?"

The reply came, "I was hoping that when my parents realised what you mean to me, they might relent. I can't go against my parents' wishes."

His mother kept preparing those picnic baskets in the hope that I would lose interest in Nigel. It didn't make sense to me. I knew that many British soldiers had married German girls, many of whom wanted to escape the hardship and aftermath of the war. These women were on the other side, fighting against us in Britain, yet now these girls didn't seem to face the same problem as I did. Or was it that they were simply tougher than I was? Even today, I am still shy about admitting that I was born in Germany.

Nigel and I carried on with our friendship for another six months, but then ended it. Despite this, 1950–51 will always remain my "Festival Year" as it shaped my life. I was to teach for thirty-five years, not just the three years that were expected of us. After applying for several positions, I was finally appointed to start a catering department at a college in Cambridge. I was assured that my nationality would never be a stumbling block. For the first time in my life I received a good salary. I was able to save up to pay a solicitor and apply for naturalisation, swearing allegiance to the king. This was to be a happy day for me, because I would then feel that I belonged. I had known the hardship and terror caused by a dictator, but in 1951, thirteen years after escaping to these shores in a trawler, I became a citizen of England, a land that cares for and offers hope to oppressed people. 1951. My life's dream of becoming a teacher was about to be fulfilled. At last, I could happily say, "The sparrow has landed."

The Perilous Road to Rome and Beyond

Edward Grace MC

The cold bleak mountain top in Tunisia was the last place one would want to spend the night. Yet here we were, with the prospect of enduring perhaps many days and nights.

The author fought with the 6th Battalion of the Gordon Highlanders during the campaigns of the 1st Army in Tunisia and Italy. As a young platoon commander he and his men were in the forefront of the action. Matters came to a head during the desperate fighting on the Anzio beach-head. Severely wounded, Grace was evacuated and, once sufficiently recovered, he wrote notes of all that had happened in exact detail.

The Perilous Road to Rome and Beyond captures in dramatic style the comradeship, the dangers, the fear and the elation of war.

ISBN 978-0-7531-9476-8 (hb)
ISBN 978-0-7531-9477-5 (pb)

Aintree Days

Alexander Tulloch

If the sound of Sunday was church bells, the smell of Sunday was cabbage.

Alexander Tulloch effortlessly evokes life in Liverpool from 1945 to 1962, when he was growing up with his parents, sister and grandparents in a small terraced house in Aintree. He conjures up a world, to today's children as alien as Victorian England, in which all adults seemed to smoke for England, a pint of beer cost a few pence, where frost painted patterns on the inside of windows every winter, where the "lav" was a trek across the yard and where you always went on holiday to Llandudno — an exciting 60 miles away.

ISBN 978-0-7531-9430-0 (hb)
ISBN 978-0-7531-9431-7 (pb)

Dangerous Devotion

Christopher Portway

In silence we watched her go, a slight figure pushing her bicycle. I was convinced, even then, that meeting her had changed the course of my life.

As a prisoner-of-war, 20-year-old Christopher Portway found himself a virtual slave in the mines of Silesia, working for the Nazis in the most inhumane conditions imaginable. A born survivor, Christopher escaped three times, and it was during his second period on the run that he met Anna, the daughter of a Czech family who offered him shelter.

Although determined to be together after the turmoil of the war, Anna and Christopher found their plans thwarted as the Iron Curtain descended to divide Europe. But Christopher refused to give up the thought of being with Anna, and in a show of remarkable resilience, spent the next ten years risking everything in order to reach her.

ISBN 978-0-7531-9434-8 (hb)
ISBN 978-0-7531-9435-5 (pb)

Bockety

Desmond Ellis

The only people who aren't bockety are the ones who don't worry about anything. And the only people who don't worry about anything are simple-minded, and you can't get more bockety than that, can you?

Born in 1944, Desmond Ellis grew up on the banks of the Grand Canal in Dublin. This slightly awkward first-born child romps through his childhood like a bockety bicycle that won't quite go where it is steered. His playground is the Grand Canal, where he goes crashing through the reeds with fishing nets. At home he washes off the inevitable grime in a tin tub by the fire, and the toilet is a draughty shed in the yard.

Bockety is a tale of a time of few cars and many bicycles. Gratification was to be had in Cleeve's toffee and gobstoppers. And then there was the terrible confusion of girls . . .

ISBN 978-0-7531-9424-9 (hb)
ISBN 978-0-7531-9425-6 (pb)

Dreams of Hope

Lily O'Connor

I watched him. He led the floor with the best dancers, the girls who knew his every step.

This sparkling memoir is a remarkable personal account of the emigrant lives of one Irish couple amongst the hundreds upon thousands forced to emigrate in the 1950s.

The book centres on Lily O'Connor's married life with Paddy in Dublin, Luton and Australia. At its heart is the story of a man who always wanted too much and a woman whose resilience saw her coping courageously, often on her own, with a large family and difficult circumstances. This is a resonant tale of one woman's life in three countries with a man torn between the contentment of family life and the pursuit of ambition and adventure as a single man.

ISBN 978-0-7531-9426-3 (hb)
ISBN 978-0-7531-9427-0 (pb)

ISIS publish a wide range of books in large print, from fiction to biography. Any suggestions for books you would like to see in large print or audio are always welcome. Please send to the Editorial Department at:

ISIS Publishing Limited
7 Centremead
Osney Mead
Oxford OX2 0ES

A full list of titles is available free of charge from:

Ulverscroft Large Print Books Limited

(UK)
The Green
Bradgate Road, Anstey
Leicester LE7 7FU
Tel: (0116) 236 4325

(Australia)
P.O. Box 314
St Leonards
NSW 1590
Tel: (02) 9436 2622

(USA)
P.O. Box 1230
West Seneca
N.Y. 14224-1230
Tel: (716) 674 4270

(Canada)
P.O. Box 80038
Burlington
Ontario L7L 6B1
Tel: (905) 637 8734

(New Zealand)
P.O. Box 456
Feilding
Tel: (06) 323 6828

Details of **ISIS** complete and unabridged audio books are also available from these offices. Alternatively, contact your local library for details of their collection of **ISIS** large print and unabridged audio books.